CULTIVATING BELIEF

Cultivating Belief

Victorian Anthropology, Liberal Aesthetics,
and the Secular Imagination

SEBASTIAN LECOURT

OXFORD
UNIVERSITY PRESS

OXFORD
UNIVERSITY PRESS

Great Clarendon Street, Oxford, OX2 6DP,
United Kingdom

Oxford University Press is a department of the University of Oxford.
It furthers the University's objective of excellence in research, scholarship,
and education by publishing worldwide. Oxford is a registered trade mark of
Oxford University Press in the UK and in certain other countries

© Sebastian Lecourt 2018

The moral rights of the author have been asserted

First Edition published in 2018
Impression: 1

Published in the United States of America by Oxford University Press
198 Madison Avenue, New York, NY 10016, United States of America

British Library Cataloguing in Publication Data
Data available

Library of Congress Control Number: 2017954408

ISBN 978–0–19–881249–4

Printed and bound by
CPI Group (UK) Ltd, Croydon, CR0 4YY

Acknowledgments

This book had its beginnings as a dissertation at Yale University. But it has also been shaped by intellectual encounters at other institutions that have hosted me as a teacher and a researcher: Brandeis University, Rutgers University, Universität Konstanz, the Johns Hopkins University, and now the University of Houston.

At Yale I learned much from the advising of Katie Trumpener and the late, great Linda Peterson, as well as from conversations with Tanya Agathocleous, Jon Butler, Janice Carlisle, Emily Coit, Paul Fry, Jeff Glover, Andrew Goldstone, Amy Hungerford, Stefanie Markovits, Aaron Pratt, Frank Turner, R. John Williams, Andrew Willson, and Ruth Yeazell.

At Brandeis Billy Flesch, Tom King, and John Plotz provided sympathetic ears and sage advice. Rutgers, meanwhile, welcomed me into a tremendous nineteenth-century cohort that included Brad Evans, Billy Galperin, Colin Jager, John Kucich, David Kurnick, Meredith McGill, Jonah Siegel, Barry Qualls, and Carolyn Williams. I would also like to thank Sean Barry, Naomi Levine, Kyle McAuley, John Miller, Mimi Winnick, and the other members of an excellent RU English graduate cohort for a rich exchange of ideas.

The Kulturwissenschaftliche Kolleg at Universität Konstanz provided a beautiful year of quiet and concentration along the edge of the Alps. I'm deeply indebted to Fred Girod, Daniela Göpfrich, Nina Kück, Svenia Schneider-Wulf, and Christina Thoma, and the hardworking KuKo Hiwis for that gift.

At Johns Hopkins I had the privilege of participating in conversations both at the Humanities Center, where I was housed as a Mellon Fellow, and within the English Department. Special thanks should go to Hent de Vries, Jared Hickman, Jeanne-Marie Jackson, Leonardo Lisi, Douglas Mao, Anne Eakin Moss, Yi-Ping Ong, Gabby Spiegel, and Jesse Rosenthal, for a rewarding year in Baltimore.

I have not been at the University of Houston long, but I have already found intellectual companionship among Hosam Aboul-Ela, Margo Backus, Jason Berger, Lauren Brozovich, Sally Connolly, Ann Christensen, Sarah Ehlers, Karen Fang, J. Kastely, Auritro Majumder, David Mazella, Kavita Singh, Lynn Voskuil, Jen Wingard, Lauren Zentz, and many others.

From the outset, this project was driven by my desire to think across several areas of academic inquiry and was stimulated by opportunities to speak with scholars outside of my immediate field. A special colloquium on Charles Taylor's *A Secular Age* (2007), held at Yale in April of 2008, helped jumpstart my thinking about several crucial issues. I would also like to thank Phil Gorski and Yale's Religion and Politics Colloquium for allowing me to present an early version of Chapter 4 before a room of sociologists and political scientists, as well as Charles Mathewes and Kurtis Schaeffer for organizing a 2014 NEH Summer Seminar at the University of Virginia that let me discuss questions of theory and method in the study of religion with a fantastic cross-disciplinary group: Ata Anzali, Elliott Bazzano, Joe Blankholm, Annie Blazer, Sarah Dees, Eric Hoenes, Todd LeVasseur, Beatrice Marovich, Jotham Parsons, Nathan Rein, Audrey Truschke, Emma Wasserman, Bill Wood, Peter Woodford, and Jamie Yeo.

There are several other institutions to which I am indebted. Funding for dissertation completion came from the Mrs. Giles Whiting foundation, while postdoctoral support came from the American Council of Learned Societies and the Andrew W. Mellon Foundation. Meanwhile I was able to present early versions of several chapters thanks to the North American Victorian Studies Association's annual conference, the Northeast Victorian Studies Association's annual conference, Yale's British Studies Colloquium, UC Berkeley's Nineteenth-Century Colloquium, Rutgers's Nineteenth-Century Colloquium, and P19, the Philadelphia nineteenth-century working group.

Wendy Wood and Anya Hastwell helped with final proofreading, while sustaining encouragement along the way came from James Eli Adams, Jo Briggs, Ian Duncan, Elaine Freedgood, Michael Gamer, Jonathan Grossman, Charlie LaPorte, Douglas Mao, Meredith Martin, Anne McCarthy, Kent Puckett, Rachel Teukolsky, and others. Eleanor Collins and Aimee Wright at OUP have offered ongoing guidance and patience as editors.

Portions of Chapter 2 appeared in *Victorian Literature and Culture* 38.2 (September 2010) as "Matthew Arnold and Religion's Cosmopolitan Histories"; an early version of Chapter 4, meanwhile, was published as "'To surrender himself, in perfectly liberal inquiry': Walter Pater, Many-Sidedness, and the Conversion Novel" in *Victorian Studies* 53.2 (Winter 2011). I'd like to thank both journals for their permission to reprint these materials.

Stepping back a bit, I cannot extend enough gratitude to Steph Burt, Paula Cooey, Eleanor Courtemanche, Jim Dawes, Jeanne Kilde, Kiarina Kordela, Stuart Y. McDougal, David Wilson-Okamura, Michelle Wright, and other excellent professors I had at Macalester College around the turn of the millennium, who showed me an image of what I wanted to do with my career and helped me get started.

A few special cats provided company at key moments in the revision process: Gracie, my landlord's cat in Princeton, NJ; Ivan the Terrible, who stalked my apartment building in Konstanz, Germany; Max and Morris and Steve, who helped me adjust during my first year in Houston; and Magnus the kitten, who washed up in a Texas thunderstorm in the bushes outside my apartment during the final weeks of revision.

Finally, I'd like to thank my parents, Nancy and Patrick Lecourt, for their encouragement and support as I pursued employment in an ever-winnowing field. Thanks for letting me decide what I wanted to do with my life and offering me the space to learn by trial and error.

Table of Contents

Introduction
Victorian Anthropology and Victorian Secularity

Recent years have seen a significant shift in how academic commentators discuss secularization. Where debates on the subject once focused upon questions of empirical religious decline—does modernization entail the progressive disappearance of religion or not?—critics such as Talal Asad have since initiated a more self-conscious exploration of how Western modernity reshapes the category of religion itself.[1] What distinguishes the contemporary West, they argue, is not the relative presence or absence of religion but rather its habit of imagining "religion" to be a special zone of human life that can be separated from art, or sex, or politics. In turn, different constructions of this generic human religiosity have come to anchor different political and ethical projects. Liberal states draw a line segregating religion, construed as private faith, from public norms; insurgent nationalisms identify religion with the bonds of ethnic solidarity; radical secularists deride religion as an inferior form of knowledge that has been superseded by science. Understanding the secular, by this account, requires that we study explicitly what people think religion is and where they locate it. Secularity is a discourse about religion, not its lack.

---

[1] Major studies in this vein include Talal Asad, *Formations of the Secular: Christianity, Islam, Modernity* (Stanford, CA: Stanford UP, 2003); Saba Mahmood, *Politics of Piety: The Islamic Revival and the Feminist Subject* (Princeton, NJ: Princeton UP, 2005); Callum Brown, *The Death of Christian Britain: Understanding Secularisation, 1800–2000* (New York, NY: Routledge, 2001). Within the sphere of nineteenth-century literary studies, see Vincent P. Pecora, *Secularization and Cultural Criticism: Religion, Nation, and Modernity* (Chicago, IL: U of Chicago P, 2006); Colin Jager, *The Book of God: Secularization and Design in the Romantic Era* (Philadelphia, PA: U of Pennsylvania P, 2007); William R. McKelvy, *The English Cult of Literature: Devoted Readers, 1774–1880* (Charlottesville, VA: U of Virginia P, 2007); John Lardas Modern, *Secularism in Antebellum America* (Chicago, IL: U of Chicago P, 2010); Sara Lyons, *Algernon Swinburne and Walter Pater: Victorian Aestheticism, Doubt, and Secularization* (London, UK: Legenda, 2015). For an overview of developments in literary studies, see Michael W. Kaufmann, "The Religious, the Secular, and Literary Studies: Rethinking the Secularization Narrative in Histories of the Profession," *New Literary History* 38.4 (2007): 607–28.

Cultivating Belief proposes that this way of thinking about the secular offers a more useful approach to Victorian literature. The Victorian period, with its overlapping forces of industrialism, urbanization, and Darwinism, has long been central to narratives of modern religious decline. But in fact, I argue, it is better understood as a moment in which an ever-widening range of writers, responding to the twin pressures of sectarian dispute at home and colonial encounters abroad, became preoccupied with defining the nature of religion and its function in the world. Competing claims about what religion was and what it did animated parliamentary debates, evangelical reform movements, literary criticism, and the emerging social sciences, all of which were available to readers through a burgeoning periodical press.

At the same time, *Cultivating Belief* ventures that Victorian literature can challenge what has become a central claim of the new secularity studies: the idea that modern liberalism has primarily constructed religion as a zone of inward belief. Many of the recent commentators on secularism have shown how Anglo-American liberals since Locke have used the term religion to designate a species of sincere conviction—the epitome of all those inward matters that the state cannot coerce and that individuals must determine for themselves. The reality, however, is that the 1860s also saw a number of liberal writers become interested in more embodied conceptions of religion as a matter of racial or ethnic identity. Drawing upon the emerging field of anthropology, a group of writers that included Matthew Arnold, George Eliot, Walter Pater, and Andrew Lang began to suggest that religion could actually do the most for individuals when it came embedded in the unconscious inheritances of the past. As they saw it, religious identities that preceded any personal belief could build up a liberal self by giving it a quality of aesthetic heterogeneity. In texts such as Eliot's *Daniel Deronda* (1876), Pater's *Marius the Epicurean* (1885), and Arnold's *Culture and Anarchy* (1869), the self that can be reduced to mere personal convictions risks becoming parochial and narrow, while the self that can gather its many contradictory histories into a heterogeneous free play will develop a many-sided individuality.

It is no longer customary to make writers like Arnold and Pater central to discussions of Victorian secularization. Doing so would seem to smack of an old-fashioned intellectual history that privileges the mental crises of elite thinkers over wider social trends. *Cultivating Belief*, however, contends that exploring how and why these literary liberals rethought the nature of religion can illuminate some important currents within modern secularity. For one thing, it lets us explore how liberal thinkers in the Anglo-American world began to turn away from their traditional (and markedly Protestant) emphasis on abstract individualism and toward models that valued inheritance and identity as resources for the self. By reimagining religion, Arnold, Eliot, and Pater were in fact reimagining liberal subjectivity altogether, supplanting a self that was defined by its capacity to pick and choose with one that acquired its full individuality by bringing the varied heritages of race, culture, and religion into a kind of aesthetic play.

More broadly, I argue, these writers reveal an emerging split between two versions of secularism—two ways of mapping the relationship between individualism, religion, and global difference that continue to divide liberal thinking. Against a classical Protestant secularism centered upon private commitment and freedom of conscience, Arnold and Eliot were picturing an aesthetic secularism that emphasized hybridity, diversity, and the ability to balance multiple values. Like many critics in our own day, they were rejecting a secular subject who maintains clear boundaries between private and public, belief and reason, for an eclectic subject who could draw upon both choice and inheritance in cultivating a complex personality. In so doing, they opened up a set of questions that continue to vex us a century and a half later. Can secularism define an expansive framework of values that encompasses narrower ones, or must it at some point become exclusionary too? Can we successfully envisage secularism beyond Protestant conceptions of sincerity and interiority? Above all, Arnold, Eliot, and my other figures illuminate the curious way in which pluralistic secularism can become hostile toward the very things that it seeks to accommodate. Arnold's essays on Islam and Judaism cast those traditions as embodiments of a pure, racialized religiosity that liberalism must internalize even as they antagonize liberalism from within. Similarly, Eliot's *Deronda* endeavors to recuperate ethnic religion as a moral resource for a complex modern selfhood, only to reinstate an implicitly hierarchical relationship between the many-sided Western individual who can dally with different identities and the colonized peoples who supposedly embody those identities on the ground. Crucially, all of these figures show how such difficulties often stem from the attempt to project an aesthetic understanding of differences onto the realms of politics, ethics, and history.

This introductory chapter is divided into three parts. In the first part, I survey some of the major anthropological accounts of religion that were developed during the eighteenth and nineteenth centuries and consider how they disseminated within the world of Victorian print culture. In the second, I explore what it meant for Victorian liberals such as Arnold, Eliot, and Pater to take up racialized models of religion usually favored by conservative thinkers—what historical patterns it pushed against and what new imaginaries it offered. The final section asks how exploring these debates over the meaning of religion as a category can offer us a new perspective on secularization as a keyword for Victorian studies.

VICTORIAN ANTHROPOLOGY AND RELIGION *SUI GENERIS*

One of the first achievements of the Age of Reason was to discover religion. Where for centuries that word had designated only the particular forms of worship prescribed by the Roman Catholic Church, writers of the European Enlightenment began using it to signify an analytically distinct department of human life that could be seen in all societies. In so doing they were responding to a complex web of concerns. Locally, they were seeking new terminology that could mediate the bloody conflicts instigated by the Reformation and Wars of Religion. Globally, they were aiming to make sense of the various forms of non-Christian worship being described by missionaries, explorers, and colonial administrators.[2] In this sense the transformation of religion into a cross-cultural category reflected the emergence of what Mary Louise Pratt calls Europe's "planetary consciousness," its new understanding of the globe as a single space to be mapped and ordered.[3]

During the early modern period, for instance, Neoplatonists such as Marsilio Ficino and the so-called Cambridge Platonists in England sought to pare Christianity down to a set of simple tenets, derived from the objective facts of human nature, upon which all Christians could agree. Christianity, by their account, was simply the finest expression of a "natural religion" that was everywhere self-evidently true.[4] In turn, a more radical group of thinkers known as Deists went further by venturing that this natural religion had preceded *all* known creeds, even Christianity, and could therefore critique the latter's claims. According to Lord Herbert of Cherbury's *De Veritate* (1624), true religion consisted of a set of general intuitions—the existence of an ultimate deity, the necessity of worshiping it, the centrality of moral practice to worship—which particular creeds

---

[2] On the European sectarian context, see Peter Harrison, *"Religion" and the Religions in the English Enlightenment* (New York, NY: Cambridge UP, 1990), 19–28. For the imperial context, see Tomoko Masuzawa, *The Invention of World Religions* (Chicago, IL: U of Chicago P, 2005) and David Chidester, *Empire of Religion: Imperialism and Comparative Religion* (Chicago, IL: U of Chicago P, 2014).

[3] Mary Louise Pratt, *Imperial Eyes: Travel Writing and Transculturation* (New York, NY: Routledge, 1992), 11.

[4] Harrison, 10–98.

inevitably tended to distort.[5] Hence Deist texts like John Toland's *Christianity Not Mysterious* (1696) and Matthew Tindal's *Christianity as Old as the Creation* (1730) narrated the history of religion as a history of its corruptions, whether by priestly machinations or through the imperfect media of custom, climate, and bodily humor.[6] As Thomas Blount put it, "the great Variety of Mens Actions and Opinions cannot proceed from the Diversity of their Souls, which are accounted all equal, but from that of the Bodies; wherein according to the various Tempers thereof, the soul produces that variety of Manners.... For so long as Mens Organs are of several makes, and we live under divers Climats, we must necessarily have different Sentiments, and Apprehensions of things."[7]

In short, the Deists and Cambridge Platonists refashioned religion into a cultural universal by disembodying it. Religion as such, to their minds, was something that preceded and was inevitably diminished by the particulars of any historical religion. Subsequent writers of the Enlightenment, in turn, responded to this "negative anthropology" by mapping out religion's concrete social development.[8] In both Scotland and France, the eighteenth century saw the emergence of what is often called stadial or conjectural history: evolutionary accounts of human society as progressing through a series of predictable stages from hunting and gathering to agriculture and finally to modern industrialism.[9] While all cultures were obliged to pass through these stages in roughly the same order, the claim went, they inevitably did so at different speeds, and this developmental lag allowed for a comparative methodology whereby first-hand accounts of modern-day Africans or Australians could substitute for the absent data on the religion of ancient European hunter-gatherers. Hence the "denial of coevalness" that Johannes Fabian sees running through much modern anthropology—the construct of "*anachronistic space*" that, in Anne McClintock's phrase, locates "colonized people ... in a permanently anterior time within the geographic space of the modern empire as anachronistic humans."[10]

Stadial history, as George Stocking has shown, took shape as a coherent tradition in the decades following the publication of Montesquieu's *Of the Spirit of the Laws* (1748). Other major examples of the genre include

[5] Ibid., 67–8.

[6] Ibid., 160–8; J. S. Preus, *Explaining Religion: Criticism and Theory from Bodin to Freud* (New Haven, CT: Yale UP, 1996), 23–39.

[7] Quoted in Harrison, 118.   [8] Ibid., 102.

[9] George Stocking, *Victorian Anthropology* (New York, NY: Free P, 1987), 9.

[10] Johannes Fabian, *Time and the Other: How Anthropology Makes Its Object* (New York, NY: Columbia UP, 1983), 31; Anne McClintock, *Imperial Leather: Race, Gender, and Sexuality in the Colonial Contest* (New York, NY: Routledge, 1995), 30.

Adam Ferguson's *Essay on the History of Civil Society* (1767), Adam Smith's *Sketches of the History of Man* (1774), Lord Monboddo's *Origin and Progress of Language* (1773–92), as well as treatises by Lord Kames, Condorcet, and John Millar.[11] The groundwork for stadialist accounts of religion, however, had been established slightly earlier in the century by the French writer Bernard Fontenelle, whose *Of the Origin of the Fables* (1724) argued that early humans, lacking a scientific epistemology, had accounted for natural phenomena by postulating the actions of immanent gods and spirits. Over time, the human mind's growing capacity for abstraction allowed it to consolidate all of these different gods into one omnipotent deity.[12] Charles de Brosses of the Académie des Inscriptions et Belles-Lettres would dub the belief in universal animation "fétichisme" in 1760, and its importance to the history of religion would be described over the rest of the eighteenth century by Christoph Meiners, Philip Christian Reinhard, J. A. Dulaure, and Charles Dupuis.[13]

In many ways the Deists and the stadial historians shared a common goal of criticizing, or at least relativizing, Christian orthodoxy by framing it as an instance of generic human religion. Ostensibly, of course, stadial history attained these critical ends by radically different means. In contrast with Deism's Idealist take on cognition and its view of cultural development as a process of gradual corruption, it offered a materialist, progressivist story of the human mind positively accumulating knowledge over time.[14] The truth is, however, that stadial history was very much a kind of negative anthropology in its own right, a "sociology of error" that treated religion mostly as a vestige of primitive intellectual confusion.[15] No less than the Deists, the stadial historians paid scant notice to the constitutive role that individual religions had played in actual historical societies. This Enlightenment inattention to the local and the particular would, by the end of the eighteenth century, become the primary target of a new Romantic anthropology that valorized the idiosyncrasies of different peoples and their organic religious formations. In Germany particularly, writes Stocking, the "reaction against the cultural imperialism of the French Enlightenment, and a growing sense of economic and political backwardness to France and England," inspired some of the foundational theorizations of what we would call race or ethnicity.[16] Perhaps the seminal figure here was the poet-philosopher Johann Gottfried von Herder, whose *Ideas for a Philosophy of Mankind* (1784–91) argued that

---

[11] Stocking, 13–15.
[12] Peter Melville Logan, *Victorian Fetishism: Intellectuals and Primitives* (Albany, NY: SUNY P, 2009), 24; Preus, 40–55.
[13] Logan, 28–9. [14] Stocking, 15–19. [15] Ibid., 19. [16] Ibid., 20.

the unique historical experience of a people molded it over time into a *Volk*, "one people, having its own national form, as well as its own language."[17] Herder's thought was, in Stocking's phrase, "pluralistic, relativistic, and historicist" to a degree that stadial history had never been, "emphasiz[ing] the variety of national characters, seeing each as the unique outcome of a people's environmental and historical experience, embodied in its own mythology, which was the characteristic religious, esthetic, and ethical expression of the *Volksgeist*."[18] In a similar vein, the Savoyard anti-Jacobin Joseph de Maistre argued in his *Study on Sovereignty* (1793–98) that the function of religion was not to express individual conscience but rather to bind the individual to a "national mind" that emanated organically from the collective. "Do not talk ... of scrutiny, choice, discussion," Maistre warned the partisans of the Enlightenment, for "let everyone rely on his individual reason in religion, and you will see immediately the rise of anarchy of belief."[19] "It is a basic mistake to represent the social state as an optional state based on human consent," for on the contrary "[m]an's primary need is that his nascent reason" should "lose itself in the national mind, so that it changes its individual existence for another communal existence, just as a river which flows into the ocean."[20]

This anti-Enlightenment model of religion as the gravity binding a social group together would have a wide influence across the nineteenth century. Increasingly, as we will see in Chapter 1, many thinkers developed Herder's notion of the *Volk* into a concept of biological race that derived a people's religion, language, customs, and institutions from a unique blood-essence. "Race," writes Colin Kidd, came to stand for "the ultimate reality in human affairs," and "religious diversity [for] an expression of the deeper underlying truth of racial differences."[21] In Germany, most accounts of race following Herder came from comparative philologists who traced an ancient struggle between Semitic religions, built around authoritarian monotheism, and Indo-European religions, which expressed themselves through an imaginative and highly poetic

[17] Johann Gottfried Herder, *Reflections on the Philosophy of the History of Mankind* (1784–91), trans. Frank Manuel (Chicago, IL: U of Chicago P, 1968), 7.

[18] Stocking, 20. For more on Herder as a forerunner of anthropological relativism, see Isaiah Berlin, *The Roots of Romanticism*, ed. Henry Hardy (Princeton, NJ: Princeton UP, 1999), 57–67; Michael F. Brown, "Cultural Relativism 2.0," *Current Anthropology* 49.3 (2008): 365.

[19] *The Works of Joseph de Maistre*, ed. and trans. Jack Lively (1965; New York, NY: Schocken, 1971), 109, 108.

[20] Ibid., 96, 109.

[21] Colin Kidd, *The Forging of Races: Race and Scripture in the Protestant Atlantic World, 1600–2000* (New York, NY: Cambridge UP, 2006), 171.

polytheism. From the contrast between the structures of Semitic and Indo-European languages, philologists such as Friedrich Schlegel, Wilhelm von Humboldt, and Franz Bopp extrapolated a larger civilizational rift between two different philosophies of life: the moral and the aesthetic, the practical and the disinterested, the monological and the dialectical. The Indo-European peoples, flowering most conspicuously in classical Greece, stood for the expansion of the imagination and the philosophical, scientific, and artistic exploration of nature. The Semites, by contrast, embodied a utilitarian and moralistic outlook on nature as the theater for man's striving with an absolutely transcendent deity.[22] For this reason Tomoko Masuzawa portrays Indo-European philology as an attempt to forge a new, secular understanding of Europeanness "apart from the hitherto defining notion of Christendom," one grounded in racial and linguistic affinity more than in theological confession.[23]

In Britain and France, meanwhile, race-driven readings of religion were often articulated through the study of comparative anatomy. Robert Knox's profoundly controversial *The Races of Men* (1850), for example, argued that the Englishman, the Irishman, and the African were separate species with incompatible spiritual outlooks. "[H]uman character," wrote Knox, "is traceable solely to the nature of that race to which the individual or nation belongs," which meant that race was the undergirding principle even of religion.[24] Christianity, for instance, "presents . . . a variety of forms essentially distinct: with each race its character is altered; Celtic, Saxon, Sarmatian, express in so many words, the Greek, Roman, Lutheran forms of worship."[25] Like Herder, mid-Victorian theorists found the idea of racially embodied religion appealing as a rebuke to Enlightenment universalism, but for very different political reasons. Instead of offering a localist critique of Napoleonic empire, it expressed disenchantment with the imperial civilizing mission following the colonial uprisings in India (1857) and Jamaica (1865), as well as the ongoing troubles in Ireland. To those who hoped that Anglo-Protestant moral suasion could civilize the Irishman or the African, Knox warned that "all abstractions, neglecting or despising this great element, the physical character and constitution of

---

[22] See Raymond Schwab, *Oriental Renaissance: Europe's Rediscovery of India and the East, 1680–1880* (New York, NY: Columbia UP, 1984), 11–336; Bruce Lincoln, *Theorizing Myth: Narrative, Ideology, and Scholarship* (Chicago, IL: U of Chicago P, 1999), 47–75; Masuzawa, 147–78.

[23] Masuzawa, 148.

[24] Robert Knox, *The Races of Men: A Fragment* (Philadelphia, PA: Lea and Blanchard, 1850), 7.

[25] Ibid., 11.

man, his mental and corporeal attributes must, of necessity, be at least Utopian, if not erroneous."[26]

Although these racialist models of religion, as we will see in Chapter 1, had a significant impact upon mid-Victorian historiography, they were soon to be challenged by a revival of stadial history during the 1860s and '70s. Thanks partly to the vogue for evolutionary theories created by Auguste Comte, Charles Darwin, and Herbert Spencer, and partly to the aggressively self-universalizing outlook of the New Imperialism, writers such as John Lubbock, J. F. McLennan, E. B. Tylor, W. Robertson Smith, and James Frazer revived the thesis that every human society passed through a regular sequence of developmental stages, with Great Britain currently occupying the vanguard position. The first significant works of the new evolutionary anthropology were Lubbock's *Prehistoric Times* (1865) and *The Origin of Civilization* (1870), both of which charted the evolution of humankind's religious ideas from an original state lacking philosophical or mythological conceptions through fetishism (the worship of objects), totemism (the worship of animals), anthropomorphic poly-theism, and finally ethical monotheism.[27] But its seminal elaboration would arguably arrive in the work of Tylor, a son of prosperous Quaker manufacturers who developed an interest in anthropology during a trip to Central America in 1855.[28] In *Primitive Culture* (1871), Tylor defined "Culture, or Civilization" as "that complex whole which includes knowledge, belief, art, morals, law, custom," and which advances in "uniform . . . stages of development or evolution" around the world.[29] Like Montesquieu and Smith before him, Tylor drew a basic parallel between the stages of cultural evolution, the different levels of civilization apparent in the contemporary world, and the phases of individual psy-chological maturation. The concept of a deity, he argued, had evolved from the idea of individual spirits, which early humans had developed by pondering the body's loss of animation upon death, as well as the origins of dreams. Over time, human beings had begun to project this soul-idea outward, thus arriving at the belief that every living thing possessed an animating spirit, a notion that eventually grew into the belief in a single, all-powerful creator.[30] In this respect modern religion was what Tylor called a "survival," one of many "customs, opinions, and so forth" that had

[26] Ibid., 9.

[27] See Eric Sharpe, *Comparative Religion: A History* (La Salle, IL: Open Court, 1986), 52.

[28] Stocking, 156–64.

[29] E. B. Tylor, *Primitive Culture: Researches into the Development of Mythology, Philoso-phy, Religion, Language, Art, and Custom* (2 vols.; London, UK: John Murray, 1871), 1: 1.

[30] See E. E. Evans-Pritchard, *Theories of Primitive Religion* (Oxford, UK: Clarendon P, 1965), 23–6.

been "carried on by force of habit into a new state of society different from that in which they had their original home."[31]

If Tylor's version of stadial history rehashed the largely intellectualist view of religion advanced by his eighteenth-century predecessors, other evolutionary anthropologists would lay aside the thesis that religion primarily expressed mistaken ideas and consider instead how religion might have originated in social practices.[32] The Scottish lawyer McLennan, for instance, argued in a series of essays in the *Fortnightly Review* (1869–70) that Tylor's animism had actually served as the original basis of social organization insofar as it had encouraged early tribes to select a totem animal to stand for the group's collective identity.[33] Even in modern Australia, he wrote, "the natives represent their family names as having been derived from some vegetable or animal common in the district they inhabited"; there is "an Opossum tribe, an Emu tribe, a Swan tribe, a Duck tribe, a Fish tribe, and three water-fowl tribes."[34] Following McLennan's lead, the theologian and biblical scholar William Robertson Smith's *Lectures on the Religion of the Semites* (1889) maintained that "it is of the first importance to realise ... that ritual and practical usage were, strictly speaking, the sum-total of ancient religions."[35] By killing and eating their totem animals, Smith showed, ancient tribes had made themselves, at least performatively, the blood-kin of their gods. In this respect mankind's religious traditions were originally not beliefs so much as "parts of one whole of social custom."[36]

This ritualist turn within late-Victorian anthropology would have its most celebrated effects beyond Victorian Britain. On the one hand, it provided the basis for Frazer's claim that Christianity was part of an elaborate misremembering of ancient priest-king sacrifices—a thesis that, thanks to his twelve-volume *Golden Bough* (1890–1915), would become a great code of art for literary modernism.[37] On the other hand, the French sociologist Émile Durkheim's *Elementary Forms of the Religious Life* (1912)

---

[31] Tylor, 1: 16.

[32] Sharpe, 72–3; Evans-Pritchard, 53–4. For a wider survey, consult Robert Ackerman, *The Myth and Ritual School: J. G. Frazer and the Cambridge Ritualists* (New York, NY: Garland, 1991).

[33] J. F. McLennan, "The Worship of Plants and Animals," *Fortnightly Review* 6 (1869): 422.

[34] McLennan, 409, 411.

[35] W. Robertson Smith, *Lectures on the Religion of the Semites* (New York, NY: D. Appleton, 1889), 21.

[36] Ibid., 22. On Smith and his challenge to anthropology's largely Protestant assumptions, see Ackerman, 40–5.

[37] See John B. Vickery, *The Literary Impact of the Golden Bough* (Princeton, NJ: Princeton UP, 1973).

would draw heavily upon the technical vocabulary of writers like Tylor and McLennan—fetishes, totems—and parlay it into a holistic vision of the social more reminiscent of Herder. Religion by Durkheim's account represented "a unified system of beliefs and practices... which unite[s] into one single moral community... all those who adhere to them."[38] Durkheim, however, was not a Romantic reactionary but rather a socialist whose collectivist understanding of religion offered a critique of liberal individualism from the left instead of from the right. Like Comte a half-century before him, Durkheim hoped that by reconstructing the ancient social basis of religion he might lay the groundwork for postliberal, postindustrial forms of solidarity in the future.[39]

In short, by the end of the nineteenth century there had emerged in Great Britain a well-developed scholarly conversation about the social origins and function of religion. In retrospect, we call this discourse the anthropology of religion, although at the time it was far more disparate. Not only did it overlap ambiguously with several other emerging intellectual projects, such as linguistics and sociology, but it also had scattered institutional bases. The United States and France established government centers of anthropology or ethnology (a distinction that we will examine in Chapter 1), but in Britain such research remained the concern of amateurs and made only minor inroads within academia.[40] In 1896, after more than a decade as the Keeper of the University Museum and also as a Reader in Anthropology, E. B. Tylor was promoted to the position of Oxford's first professor of the subject and became, in effect, Britain's first professional anthropologist. Arthur Thomsen soon joined the teaching staff as Lecturer in Human Anatomy, while at Cambridge an unsuccessful attempt to hire McLennan would find some compensation in the hiring of A. C. Haddon in 1895.[41] On the whole, however, by the end of Victoria's reign "there were probably no more than a dozen men" in England, most of them museum employees, "whose professional life was given over solely to anthropological activity."[42] Most of the British writers surveyed here remained dilettante enthusiasts preoccupied with other lines of work: Lubbock was a banker; McLennan a lawyer; Andrew Lang a prolific literary journalist and children's writer.

The upshot of this situation was that Victorian anthropological theorists of religion found their audiences not just in the academy but also among the readers of *Fraser's*, *Cornhill*, the *Fortnightly Review*, and other

---

[38] Émile Durkheim, *The Elementary Forms of the Religious Life* (1912), trans. Joseph Ward Swain (London, UK: Allen and Unwin, 1915), 47.

[39] See Preus, 107–9, 157–77; Evans-Pritchard, 64.

[40] Stocking, 267–8.   [41] Ibid., 264–5, 300.   [42] Ibid., 267.

journals that offered a mixture of literary and scientific knowledge to the educated middle classes.[43] A twenty-first-century reader, accustomed to hard divisions between academic disciplines, might be surprised to open the *Fortnightly* for November 1, 1869, and find McLennan's pioneering essay on totemism next to Algernon Charles Swinburne's poem "Intercession" and Walter Pater's "Notes on Leonardo da Vinci."[44] But in fact it was in the very nature of Victorian anthropology to circulate through multiple publics and to inform the thinking of a variety of intellectuals. As a result, anthropology became a sounding board for larger cultural issues, and it is to one such area of concern that we now turn.

RELIGION, RACE, AND THE CULTIVATED SELF

The foregoing summary has only skimmed the surface of a complex history. One thing that it highlights, however, is the striking way in which religion, once it had been reimagined as a cultural universal, also became a proxy for different theorists' views regarding politics, ethics, and human agency. Even as writers employed the term *religion* to name a narrower and narrower sphere of human life, where they located that sphere became increasingly significant for their understandings of subjectivity and the social. On the one hand, anthropologists who belonged to the emerging tradition called liberalism tended to treat religion as a matter of mental beliefs that individuals needed to choose freely. Although they differed on many points, including in their overall attitudes toward religion itself, the Deists and the stadial historians all agreed that the seminal event of modernity had been the disembedding of religion from custom and collectivity and its transfer to the domain of private conscience. As Robertson Smith (a liberal theologian by trade) put it, "the oldest religious and political institutions... were parts of one whole of social custom," "handed down from father to child, and therefore... in great measure an affair of race."[45] Only after centuries had these ethnic creeds been superseded by "*positive* religions" such as Islam and Christianity,

[43] See Walter E. Houghton, "Victorian Periodical Literature and the Articulate Classes," *Victorian Studies* 22.4 (1979): 389–412. For periodicals in relation to the emergence of specialized academic discourse, see Stefan Collini, *Public Moralists: Political Thought and Intellectual Life in Britain* (Oxford, UK: Clarendon P, 1991), 50–7; and for Victorian print culture and the creation of religious imaginaries, see Joshua King, *Imagined Spiritual Communities in Britain's Age of Print* (Columbus, OH: Ohio State UP, 2015).

[44] Robert Crawford, "Pater's Renaissance, Andrew Lang, and Anthropological Romanticism," *ELH* 53.4 (1986): 849.

[45] W. R. Smith, 22, 5.

which "did not grow up...under the action of unconscious forces operating silently from age to age, but trace their origin to the teaching of great religious innovators, who...deliberately departed from the traditions of the past."[46] To be modern, for such thinkers, was to hold religion as an object of belief, while inheriting one's religion from the ethnic past remained the provenance of premodern "savages," Orientals, Catholics, or Jews.

On the other hand, social theorists critical of the Enlightenment, from both the left and the right, tended to valorize religion precisely insofar as it belonged to Smith's "one whole of social custom." Conservative Romantics such as Maistre repudiated the association of religion with personal faith and instead sacralized the pull of collective heritage upon the individual. Left-wing critics of industrial society from Comte to Durkheim, meanwhile, would argue that religion represented a force by which subjects developed some sense of solidarity with a larger social body. (The difference between these two camps was understandably lost on some, especially around the time of the Second World War; as the French philosopher Raymond Aron reportedly remarked to Léon Brunschvicg during the 1930s, "Nuremberg is religion according to Durkheim, society adoring itself."[47])

In recent years, a number of commentators have set about sketching this political history of the concept of religion. In particular, Saba Mahmood, Webb Keane, and others have illuminated the deep links between modern liberal individualism and the construction of religion as belief. Classical liberal values such as individual autonomy and the private–public distinction, they argue, not only took shape within the milieu of British Dissent but were also modeled upon a markedly Protestant understanding of religion as an affair of "inward sincerity" (John Locke).[48] For a figure like Locke, entering the modern political sphere depends upon being religious in a particular way—being able to arrive at firm convictions

---

[46] Ibid., 1. See Christopher Herbert, *Culture and Anomie: Ethnographic Imagination in the Nineteenth Century* (Chicago, IL: U of Chicago P, 1991), 64–5; Evans-Pritchard, 52–3.

[47] Quoted in Pecora, 115.

[48] John Locke, *Two Treatises of Government and a Letter Concerning Toleration*, ed. Ian Shapiro (New Haven, CT: Yale UP, 2003), 232. For versions of this narrative, see Mahmood, "Secularism, Hermeneutics, and Empire: The Politics of Islamic Reformation," *Public Culture* 18 (2006): 323–47; Webb Keane, *Christian Moderns: Freedom and Fetish in the Mission Encounter* (Berkeley, CA: U of California P, 2007), 1–25; Asad, *Genealogies of Religion: Discipline and Reasons of Power in Christianity and Islam* (Baltimore, MD: Johns Hopkins UP, 1993), 28, 40–3. For historical background, see Ingrid Creppell, *Toleration and Identity: Foundations in Early Modern Thought* (London, UK: Routledge, 2003); Jeremy Waldron, *God, Locke, and Equality: Christian Foundations in Locke's Political Thought* (New York, NY: Cambridge UP, 2002).

through inward reflection—which is why he famously refuses to extend religious toleration to Catholics, who perform rituals instead of believing, or to atheists, who do not believe in any higher authority. This view of religion would become a persistent motif across different strains of eighteenth-and nineteenth-century liberal thought, from Idealism to utilitarianism.[49] In Immanuel Kant's *Religion within the Limits of Reason Alone* (1793), religion embodies a private moral reason which, "since it is based upon pure moral faith... has no public status."[50] For Kant, one effect of *Aufklärung* will be the gradual emancipation of religion "from all empirical determining grounds and from all statutes which rest on history," until "at last the pure religion of reason will rule over all."[51] Published a year later, the first part of Thomas Paine's *The Age of Reason* (1794) similarly uses religion as a term of art for the universal moral faculty that each individual possesses and that the state must respect. "The belief of a God and the practice of moral truth," Paine argues, cannot be meddled with by the state, since it is only by "let[ting] every man follow, as he has a right to do, the religion and the worship he prefers," that religion will be "rid of redundancies" and revert to the "universal religion... as man believed at first."[52] John Stuart Mill's *On Liberty* (1859), although far more wary toward Christianity specifically, nevertheless makes religion its paradigm for the sort of conviction that must withstand constant testing against competing views in order to become authentic. Only when individuals are obliged to defend their beliefs before others, Mill writes, do these beliefs have their "full effect on the character," animating "the inner life of the human being" and becoming a "living belief which regulates conduct."[53]

As influential as critics like Mahmood and Keane have been, however, their accounts remain curiously silent on the ways in which liberalism

---

[49] As Lauren Goodlad notes, the evolving tradition called liberalism has meant a number of things in different contexts: "a theory of progress, freedom, equality, or tolerance; a universalizing perspective; a cosmopolitan ethics; a procedural ethics rooted in theories of democratic consent; or an ideological basis for globalizing capital and/or promoting (or rejecting) imperial pursuits." "Liberalism and Literature," in Juliet John (ed.), *The Oxford Handbook of Victorian Literary Culture* (New York, NY: Oxford UP, 2016), 105.

[50] Immanuel Kant, *Religion Within the Limits of Reason Alone*, trans. Theodore M. Greene and Hoyt H. Hudson (1793; New York, NY: Harper, 1960), 115.

[51] Ibid., 112.

[52] Thomas Paine, *The Age of Reason* (1794–1807; Amherst, NY: Prometheus, 1984), 62, 70.

[53] John Stuart Mill, *On Liberty* (London, UK: Parker, 1859), 73, 75. Timothy Larsen has shown how there was something of a revolving door connecting the evangelical churches to the Secularist and Freethought movements during the 1830s–60s because both camps tended to share basic ethical terms, particularly an emphasis upon sincere conviction. See *Crisis of Doubt* (New York, NY: Oxford UP, 2006).

since Locke has developed an interest in *non*-voluntaristic concepts of religion. In their determination to demystify a liberal self that normativizes Protestant belief as the lodestone of political authenticity, they pass over the fact that, by the mid-Victorian years, affirming religion's rootedness in cultural or racial identity had become the preoccupation not just of Romantic authoritarians but also of writers wedded to traditional liberal ideals of self-cultivation, disinterestedness, and cosmopolitanism. George Eliot, for example, wrote two major narrative works—*The Spanish Gypsy* (1867) and *Daniel Deronda* (1876)—that derived religion's power from a people's collective memory. Matthew Arnold would paint the different religions of the world not as rival doctrines but rather as distinct racial inheritances that could be incorporated by a cosmopolitan self. Walter Pater's essays on Greek mythology and his historical novel, *Marius the Epicurean* (1885), portrayed religion as a vital resource for self-cultivation insofar as it represented a fabric of "usages and sentiment rather than of facts and belief."[54] The folklorist and popular reviewer Andrew Lang valorized the unconscious survivals of primitive religion as things that gave modern literature a special eclecticism and allowed contemporary readers to cultivate a taste that blended high and low, intellect and sensibility.

Nor was this phenomenon a strange Victorian outlier. On the contrary, notes Wendy Brown, treating "ethnicity, race, religion, and culture" as "interchangeable" categories has become a standard liberal move in the age of multiculturalism.[55] Two decades ago, David Hollinger noted how odd it is that liberal governance, which was invented largely to solve the problem of sectarian struggle, now finds itself focused on managing group identities instead.[56] Brown, however, shows how "personalizing" differences and "culturalizing" them have effectively become parallel strategies by which multicultural liberalism construes differences as supplements to individuality.[57] Treating religion or race or culture as things that individuals choose and treating them as things that precede choice,

---

[54] *The Works of Walter Pater* (8 vols.; London, UK: Macmillan, 1900–1), 2: 8.

[55] Wendy Brown, *Regulating Aversion: Tolerance in the Age of Identity and Empire* (Princeton, NJ: Princeton UP, 2006), 19; see 19–24.

[56] David A. Hollinger, *Postethnic America: Beyond Multiculturalism* (New York, NY: HarperCollins, 1995), 120–1. Cf. Kwame Anthony Appiah, "Identity, Authenticity, Survival: Multicultural Societies and Social Reproduction," in Amy Gutmann (ed.), *Multiculturalism: Examining the Politics of Recognition* (Princeton, NJ: Princeton UP, 1994), 149–50.

[57] W. Brown, 15. For example, Brown shows how in nineteenth-century France treating Jews as members of a race, rather than as holders of a creed, had the effect of compartmentalizing Jewishness as something that would not compromise allegiance to the Third Republic (50–8).

she argues, *both* allow the state to separate them from the individuals who are subject to its power.

Cultivating Belief does not attempt a comprehensive genealogy of this shift. It does, however, argue that Victorian writers like Arnold and Eliot offer a useful case for examining why liberal writers might wish to align religion with ethnic identity instead of with private belief, one that speaks to our contemporary moment in surprising ways. The past decade has seen a number of critics explore how liberal writers beginning in the late-Victorian period discovered uses for the inherited, the embodied, and the particular.[58] None, however, has asked how this turn entailed a revision of the paradigmatic figure of the religious believer in the British liberal imagination. What would a liberal writer find attractive in the image of a religious subject comprised of commitments it did not choose? How did that image open up a deeper rethinking of liberal agency, along with a host of related concepts, such as the private–public division, the ethics of sincerity, or the significance of personal change and transformation?

My specific historical argument is that, by relocating religion within the sphere of ethnicity, these Victorian writers were trying to conceptualize an alternative to the austerity and abstraction of classical Protestant liberalism. In reaction to the rising clout of a Dissenting middle-class liberalism that valorized individual belief and what Arnold called "doing as one likes," they sketched out an aesthetic liberalism that was grounded in a practice of balancing multiple non-chosen inheritances.[59] As they saw it, the self that could keep its contradictory pasts in play would develop a complex individuality, while the self that insisted upon selecting its own commitments would over time become impoverished and narrowed.

---

[58] For liberal turns toward embodiment in Victorian literature, see Amanda Anderson, *The Powers of Distance* (Princeton, NJ: Princeton UP, 2001); Daniel G. Williams, *Ethnicity and Cultural Authority: From Arnold to DuBois* (Edinburgh, UK: Edinburgh UP, 2006); Elaine Hadley, *Living Liberalism: Practical Citizenship in Mid-Victorian Britain* (Chicago, IL: U of Chicago P, 2010), 13–20; Regenia Gagnier, *Individualism, Decadence, and Globalization: On the Relationship of Part to Whole, 1859–1920* (London, UK: Palgrave, 2012). On the natural sciences as an influence upon such thinking, see Douglas Mao, *Fateful Beauty: Aesthetic Environments, Juvenile Development, and Literature 1860–1960* (Princeton, NJ: Princeton UP, 2010) and Kathleen Frederickson, *The Ploy of Instinct: Victorian Sciences of Nature and Sexuality in Liberal Governance* (New York, NJ: Fordham UP, 2014). On liberal turns toward collectivity in the domain of political theory, see Michael Freeden, *The New Liberalism: An Ideology of Social Reform* (New York, NY: Cambridge UP, 1978); Stephen Collini, *Liberalism and Sociology* (New York, NY: Cambridge UP, 1979); Nancy L. Rosenblum, *Another Liberalism: Romanticism and the Reconstruction of Liberal Thought* (Cambridge, MA: Harvard UP, 1987).

[59] *The Complete Prose Works of Matthew Arnold*, ed. R. H. Super (11 vols.; Ann Arbor, MI: U of Michigan P, 1960–77), 5:115.

Their primary model was the German aesthetic ideal of many-sidedness (*Vielseitigkeit*), which proposed that the human personality was a multi-faceted thing whose various drives needed to be brought into some kind of harmony.[60] In his *Ideen zu einem Versuch, die Gränzen der Wirksamkeit des Staats zu bestimmen* (1791–92)—translated for the Victorians as *The Sphere and Duties of Government* (1854)—Wilhelm von Humboldt argued that "the true end of Man ... is the highest and most harmonious development of his powers to a complete and consistent whole," while Friedrich Schiller's *On the Aesthetic Education of Man* (1794) exhorted readers to gather their different energies into a harmony that he termed *Spiel*.[61] In England, Mill would draw upon such figures to argue that a willingness to countenance myriad "modes of life" and "varieties of character" could protect individuals from the homogenizing effects of mass culture.[62]

Yet where Mill was essentially using the idea of many-sidedness to buttress a familiar liberal argument for free discussion,[63] Eliot and Arnold imagined the different "sides" that needed to be harmonized not as competing opinions but rather as different strains of racial character. In *Culture and Anarchy* (1869) and *The Study of Celtic Literature* (1867), for example, Arnold describes modernity as the heir to a number of racial energies that can neither be denied nor be reconciled but must instead be played off against each other aesthetically:

> So long as we are blindly and ignorantly rolled about by the forces of our nature, their contradiction baffles us and lames us; so soon as we have clearly discerned what they are, and begun to apply to them a law of measure, control, and guidance, they may be made to work for our good and to carry

---

[60] Good overviews of this cluster of concepts and their pathway from German philosophy into Victorian thought can be found in J. W. Burrow's introduction to Wilhelm von Humboldt, *The Limits of State Action*, ed. and trans. Burrow (New York, NY: Cambridge UP, 1969), vii–xliii; Burrow, *Whigs and Liberals: Continuity and Change in English Political Thought* (New York, NY: Oxford UP, 1988), 77–100; David Wayne Thomas, *Cultivating Victorians: Liberal Culture and the Aesthetic* (Philadelphia, PA: U of Pennsylvania P, 2004), 3–48; Linda Dowling, *Hellenism and Homosexuality in Victorian Oxford* (Ithaca, NY: Cornell UP, 1994); Tobias Boes, *Formative Fictions: Nationalism, Cosmopolitanism, and the Bildungsroman* (Ithaca, NY: Cornell UP, 2012), 46–53.

[61] Wilhelm Von Humboldt, *The Sphere and Duties of Government*, trans. Joseph Coulthard (London, UK: John Chapman, 1854), 11.

[62] Mill, 122, 102.

[63] For Mill, many-sidedness strengthens individuality by obliging individuals to decide and choose constantly, a process that he describes in a familiar liberal language of decision and ownership: "The human faculties of perception, judgment, discriminative feeling, mental activity, and even moral preference, are exercised only in making a choice," while "[h]e who does anything because it is the custom ... gains no practice either in discerning or in desiring what is best" (105).

us forward. Then we may have the good of our German part, the good of our
Latin part, the good of our Celtic part . . .[64]

In an essay on Victorian theories of pedagogy, Sarah Winter has argued
that early Victorian liberals like Harriet Martineau and James Mill saw
ethnographic knowledge of foreign cultures as something that could build
up a many-sided character.[65] This passage sees Arnold turn that move on
its head by venturing that we might achieve the same end by reflectively
grasping our own inscription within multiple historical legacies. In this
respect he is exploiting an ambiguity that David Wayne Thomas sees as
endemic to the foundational liberal ideal of self-cultivation: the fact that
"cultivation" can be figured as either an active process or a passive one. To
cultivate the personality might be an act of deliberate self-help, a prin-
cipled jettisoning of everything that does not agree with our own desires.
But it might also entail nurturing an openness to influences that work on
us quite apart from choice. "[W]e can easily privilege either agency or
passivity in imagining this figure of cultivation. Will we envision Victorians as cultivating or cultivated?"[66] The reason why so many Victorian
liberals found themselves drawn to the idea of many-sidedness, according
to Thomas, is that, in the wake of the 1848 revolutions and the Second
Reform Bill, when "the revolutionary dimensions of romantic agency
became incendiary in a way that was not congenial" and "the most
pressing concern for the dominant middle-class culture was no longer
how to valorize . . . agency but how to cultivate its forms along specific
lines among plebians," many-sidedness seemed to reinvent liberal individualism as a practice of "modesty" that would "bracket one's own
viewpoint to a profound extent."[67]

Applied to religion, this way of thinking transformed that term from a
byword for individual sincerity into the epitome of all those strong,
narrow commitments whose very intransigence, paradoxically, played a
crucial role in giving the self a tolerant complexity. Eliot's *Impressions of
Theophrastus Such* (1878), for example, takes Judaism as the model of a
religion that enlarges the liberal personality precisely because it brings with
it a whole history of involuntary inheritance and memory:

> An individual man, to be harmoniously great, must belong to a nation of this
> order, if not in actual existence yet existing in the past, in memory, as a
> departed, invisible, beloved ideal, once a reality, and perhaps to be restored.

---

[64] Arnold, 3: 383.
[65] Sarah Winter, "Mental Culture: Liberal Pedagogy and the Emergence of Ethnographic Knowledge," *Victorian Studies* 41.3 (1998): 427–54.
[66] Thomas, 5.   [67] Ibid., xiv, 31.

A common humanity is not yet enough to feed the rich blood of various activity which makes a complete man.[68]

According to Eliot, the traditional narratives and memories built into Judaism feed a "rich blood of various activity" by creating, as it were, a dissonance between our rational selves and our inherited instincts. Realizing that we contain such layers obliges us to appreciate that humanity is a multiform thing, and feeds a cosmopolitan consciousness by reminding us that we are located within a wider world of differing histories and viewpoints. By the same token, however, religion becomes a kind of aporia that constantly reminds many-sided liberalism of its own potential intolerance. It represents that which many-sidedness needs to incorporate in order to be what it claims to be, but also something that fights against many-sidedness from the inside, and therefore a mirror-image of what it ultimately fears to become: a totalizing and exclusionary set of values in its own right. Arnold's essays, for instance, tag humankind's religious impulse as "Hebraism," a historical legacy of the Semitic peoples that can contribute to human development if it is balanced against the Greek genius for art and knowledge, the Celtic genius for beauty and sentiment, and so on. At the same time, Hebraism comes to represent for Arnold not just one side of human life but also an *ideal* of one-sidedness that positively rejects pluralism. In this way, as I show in Chapter 2, Hebraism reveals many-sidedness itself to have a highly particular and often exclusionary sense of what can contribute to free play. Arnold's doctrine of many-sidedness aspires to define a capacious framework of values that can include narrower ones, but as a result tends to ossify into yet another oppositional stance.

Alongside this political paradox, we might also list an ethical one: the fact that many-sidedness was an anti-ascetic ethos that often behaved like a species of asceticism. Ostensibly Arnold and Eliot were disavowing the Protestant valorization of individual belief—the "moment of choice or decision," which, in Lionel Gossman's words, is "always, by definition, exclusive and limiting"—because it reproduced the sacrificial logic of asceticism.[69] As Pater puts it, attacking Victorian Dissent by way of second-century monasticism, "the ideal of asceticism represents moral effort as essentially a sacrifice, the sacrifice of one part of human nature to another, that it may live that more completely in what survives of it; while the ideal of culture represents it as a harmonious development of all

---

[68] George Eliot, *Impressions of Theophrastus Such*, ed. Nancy Henry (1878; London, UK: Pickering, 1994), 147.

[69] Lionel Gossman, "Philhellenism and Antisemitism: Matthew Arnold and his German Models," *Comparative Literature* 46.1 (1994): 25.

the parts of human nature, in just proportion to each other."[70] The reality, however, is that many-sidedness quite easily becomes ascetic in its refusal to say no to any facet of experience. Many-sidedness frames the Kantian gesture of declaring independence from the past as profoundly impoverishing, and asserts instead that the individual who remains open to all of his or her external determinants is more likely to cultivate a variegated individuality. In J. W. Burrow's words, the preservation of "the free, self-determining, self-conscious moral agent which was an intrinsic part of the ideals of late eighteenth-century German humanism" involved "an endless endeavour to reconcile a coherent individuality with the utmost receptivity to the most diverse experience, an acceptance of an eternal tension between the need to be uniquely and harmoniously oneself and the duty to assimilate as much as possible of life's emotional and intellectual possibilities."[71] Eliot's *Deronda*, for instance, pictures a liberal openness to experience as requiring a "submissive expectancy" and a capacity for "difficult obedience."[72] Even more strikingly, the protagonist of Pater's *Marius* rejects Protestant asceticism for an aesthetic Anglo-Catholicism that can incorporate diverse elements of past culture but which also asks him to "surrender himself, in perfectly liberal inquiry about it, to anything that, as a matter of fact, attracted or impressed him strongly."[73]

At one level, the presence of this ethical paradox corroborates Jonathan Freedman's claim that British aestheticism partook of the very middle-class culture it protested against.[74] But it also brings us to the wider dialectic, described by Robert Pippin and others, between bourgeois and aesthetic liberalisms: on the one hand, a classical Protestant liberalism of abstract individuality, *laissez faire* freedom, and personal striving within the marketplace, and on the other hand a counter-liberalism that aims to check the former by emphasizing the free exploration of diverse cultural styles.[75] One is the liberalism of Locke, Kant, and Adam Smith, while the

---

[70] Pater, 3: 122.

[71] Burrow, "Introduction" to *Limits*, xvii, xviii. David Russell, meanwhile, perceives a basic tension between self-cultivation imagined as a progressive teleology and self-cultivation as an actual practice of openness and self-development. For Russell, the image of a self steadily advancing toward higher and higher states is practically in conflict with any ideal of "diversity of inclination and experience," which resists the streamlining impulses of progressivist narratives. "Aesthetic Liberalism," *Victorian Studies* 56.1 (2013): 16.

[72] George Eliot, *Daniel Deronda*, ed. Graham Handley (1876; New York, NY: Oxford UP, 1986), 423, 466.

[73] Pater, 3: 110.

[74] See Jonathan Freedman, *Professions of Taste: Henry James, British Aestheticism and Commodity Culture* (Stanford, CA: Stanford UP, 1990), 47–78.

[75] Robert Pippin, *Modernity as a Philosophical Problem* (Cambridge, MA: Basil Blackwell, 1991); Amanda Anderson, "Victorian Studies and the Two Modernities," *Victorian*

other is the liberalism of aesthetic curiosity and personal eccentricity through which Baudelaire, Nietzsche, and their descendants in *fin de siécle* aestheticism and the twentieth-century avant-garde denounced the constraints of Victorian culture. As Amanda Anderson points out, however, aesthetic liberalism should be seen less as a wholesale break from bourgeois liberalism than as an indictment of it for not living up to its own goals. Both bourgeois and aesthetic liberalism "celebrate the freedom of autonomous self-authorization," but where the former seeks to attain this end through "the self-authorization of belief through the use of reason," the latter does it by pursuing heterogeneous styles of life.[76] More to the point, the aesthetic critique of bourgeois liberalism contained a deep irony, as did the solution that it proposed. Arnold and Eliot were at once faulting Protestant liberalism for narrowing the self's horizons and for encouraging forms of anarchic violence; in response, their version of many-sidedness located self-development in a rigorous form of restraint. According to Gregory Castle, such writers sought alternatives to the "socially pragmatic Bildung... of upward mobility, socialization, 'getting on'" in a practice of aesthetic cultivation that demanded what T. S. Eliot would call "continual self-sacrifice, a continual extinction of personality."[77]

Ultimately, I argue, Arnold, Pater, Eliot, and my other figures illustrate the difficulties inherent in rewriting the script of liberal selfhood in a way that transcends Protestant *askesis*. They remind us that the aesthetic injunction to escape the strictures of bourgeois morality by dallying with unfamiliar ideas or by embracing sensory pleasures has come to function as a moral obligation within what Thomas calls the "liberal heroics of self-management."[78] This is something we are prone to forget in a post-Reagan Anglosphere that has seen bourgeois and aesthetic liberalism become, respectively, the languages of left and right. What we call liberalism today describes itself the language of pleasurable self-expansion and the pursuit of multiple desires, often forgetting its kinship with the ethos of negative liberty and self-discipline that now goes by the name of conservatism. But in fact the aesthetic was conservative, strictly speaking, until quite recently—the edifice of old cultural capital that democratic individualism sought to overturn—and its conscription into the cause

---

Studies 47.2 (2005): 195–203; see also Matei Calinescu, *Five Faces of Modernity* (1977; Durham, NC: Duke UP, 1987).

[76] Anderson, "Two Modernities," 197.

[77] Gregory Castle, *Reading the Modernist Bildungsroman* (Gainesville, FL: UP of Florida, 2006), 71, 67. Along similar lines, Linda Dowling shows how the Victorian rhetoric of "Hellenism" performed double-duty as a language of manly civic virtue *and* a counter-ethos of passivity and receptivity (see 31, 35–6).

[78] Thomas, 33.

of liberal individualism was a distinctive innovation of late-Victorian liberalism. Meanwhile contemporary liberalism still trades in forms of self-discipline not unrelated to their Protestant prototypes, from the well-regimented hedonism of workout culture to the sense of moral duty that we attach to learning about other cultures. We imagine that all aestheticism is liberal and self-restraint reactionary, but the two are closer than we realize.

In tracing this Victorian revision of religion as a liberal category, *Cultivating Belief* has three main goals. The first is to develop a more complex sense of how Victorian liberals took up anthropological theories of racial or cultural difference. Since the 1980s, a number of major studies have explored how the Victorians constructed our modern notions of race, culture, and ethnicity.[79] Although their exact arguments vary, most of these studies agree that Victorian liberal writers used this nascent vocabulary to project a gulf between the reflective, creative metropolitan self and non-Western peoples supposedly imprisoned by custom and collectivity. As Wendy Brown paraphrases it, "'we' have culture while culture has 'them,' or we *have* culture while they *are* a culture."[80] *Cultivating Belief* argues that in fact concepts of embodied or inherited identity could be deployed toward a number of ends. The idea that humankind was divided between organically different peoples could be used to assert the superiority of European civilization, but also to dismantle the idea of a single civilizational narrative and situate Europe within a fractured and relativized world. Indeed, this very relativism could itself operate both as a moral critique of colonialism and as an isolationist assertion of English preeminence over the rest of humankind. In exploring these ambiguities within a study of literary liberalism, I am therefore taking up the question that Uday Mehta broached in *Liberalism and Empire* (1999) and which still vexes the politics of our own moment: When does liberalism want to assert sameness, when does it want to assert difference, and to what ends? When is saying that we are all intrinsically different a gesture of othering and subjugation, and when might it be an attempt to define grounds for mutual respect?[81] My guiding principle throughout will be that there is inevitably a gap between the construction of difference and the elaboration of some narrative about why that difference is meaningful. If race

---

[79] Herbert; Adam Kuper, *Culture: The Anthropologists' Account* (Cambridge, MA: Harvard, 1999), 5–9; Marc Manganaro, *Culture, 1922* (Princeton, NJ: Princeton UP, 2002); David Amigoni, *Colonies, Cults, and Evolution: Literature, Science, and Culture in Nineteenth-Century Writing* (New York, NY: Cambridge UP, 2010).

[80] W. Brown, 150–1.

[81] Uday Mehta, *Liberalism and Empire: A Study in Nineteenth-Century British Liberal Thought* (Chicago, IL: U of Chicago P, 1999).

and ethnicity are, axiomatically, social constructs, then they can be con-scripted into telling multiple stories and performing multiple kinds of work.

Second, *Cultivating Belief* offers a positive account of the multigeneric as a literary mode through which Victorian writers engaged the secular. Critics have, interestingly, tended to associate both theological and secu-larist projects in the Victorian period with a strong use of particular literary forms. Kirstie Blair and Charles LaPorte, for instance, have stressed how verse in particular became associated with the rigors of liturgy, ritual, and scripture.[82] A critical tradition going back to Lukács, meanwhile, has depicted the novel as a literary form through which nineteenth-century writers forged a sense of coherence in a world grown bereft of religious consolation.[83] In both cases, religion is read as a source of unified meaning and secularity as a condition of entropy that must turn to literary form for a substitute principle of order. This study ventures a different spatial metaphor for the secular—the play of differences, rather than the absence of fixed meaning—and thus a new formal figure for it as well: eclecticism. By experimenting with modes as various as the critical essay, the long poem, the *Bildungsroman*, and the folk tale anthology, writers like Eliot pictured a modern self whose relationship to the cultural past needed to be viewed through multiple optics. Eliot wrote a novel (*Daniel Deronda*) and a verse tragedy (*The Spanish Gypsy*) with roughly the same plot in order to dramatize two possible relationships to heritage; one in which race becomes a resource for personal vocation, and one in which it stifles vocation. Arnold's essays reflected upon the strife between church and state by staging a clash between critical and prophetic voices. And Andrew Lang regarded his fairy-tale anthologies as exercises in belated forms: collections of narrative relics that modern authors could take up and rearrange but never consciously invent. This impulse toward formal eclecticism was especially well suited to the predisciplinary landscape of the 1870s–90s, when literary criticism, political theory, and the social sciences, none of them specialized academic disciplines yet, appeared side by side in journals such as *Cornhill* and the *Fortnightly Review*. But it also

[82] Kirstie Blair, *Form and Faith in Victorian Poetry and Religion* (New York, NY: Oxford UP, 2012); Charles LaPorte, *Victorian Poets and the Changing Bible* (Charlottesville, VA: U of Virginia P, 2012).

[83] Georg Lukács, *Theory of the Novel* (1916/1920), trans. Anna Bostock (Cambridge, MA: MIT P, 1971), 62–4. For a recent study in this vein, see Norman Vance, *Bible and Novel: Narrative Authority and the Death of God* (New York, NY: Oxford UP, 2013). Lukács arguably also looms large over recent work that depicts the novel as the main literary form through which Victorian literary writers engaged social theory; see James Buzard's *Disorienting Fictions* (Princeton, NJ: Princeton UP, 2005) and Catherine Gallagher's *The Body Economic* (Princeton, NJ: Princeton UP, 2008).

performed what Freedman sees as a broader philosophical move of aestheticism: taking modernity's "experience of fragmentation, loss, and
disintegration" as a new site of moral commitment by embracing "hateful
contraries" and "cultural contradictions...without abandoning the
option of contradicting contradiction itself, without the loss of the nostalgia for a lost unity and the desire to project such a unity into the vision
of a future consummation."[84]

THE SECULAR IMAGINATION

The third and broadest goal of *Cultivating Belief* is to shift how secularization itself is discussed within Victorian studies. The term is a familiar
one for Victorianists, yet recent years have seen considerable debate as to
its precise meaning and usefulness. Half a century ago, critics regularly
painted Victorian literature as a record of declining religious faith. Georg
Lukács, for instance, described the nineteenth-century novel as "the epic
of a world that has been abandoned by God," while J. Hillis Miller argued
that Victorian writers increasingly experienced God as a "terrifying
absence."[85] More recent commentators, however, have questioned this
narrative on the grounds that religion, whether in the form of evangelical
revivals, Anglican politics, or spirit photography, clearly maintained considerable public importance during the period. As Frank Turner put it in a
1993 essay entitled "The Religious and the Secular in Victorian Britain,"
the longstanding "agreement among historians and literary scholars of
Victorian Britain that secularization or the movement from a culture in
which theological thinking, religious activity, and clergy were important
or dominant to one in which they were much less important explained
many of the most significant religious and intellectual developments of
the era" offered precious little insight into "the Victorian Nonconformist
and Roman Catholic Revivals, the political and spiritual resurgence of
the Church of England, the liveliness of religion in both Ireland and
Scotland, [or] the strong religious alignments in nineteenth-century

[84] Freedman, 9. See also Christine Bolus-Reichert, *The Age of Eclecticism: Literature and Culture in Britain, 1815–1885* (Columbus, OH: Ohio State UP, 2009).
[85] Lukács, 88; J. Hillis Miller, *The Disappearance of God: Five Nineteenth-Century Writers* (1963; Cambridge, MA: Harvard UP, 1991), 2. See also Richard J. Helmstadter and Bernard Lightman (eds.), *Victorian Faith in Crisis: Essays on Continuity and Change in Nineteenth-Century Religious Belief* (Stanford, CA: Stanford UP, 1990) and, more recently, George Levine, *Realism, Ethics and Secularism: Essays on Victorian Literature and Science* (New York, NY: Cambridge UP, 2008), 14.

British politics."[86] Similarly, in *Nineteenth-Century Religion and Literature* (2006), Mark Knight and Emma Mason contend that we should be "skeptical about the notion that a linear and inescapable erosion of faith was at an advanced stage by the second half of the nineteenth century," pointing to, among other things, "the multitude of writings" from the period "pertaining to the supernatural."[87]

This empirical critique of the secularization-narrative holds a deep appeal for critics whose own era has witnessed multiple resurgences of public religion, from the proliferation of syncretic spiritualities in global media to the rise of Islamic State. As Vincent Pecora reminds us, "the end of the cold war and the dissolution of its opposed stabilizing blocs of political hegemony" has "helped usher in a variety of global religious revivals, especially Islamist, Hindu nationalist, and Christian fundamentalist," obliging scholars to re-examine the narrative of secularization "in what Edward Said would have called contrapuntal terms, with one eye on Europe and America, and with the other on the formerly colonized worlds of the Middle East, India, Africa, and Asia."[88] Such a critique, however, is limited in that it tends to leave the category of religion itself outside the analysis. What exactly was this thing that was by some accounts waning and by others waxing? Was it always the same thing, or is the blanket term *religion* misleading? Indeed, one might note that, although Turner, Knight, and Mason all stress religion's ongoing importance to the Victorians, they use that word to mean very different things. For Turner, "religion" means matters of official church ritual and liturgy, while for Knight and Mason it refers to a broader fascination with the supernatural and the non-empirical.

As it happens, the most important work on secularization since Hillis Miller's day has investigated precisely this semantic slipperiness by replacing the quantitative question of decline with a nuanced analysis of how modernity has refashioned dominant constructions of religion. During the 1960s, social scientists such as Thomas Luckmann, Peter Berger, and Bryan Wilson began to describe secularization as the process whereby religion became disaggregated from politics and consigned to a special, limited sphere. As Berger put it, secularization may be conceptualized as "the process by which sectors of society and culture are removed from the

---

[86] Frank Turner, *Contesting Cultural Authority* (New York, NY: Cambridge UP, 1993), 3, 4.

[87] Mark Knight and Emma Mason, *Nineteenth-Century Religion and Literature: An Introduction* (New York, NY: Oxford UP, 2006), 152. See also Jude M. Nixon's introduction to *Victorian Religious Discourse: New Directions in Criticism*, ed. Jude M. Nixon (London, UK: Palgrave, 2004), 1–24.

[88] Pecora, 31, 28.

domination of religious institutions and symbols."[89] The paradox of
secularization thus defined is that it simultaneously marginalizes religion
by severing it from traditional channels of public power *and* opens up new
avenues of religious expression and experimentation. The sociologist José
Casanova, for instance, has criticized many scholars' tendency to conflate
differentiation with privatization by documenting how the compartmentalization of religion in modern societies has actually enabled new forms
of "public religion."[90]

Historians have employed this conception of secularization to reconstruct the changing role of religion in post-Restoration England, as the
Anglican Church shifted from representing the structural opposite of
Dissent to being just one more sect among many.[91] Cultural critics like
the anthropologist Talal Asad, meanwhile, have used it to explore how
such changes have reshaped popular views of religion by cordoning it off as
a special zone and then assigning political and cultural significance to its
boundaries. Secularization, as they wield the term, names not the loss but
instead "the discovery of religion" as a realm whose sequestration from the
"sphere of this-worldly individual freedoms, laws, and markets" helps
bring the latter into being.[92] One strain of this work has examined how
rubrics of religious pluralism and toleration are hardly neutral frameworks
but in fact prescribe, and enforce, distinctive understandings of religion
and its public role. The postcolonial anthropologist Saba Mahmood,
for instance, has traced how the secularization of Iraq under the
U.S. Coalition Provisional Authority involved teaching Iraqi Muslims to
understand religion as "an abstracted category of beliefs and doctrines
from which the individual believer stands apart to examine, compare, and

[89] Peter Berger, *The Sacred Canopy* (New York, NY: Anchor, 1967), 107. See also
Thomas Luckmann, *The Invisible Religion* (New York, NY: Macmillan, 1967); Bryan
Wilson, *Contemporary Transformations of Religion* (New York, NY: Oxford UP 1976);
David Martin, *A General Theory of Secularization* (New York, NY: Harper and Row, 1978);
Karel Dobbeleare, "Secularization: A Multi-Dimensional Concept," *Current Sociology* 29.2
(1981): 1–216. For surveys of secularization as a term in social and literary theory, see
Pecora, 1–66; Philip Gorski and Ateş Altınordu, "After Secularization?" *Annual Review of
Sociology* 34 (2008): 55–85.

[90] José Casanova, *Public Religions in the Modern World* (Chicago, IL: U of Chicago P,
1994), 4. For a parallel critique, see Christian Smith, *The Secular Revolution: Power,
Interests, and Conflict in the Secularization of American Public Life* (Berkeley, CA: U of
California P, 2003), 14–15. Casanova and Smith both loom large in Colin Jager's application
of secularization theory to Romantic literature; see 28–33.

[91] For example, see Richard Brown, *Church and State in Modern Britain, 1700–1850*
(London, UK: Routledge, 1991), 425–37.

[92] Timothy Fitzgerald, *The Ideology of Religious Studies* (New York, NY: Oxford UP,
2000), 5.

evaluate its various manifestations."[93] Another line of critics, exemplified by the philosopher Charles Taylor, has taken a phenomenological tack by focusing not on secularism as a political rubric, nor on secularization as a historical process, but rather on "secularity" as a new social imaginary that includes normative views as to what religion is and does. Taylor's mammoth *A Secular Age* (2007) describes Western modernity as a "nova" in which religion is reinscribed as one possible source of commitment among others, and in which even non-religious identities often depend profoundly on particular conceptions of what counts as religion.[94]

Cultivating Belief follows this way of framing the issue. I treat the Victorian period not as a moment of religious decline so much as one in which religion's nature and role were being contested in new ways by an ever-wider range of writers.[95] Instead of regarding secularity as a zero-sum question, I depict a field of competing Victorian secularities—different ways of imagining what religion was and what it did in relationship to the modern. Indeed, I trace a struggle between two secularities that diverged toward the end of the nineteenth century and continue to animate the liberal imagination. One is a classical Protestant secularity that valorizes personal privacy, freedom of conscience, and negative liberty. The other, which Arnold, Pater, and Eliot theorize, is an aesthetic secularity that emphasizes hybridity, heterogeneity, and the ability to keep multiple values in play. Both turn on different definitions of religion: for Protestant secularity, religion exemplifies the sort of sincere, personal commitment that defines the space of freedom against political authority, while for aesthetic secularity it epitomizes the many non-chosen affiliations that the self must balance. Both posit different visions of individualism: Protestant secularity pictures an individual who wins his or her identity through the

---

[93] Mahmood, "Secularism, Hermeneutics, and Empire," 341. For broader accounts of religious toleration as a secular political rubric, see W. Brown; David Fergusson, *Church, State, and Civil Society* (New York, NY: Cambridge UP, 2004); Ursula Henriques, *Religious Toleration in England, 1787–1833* (Toronto, Canada: U of Toronto P, 1961).

[94] Charles Taylor, *A Secular Age* (Cambridge, MA: Harvard UP, 2007), 1–22; Asad, *Formations*, 25. See also the many recent studies of "enchantment" as a kind of modern experience that is produced by the epistemologies of science or materialism. Alex Owen, *The Place of Enchantment: British Occultism and the Culture of the Modern* (Chicago, IL: U of Chicago P, 2007); Corinna Treitel, *A Science for the Soul* (Baltimore, MD: Johns Hopkins UP, 2004); Simon During, *Modern Enchantments: The Cultural Power of Secular Magic* (Cambridge, MA: Harvard UP, 2002); and, for an overview, Michael Saler, "Modernity and Enchantment: A Historiographical Review," *The American Historical Review* 3.3 (2006): 692–716.

[95] In focusing on anthropology as a discursive site where Victorian writers debated the nature of religion, *Cultivating Belief* has the same broad goals as Timothy Larsen's *The Slain God: Anthropologists and the Christian Faith* (New York, NY: Oxford UP, 2014), which frames the emerging anthropology of religion as a medium through which intellectuals theorized, often in surprisingly sympathetic terms, religion's place in the world.

cultivation of sincere convictions, as against the pressures of tradition and popular opinion, while aesthetic secularity valorizes one who can pull different inheritances into the orbit of a personal many-sidedness. Finally, these two secularities inhabit separate political genealogies. Protestant secularity harkens back to classical liberal figures such as Locke and Kant and extends up through Habermas's contemporary liberal theory. Aesthetic secularity, in contrast, emerges from revisions of liberalism under Humboldt and flowers in what Taylor calls the "immanent counter-Enlightenment" of Baudelaire and Nietzsche, which rejects both Christian otherworldliness and Enlightenment rationality for an ethos that refuses to "sacrifice the body, or ordinary desire, or the fulfillments of everyday life" in quest of some higher ideal.[96]

In drawing this dichotomy I have returned, of course, to the distinction between aesthetic and Protestant liberalisms that I made in the previous section. Yet once we think of them as two kinds of secularity, their entanglement opens up a new set of questions. Can we imagine a secularism beyond Protestantism? Can we detach religion from state power without relying upon the figure of the abstract individual defined largely by his or her beliefs? This is, I would argue, the deeper concern that drives the new secularity studies. By showing how the secular is not just a neutral space left behind by departed faith, but instead represents a specific formation built upon particular constructions of religion, critics such as Asad and Mahmood are asking how we might construct a secular imaginary that escapes the binaries of private-versus-public and individuality-versus-collectivity. As they see it, the warring camps that today dominate global debates about religion—liberalism and fundamentalism, modernity and traditionalism—share a common understanding of religion ultimately rooted in the Enlightenment and its imperial schemes. Their hope, in turn, is less to take one side or another than to find a better set of categories.[97] Odd as it may seem, this is the project in which Eliot and Arnold were engaged too. By entertaining non-voluntaristic modes of religion as resources for aesthetic individuality, they were seeking to eclipse the vision of the self and its possibilities shared by Calvinism and Utilitarianism, the Rev. Esau Hittal and Professor Thomas Huxley. In this sense their desires and vexations remain very much our own.

A final word should be said about my choice of authors. In some sense it is extremely old-fashioned to focus a book about Victorian literature and

---

[96] Taylor, 369, 640.

[97] Mahmood, for instance, seeks to imagine how Islam and feminism might be compatible without abstracting and de-gendering the subject into a free believer (*Politics of Piety*, 1–39).

secularization on intellectual prose writers. Such an approach was typical of Victorian studies in the 1960s, when critics sought to combat modernist caricatures of the Victorians as backward-looking prudes by portraying figures like Arnold and Eliot as brave intellectuals who confronted the biggest questions of modernity: industrialization, democratization, and the place of aesthetics. When this version of Victorian studies was upended by the New Historicism, so too was its approach to Victorian secularization. Just as New Historicism shifted our focus from intellectual prose writers toward that most populist of forms, the novel, so have more recent critics maintained that, if we look beyond the world of prose intellectuals, we discover that religion in fact led a far more varied life than the Matthew Arnolds of the age acknowledged. My goal in *Cultivating Belief* is not to reverse this widening of our perspective but rather to argue that, if we approach the secular in the way that Asad and others suggest, we rediscover the value of studying how such intellectuals talk about religion. If we treat the question of secularity as the question of how religion is redefined and circumscribed by modernity, then it becomes worthwhile to examine what literary intellectuals think religion is, what they think it is not, and what role they picture it playing in public life. We jettison a trickle-down narrative that sees intellectuals as experiencing the cold winds of disenchantment before the rest of us and instead discover them as complex theorists of their own moment.

My chapters trace an arc that runs from early Victorian anthropological theory through its appropriation by aesthetic liberals writing in the final third of the century. Following a theoretical and historical introduction, the opening chapter explores how British anthropological debates of the 1840s–60s made religion a key term for theorizing the relationship between civilization, colonialism, and human difference. Subsequent chapters then examine how concepts from those debates were taken up by aesthetic liberals in order to think about religion and political subjectivity in the domestic context.

My first chapter, "The Rubicon of Language: Max Müller, Evangelical Anthropology, and the History of True Religion," explores what it meant, politically and ethically, to identify religion with individual belief or with embodied identity during the mid-Victorian years. On the one hand, I describe a liberal and evangelical construction of religion as the common human capacity for spiritual interiority that validated missionary and colonial enterprises in Polynesia and India. On the other hand, I describe a conservative, reactionary model that interpreted religious differences as the expressions of fixed racial identities that education could not erase. Taking the Oxford philologist F. Max Müller as my primary case, I show how the former model identified religion and language as the twin enablers of self-cultivation. For Müller, language was "our Rubicon," the thing that separated human beings from animals as free, willful subjects. But I also tease out the subtle forms of determinism that were implicit in this model and which brought it closer to racialized constructions of religion. This was an ambiguity that the subsequent authors in this study would exploit as they envisioned alternative possible relationships between religion, individualism, and racial or cultural identity.

My subsequent chapters trace how major liberal writers writing in the final third of the century broke with Müller by taking up explicitly deterministic constructions of religion in order to rethink individuality as a kind of many-sidedness. Chapter 2, "Arnoldian Secularism: Race and Political Theology from *Celtic Literature* to *Literature and Dogma*," argues that Matthew Arnold's major essays established a liberal counter-paradigm for theorizing religion, race, and self-cultivation. Specifically, Arnold argued that the race-based understandings of religion opposed by Müller could lay a better groundwork for individualism. In texts such as *Culture and Anarchy* (1869) Arnold identifies the various energies of human civilization with the characters of different "races." His point in doing so is to model civilization itself as a necessarily many-sided project that must balance these different energies rather than privilege one over the other. But in fact, I argue, religion comes to assume an outsized role in Arnold's thinking, epitomizing all of those narrow values that many-sided civilization must internalize precisely because they oppose it. Religion becomes a complex other for Arnoldian secularism, both its key building block and its competitor as a way of organizing human life.

Chapter 3, "History's Second-Hand Bookshop: Self-Cultivation and Scripturality in George Eliot's *Daniel Deronda* and *The Spanish Gyspy*," shows how George Eliot followed Arnold in envisioning ethnic religion as a resource for secular individualism. But it also contends that Eliot thought more deeply than Arnold about what consequences this alternative secularism held for a key liberal fetish: reading. Comparing Eliot's *Daniel Deronda* (1876) with her 1868 verse drama, *The Spanish Gypsy*, I argue that both texts stage a character's recuperation of ethnic heritage— Jewish and Gypsy, respectively—but that only in *Deronda* does this recuperation successfully yield a many-sided individuality. The difference, Eliot suggests, is that the Gypsies are an ethnic group that lacks any religious tradition, while Judaism's scriptural dimension allows Daniel to fashion an idiosyncratic relationship to its history. Religion, for Eliot, is the best conduit through which race can feed individuality because it sees race come in the form of an interpretable text. However, this valorization of scripture as the site at which one personalizes one's relationship to tradition also jars with Eliot's longstanding wariness toward Protestant private interpretation. Like many self-proclaimed distant or descriptive readers in literary studies today, Eliot is a liberal who mistrusts absorptive private reading, yet who still wants to make reading central to ethical subjectivity. In *Daniel Deronda*, I suggest, she tries to get around this impasse by evaluating her characters, not according to how well they interpret texts, but by how they relate to books as material metonyms of the past.

Chapter 4, "A More Liberal Surrender: Aestheticism, Asceticism, and Walter Pater's Erotics of Conversion" traces how Walter Pater translated the political paradoxes of Arnoldian secularism into an ethical paradox of asceticism. Much as Arnold had struggled to define a many-sided selfhood against the Dissenting ethos of pursuing only "one thing needful," Pater imagines a many-sided religiosity that eschews the narrowness of Protest-ant asceticism. Also like Arnold, however, he finds that many-sidedness entails its own sorts of self-sacrifice. In his 1885 historical novel, *Marius the Epicurean*, Pater tells the story of a second-century Roman who embraces the new religion of Christianity because he sees in it the summation of a pagan past that has shaped his own consciousness. Thus, *Marius* becomes a kind of conversion novel against conversion, one that juxtaposes an ascetic, conversionist Christianity with a religion that embraces all the contradictory inheritances of history. Yet in his very repudiation of ascetic sacrifice, Marius also becomes the sacrificial victim of his own aesthetic openness, since it renders him the passive spectator of historical flux.

Chapter 5, "National Supernaturalism: Andrew Lang, World Litera-ture, and the Limits of Eclecticism" explores how the late-Victorian folklorist and belletrist Andrew Lang used Arnold's concept of many-sidedness to construct a new map of world literature—one that rejected racialized readings of literature, but that also taught W. B. Yeats and other Irish modernists how to recuperate the old moves of literary nationalism through a kind of globalized primitivism. Although Lang had been Matthew Arnold's student at Oxford, his seminal anthropological treatises and fairy-tale anthologies insisted that many-sidedness could best be cultivated not by sampling "the best which has been thought and said in the world" but rather by omnivorously embracing the superstitious fantasies preserved in ancient folk tales and pop adventure novels. While Lang's populist primitivism was meant to eschew race-based readings of literary history, however, in practice it also recuperated a crypto-Romantic view of folklores as talismans of an endangered authenticity out of place in the modern world. This buried essentialist rhetoric ultimately alienated

Lang from the mainstream of anthropology, especially when he began to argue that folk tales preserved actual evidence of paranormal phenomena. But the curious interchangeability of the primitive and the supernatural in Lang's work would also have a powerful influence on the young Yeats, who learned, in effect, that presenting the national as the primitive and the primitive as the occult allowed one to advertise Irish literature as being simultaneously local and cosmopolitan. In Lang's work, for better or for worse, occult religion becomes a rubric through which ethnic heritage can be liquidated into spiritual currency that anyone can use.

1

The Rubicon of Language

Max Müller, Evangelical Anthropology, and the History of True Religion

This chapter explores the politics of defining religion as belief or as race within mid-Victorian anthropology, mapping out a constellation of positions that Arnold, Eliot, and the subsequent authors in this study would ultimately reinvent. If, as many critics have argued, British liberals following Locke tended to construct religion as a mode of inward conviction, what did this move look like during those years between the Slavery Abolition Act of 1833 and the anti-colonial uprisings in India (1857) and Jamaica (1865)? To get at this question, I turn toward the so-called monogenesis-polygenesis controversy, an extended argument over the nature of race, religion, and imperialism that helped define British anthropology in the decades before its academic institutionalization.[1] On one side of this debate, a party known as the monogenists, linked both to the abolitionist movement and to various missionary societies, used the emerging tools of anthropology to defend the idea that all human beings shared a common origin and moral status. On the other side, a school of polygenists proposed that Africans, Europeans, and Polynesians all represented separate species and were therefore not equally answerable to the values of Western liberalism and Christianity. Politically, the monogenesis-polygenesis debates concerned how Great Britain ought to treat its colonized peoples. What exactly were the anthropological commonalities between white English subjects and black Africans, Polynesians,

---

[1] For major studies, see J. W. Burrow, "Evolution and Anthropology in the 1860's: The Anthropological Society of London, 1863–71," *Victorian Studies* 7.2 (1963): 137–54, and *Evolution and Society* (New York, NY: Cambridge UP, 1966), 101–36; Douglas A. Lorimer, *Colour, Class, and the Victorians: English Attitudes to the Negro in the Mid-Nineteenth Century* (Leicester, UK: Leicester UP, 1978), 131–61; George Stocking, *Victorian Anthropology* (New York, NY: Free P, 1987), 239–73; and Colin Kidd, *The Forging of Races: Race and Scripture in the Protestant Atlantic World, 1600–2000* (New York, NY: Cambridge UP, 2006), 121–67.

or (for that matter) the Irish—and how did those facts translate into norms of imperial governance? Disciplinarily, the debates asked what kind of object of study humankind was and what tools were required to examine it. Was "the human" best conceptualized as a certain quality of consciousness that could be investigated by linguists and moral philosophers, or was it a matter of biology, and therefore the domain of the comparative anatomist?

Perhaps most importantly, the monogenesis-polygenesis dispute represented a contest between two competing visions of religion and how it defined modern subjectivity. The monogenists were comprised of a mixture of radical Protestants and more secular liberals who, whatever their theological differences, understood religion as an innate capacity for spiritual interiority that made self-cultivation possible. The universality of religion, in their view, provided evidence both of humankind's shared origins and of each individual's ability to be educated into a thinking and reflective subject. For this reason it formed the lynchpin not just of the missionary enterprise but also of Britain's secular civilizing project worldwide. The polygenists, by contrast, rejected this faith in human universality by insisting that religion was merely an epiphenomenon of the deep, embodied differences that divided various peoples from each other. If the monogenists regarded human nature as characterized by spiritual agency and a capacity for growth, the polygenists (like Herder and Maistre in the eighteenth century) saw it as rooted in local ways of being that no universal values could overcome. Their camp thus attracted proponents of a more ruthless version of imperialism, one not cloaked in the rhetoric of missionary uplift or liberal humanism.

Cultivating Belief is ultimately the story of how this well-balanced ideological conflict was upset, as late-Victorian writers such as Matthew Arnold and George Eliot began to view race and religion as offering very similar resources to the cultivated self. This chapter sets out the monogenesis-polygenesis debates as the background against which that turn occurred, but also suggests that we can see such alternative possibilities already latent within the debates themselves. In particular, I argue, the work of the Oxford linguist F. Max Müller reveals how the monogenists' picture of a religious subject able to grow toward universal values could in fact harbor a hidden determinism. Müller's emphasis upon language as the chief medium of human spiritual development tended to enmesh human nature within a set of gradual, organic processes that subtly robbed it of agency. Conversely, the work of Sir Richard Burton—polygenist, sexologist, flaunter of liberal pieties—reveals how racial determinism could be parlayed into a surprising openness toward different ways of being. For Burton, the idea that different religions were racially embodied rather than freely chosen inspired an eccentric regime of self-cultivation that was willing to try on a range of different styles of life.

Finally, I want to suggest, we see an alternative liberal use for embodied religion in the new evolutionary anthropology that emerged during the 1860s. For in fact evolutionism, in the hands of E. B. Tylor and others, had a curious way of combining the values of self-cultivation and universalism with an emphasis upon involuntary inheritance. Commentators sometimes portray evolutionary anthropology (under the label of "social Darwinism") as the thing that opened the door to scientific racism on the eve of the twentieth century.[2] In reality, evolution was designed to refute polygenesis by showing that all human beings took part in the same Whiggish story of civilizational advancement. Nevertheless, evolution could also be strangely deterministic in its own right, insofar as the progress of "culture, or civilization," as imagined by Tylor, was an unconscious process over which no single human agent exercised control.[3]

In telling this story, this chapter seeks to expand upon recent accounts of what John Lardas Modern calls "evangelical secularism," or the complex intersection between nineteenth-century Protestant understandings of language and subjectivity and more secular political imaginaries, especially those that underpinned the social sciences.[4] While I agree with Modern and other critics that British evangelicalism bequeathed to secular liberalism certain notions of "immediate cognition, intentionality, and self-mastery," I also want to tease out certain illiberal possibilities lurking within the evangelical self as mapped out by missionary anthropology and linguistics.[5] Although I examine a number of characters, the central figure here is Müller, who began his public career in England as an ally of Prichard's monogenists and went on to become a fixture of British

---

[2] See, for example, Anne McClintock, *Imperial Leather: Race, Gender and Sexuality in the Colonial Contest* (New York, NY: Routledge, 1995), 44; Peter van der Veer, *Imperial Encounters: Religion and Modernity in India and Britain* (Princeton, NJ: Princeton UP, 2001), 134–57.

[3] E. B. Tylor, *Primitive Culture: Researches into the Development of Mythology, Philosophy, Religion, Language, Art, and Custom* (2 vols.; London, UK: John Murray, 1871), 1: 1.

[4] John Lardas Modern, *Secularism in Antebellum America* (Chicago, IL: U of Chicago P, 2011), 12. See also Boyd Hilton, *The Age of Atonement: The Influence of Evangelicalism on Social and Economic Thought, 1795–1865* (Oxford, UK: Clarendon P, 1988); Christopher Herbert, *Culture and Anomie: Ethnographic Imagination in the Nineteenth Century* (Chicago, IL: U of Chicago P, 1991); Callum Brown, *The Death of Christian Britain: Understanding Secularisation, 1800–2000* (New York, NY: Routledge, 2001), 1–169; Webb Keane, *Christian Moderns: Freedom and Fetish in the Mission Encounter* (Berkeley, CA: U of California P, 2007).

[5] Modern, 16.

intellectual life as Oxford's first Professor of Comparative Philology.[6] Müller's work combines a Dissenting emphasis on sincere "true religion" with liberal values of cultivated individualism and a profound aversion to race as an explanatory category. Within the arc of this study, he represents a sort of road not taken—someone who stood by a vision of religion as epitomizing the inner core of human spiritual agency, even as other writers who shared his politics began to imagine other possible relationships between religion, race, and liberal selfhood.

JAMES PRICHARD AND THE POLITICS OF MONOGENESIS

British anthropology in the decades before Darwin was largely preoccupied with the question of race. How intrinsic were the differences that appeared to separate one human group from another? Were they merely inflections of color and custom, or did they run deeper? To what extent did they represent obstacles to global projects of civilization and Christianization? Mid-Victorian writers seeking to answer such questions were able to draw upon two major lines of continental theory: Romantic historiography and comparative anatomy. Romantic race-theory, as we saw in the last chapter, took shape in the late eighteenth century as writers such as Johann Gottfried von Herder and Joseph de Maistre attempted to defend the value of local, idiosyncratic ways of life against the tyranny of the French Enlightenment. Although neither Herder nor Maistre made serious recourse to the idea of biologically inherited traits, both did give national character a quality of bodily determinacy by linking it to the peculiarities of the physical environment. Maistre, for example, wrote that "the same laws cannot suit different provinces which have different customs [and] live in opposite climates," while Herder insisted that each *Volk* was shaped by such factors as "the elevation or depression of a region, its nature and products, the food and drink men enjoy in it, the mode of life they pursue, the labors in which they are employed," and so on.[7]

---

[6] Stocking, *Victorian Anthropology*, 57. For overviews of Müller's work and career, see Nirad C. Chaudhuri, *Scholar Extraordinary: The Life of Professor the Rt. Honorable Friedrich Max Müller* (New York, NY: Oxford UP, 1974); Lourens P. van den Bosch, *Friedrich Max Müller: A Life Devoted to the Humanities* (Leiden, Netherlands: Brill, 2002); Jon Stone, "Introduction" to *The Essential Max Müller*, ed. Jon R. Stone (New York, NY: Macmillan, 2002), 1–23. For a review of scholarship, see Tomoko Masuzawa, "Our Master's Voice: F. Max Müller after a Hundred Years of Solitude," *Method and Theory in the Study of Religion* 15.4 (2003): 305–28.

[7] *The Works of Joseph de Maistre*, trans. Jack Lively (1965; New York, NY: Schocken, 1971), 100; Johann Gottfried Herder, *Reflections on the Philosophy of the History of Mankind* (1784–91), trans. Frank Manuel (Chicago, IL: U of Chicago P, 1968), 16.

By the early nineteenth century, the notion that humankind was subdivided into several organically unique groups—sometimes called nations, sometimes *Völker*, and increasingly *Rasse* or races—had gained wide popularity among German and French historians. The Roman historian Barthold Niebuhr, for example, described the conflict between racial families as a great "motor force" of world history, while Amédée Thierry portrayed the French Revolution as the outcome of a series of class antagonisms that were ultimately racial in origin.[8] But the field that would give Romantic notions of race the greatest intellectual legitimacy was the emerging discipline of comparative philology. In 1786 Sir William Jones, founder of the Asiatic Society of Bengal, announced his discovery of significant affinities between Sanskrit, the language of classical Hinduism, and European classical languages like Greek and Latin. To Jones's German readers, many of whom were steeped in Herder, his discovery suggested nothing less than the existence of an ancient Indo-European race that had migrated centuries ago from India into Europe, leaving traces of its blood and its language along the way. This narrative, most famously set forth in Karl Wilhelm Friedrich Schlegel's *On the Language and Wisdom of the Indians* (1808), would guide the next half-century of comparative philology, setting a research agenda for such figures as Wilhelm von Humboldt, Franz Bopp, Jakob Grimm, and Ernest Renan, while also having a more general influence upon neohumanist philosophers like G. W. F. Hegel and Friedrich Schelling.[9]

Although Indo-European philology would help make race a major keyword in European cultural theory, writers such as Schlegel could be remarkably unclear as to the term's concrete referent. Sometimes the word functioned as a synonym for blood or stock, while at other times it suggested something like a community of shared language or custom, a matter more of consciousness than of ancestry. For the most part, however, the major figures of German Romanticism were monogenists who held to the biblical notion that, whatever the means and media of their separation, all human groups were ultimately descended from a single original stock. Polygenesis, or the thesis that there existed permanent physical differences between various groups of people, would be theorized far less ambiguously by the discipline of comparative anatomy, which also emerged toward the end of the eighteenth century. In his seminal *Sketches*

[8] Robert J. C. Young, *Colonial Desire: Hybridity in Theory, Culture, and Race* (New York, NY: Routledge, 1995), 67, 75–6.

[9] See Raymond Schwab, *Oriental Renaissance: Europe's Rediscovery of India and the East, 1680–1880* (1950), trans. Gene Patterson-Black and Victor Reinking (New York, NY: Columbia UP, 1984), 11–336; Bruce Lincoln, *Theorizing Myth: Narrative, Ideology, and Scholarship* (Chicago, IL: U of Chicago P, 1999), 47–75; Tomoko Masuzawa, *The Invention of World Religions* (Chicago, IL: U of Chicago P, 2005), 147–78.

of the History of Man (1774), the Scottish lawyer Lord Kames proposed
that the physical and intellectual differences between Europeans, Africans,
and Asians "could not be explained by climate or other environmental
influences" but in fact had a deeper biological basis.[10] That same year,
Edward Long's widely read *History of Jamaica* (1774) went a step further
and ventured that, because the offspring of black Jamaicans and their
European masters could supposedly not produce viable offspring beyond
two generations, they should be regarded as "distinct species," as per the
French naturalist Buffon's definition of that term.[11]

Thanks to its avowed divergence from the biblical story of human
origins, polygenesis would remain a minority position in British thought
through much of the early nineteenth century. Nevertheless, the influence
of Kames and Long was sufficient to pressure writers of a humanitarian
persuasion to formulate new scientific defenses of biblical monogenesis.
By far the most significant of these was the Quaker physician James
Cowles Prichard, whose multivolume *Researches into the Physical History
of Mankind* (1813–47), along with popularizing works such as *The
Natural History of Man* (1843), argued that present day racial differences
were the effects of centuries of climatic and geographical influence. "All
mankind is the offspring of a single pair," Prichard wrote; but, as the
descendants of this pair had migrated into different regions, "each body
received modifications from the circumstances under which it existed, and
these modifications continued to accumulate as long as it continued
subject to the same conditions."[12] "The bodies reaching the torrid zone
would be deepened in colour, and thereby better adapted to bear the heat
of the sun; while such individuals as were born of lighter complexion
would not long survive the exposure"—and so on.[13] In Prichard's mind,
this process accounted both for the physical diversity of humankind and
for the differing degrees of civilization evident among contemporary
peoples. The first members of "the Adamite family," he wrote, were
"what we now term civilised": "tillers of the ground, who had a settled
habitat, and were guided by a systematic polity."[14] As Adam's descendants
had scattered, however, they gradually came to forget those basic elements
of civilization that had been humankind's possession from the beginning.

---

[10] Lorimer, 132.

[11] Ibid., 132–3; Nancy Stepan, *The Idea of Race in Science: Great Britain, 1800–1960*
(London, UK: Macmillan, 1982), 29.

[12] James Cowles Prichard, *The Natural History of Mankind; Inquiries into the Modifying
Influence of Physical and Moral Agencies on the Different Tribes of the Human Family*, ed.
Edwin Norris (1843; 2 vols.; London, UK: H. Baillière, 1855), xv–xvi.

[13] Ibid., xvi.   [14] Ibid., xv.

For Prichard, the stakes of this anthropological project were at once theological and political. By demonstrating that racial differences were largely superficial, he sought to corroborate the notion that all human beings had been created equally in God's image and thus possessed equal moral standing. "My attention was strongly excited to this inquiry," Prichard recalled, "by happening to hear the truth of the Mosaic records implicated in it, and denied, on the alleged impossibility of reconciling the history contained in them with the phaenomena of Nature, and particularly with the diversified characters of the several races of men."[15] The son of devout Bristol Quakers, Prichard had become an evangelical Anglican while studying medicine at Cambridge, and upon returning to his native city in 1808 he established a successful medical practice and became active in the temperance and anti-slavery movements.[16] His lengthy inquiries into the origins of race and ethnicity were above all, he explained, polemical—for, "if the Negro and the Australian are not our fellow-creatures and of one family with ourselves, but beings of an inferior order... [then] our relations to these tribes will appear to be not very different from those which might be imagined to subsist between us and a race of orangs."[17]

Over the next few decades Prichard would become the hub of an emerging coalition of scientists, Christian humanitarians, and political activists who all affirmed the basic tenets of mid-Victorian Whig liberalism: the universality of human nature, the freedom of the individual, and the steady progress of human civilization.[18] In 1837, four years after the British abolition of slavery, the evangelical Quaker Thomas Hodgkin and other abolitionists founded an Aborigines Protection Society (APS) in London with the goal of humanizing supposedly savage peoples before the British public through the dissemination of "authentic information concerning the[ir] character, habits and wants."[19] (The APS's motto, *ab uno sanguine*, or "from one blood," gave unmistakably Christological stakes to the question of human ancestry.[20]) Prichard was a member of the APS, and six years after its founding he and other members would establish a separate organization called the Ethnological Society of London

---

[15] James Cowles Prichard, *Researches into the Physical History of Mankind* (2 vols.; London, UK: John and Arthur Arch, 1813), 1: ii.
[16] See Stocking, "From Chronology to Ethnology," in Prichard, *Researches into the Physical History of Man*, ed. Stocking (Chicago, IL: U of Chicago P, 1973), xii–xxiv.
[17] Prichard, *Natural History*, 6.
[18] See J. W. Burrow, *Whigs and Liberals: Continuity and Change in English Political Thought* (New York, NY: Oxford UP, 1988).
[19] Quoted in Stocking, *Victorian Anthropology*, 242.   [20] Kidd, 152.

(ESL) in order to give sustained attention to certain scientific questions that the APS's agenda had raised.[21] The question of monogenesis, Prichard told the Society in an early address, was "particularly interesting to the philosopher and to men devoted to the pursuit of science," quite "independently of the claim of humanity and justice" which it entailed.[22] Nevertheless, as George Stocking and Douglas Lorimer have shown, there remained a significant overlap among the two societies, even if various individuals understood the stakes of defending human commonality somewhat differently.[23] Some ESL members took this commonality to be the special creation described in Genesis. Others, like Thomas Huxley and Francis Galton, saw it as a shared line of biological ancestry. Whether their humanism was evangelical or materialist, however, most ESL members agreed that ethnology had, in Galton's phrase, the "political value" of portraying other races "as our kinsmen, rather than as aliens."[24]

   In disciplinary terms, the most interesting move made by Prichard and the early ESL was to align their brand of ethnology with the field of comparative philology. For most of the 1830s and 1840s, papers read by Prichard, Hodgkin, and other ESL members at meetings of the British Association for the Advancement of Science (BAAS) had been placed under Section D, alongside papers on the life sciences. Prichard and his allies, however, protested this classification on the grounds that it implicitly privileged the polygenist understanding of race as a biological category.[25] Moreover, they were attracted to the way that the new comparative philology of Bopp and Schlegel described a primeval scattering of languages that was remarkably similar in outline to Genesis's story of Babel.[26] Prichard himself would venture onto philological terrain in a hefty treatise entitled *The Eastern Origin of the Celtic Nations* (1831), which sought to foster a more compassionate attitude toward Ireland by revealing the Irish to share with the English an Indo-European pedigree. At the outset of the volume, he proposed that the history of different racial groups could be settled in one of two ways: by "a survey of the natural history of the globe, and facts connected with … the multiplication and dispersion of species both of animals and plants," or by "an analysis of

---

[21] Stocking, *Victorian Anthropology*, 243–5.
[22] Quoted in Thomas Hodgkin, "Biographical Sketch of James Cowles Prichard," *The Edinburgh New Philosophical Journal* 47 (1849), 205. For more on the overlapping missions of the APS and the ESL, see Richard King, "Address to the Ethnological Society of London, Delivered at the Anniversary, 25th May 1844," *Journal of the Ethnological Society of London* 2 (1850): 9–16.
[23] Stocking, *Victorian Anthropology*, 251–3; Lorimer, 134–5.
[24] Quoted in Stocking, *Victorian Anthropology*, 252.   [25] Ibid., 245.
[26] See Burrow, *Evolution and Society*, 123.

languages, affording the means of comparing their component materials and ascertaining their affinities and diversities."[27] Although linguistic investigation, he admitted, could not definitively prove ancestry, it was preferable to physiological analysis because of its greater capacity to suggest shared origins. Thanks to the research of comparative philologists, the inhabitants of even the most remote Polynesian Islands were now known to possess a common ancestor in southeast Asia, and the Celtic peoples of Europe could be linked to the great Indo-European family that had migrated into Europe far back in remote antiquity.

Prichard's embrace of philology points toward what Webb Keane calls a distinct "semiotic ideology" animating the work of the Ethnological Society—a specific view of the relationship between words, agents, and non-human actors that united its evangelical, Anglican, and more secular liberal constituencies.[28] According to Keane, nineteenth-century Protestants and liberals alike tended to valorize religion and language as the twin bellwethers of human nature. Religion, within this formation, came to stand for humankind's special ability to freely accept or reject abstract propositions and found its most striking manifestation in the faculty of speech.[29] These interwoven capacities not only made all peoples fundamentally the same in their potential for spiritual growth, but also separated humankind, in Donovan Schaefer's phrase, from "the sticky, uneven, bestial textures of biology" and placed it upon "a flat plane in which all bodies were taken to be clones of the same free, linguistic, reasoning subject."[30]

This set of interrelated convictions can be found across the spectrum of Ethnological Society writers and allies. On one end, the evangelical Quaker Hodgkin would describe language as the key to "progressive cultivation" and thus definitive proof that a people could be civilized and Christianized.[31] On the other end, the liberal *Edinburgh Review* praised Prichard for "furnish[ing] a powerful argument" that "articulate language, relating not merely to objects of sense, but to our spiritual nature," has "every where existed from the earliest period of which we

---

[27] Prichard, *The Eastern Origin of the Celtic Nations: Proved by a Comparison of Their Dialects with the Sanskrit, Greek, Latin and Teutonic Languages* (London, UK: Sherwood, Gilbert, and Piper, and J. and A. Arch, 1831), 3.

[28] Keane, 2.

[29] Both Hilton and Modern argue that the sort of moderate evangelicals who comprised the ESL's base rejected a Utilitarian view of the mind as constituted by external impressions for a Scottish Common Sense account which "held the mind to be an active agent, endowed with various faculties and with certain intuitive knowledge" (Hilton, 165; see Modern, 22–4).

[30] Donovan Schaefer, *Religious Affects: Animality, Evolution, and Power* (Durham, NC: Duke UP, 2015), 45.

[31] Hodgkin, 210.

have any knowledge."[32] Similarly, a review essay in the *North American Review* insisted that the "inductive comparison of all the languages spoken by the various branches and tribes of the human race" stood second only to the Bible itself as a testament to humankind's common spiritual nature.[33] "Language and religion," the writer continued, "are the two poles of our consciousness, mutually presupposing each other," inasmuch as "that power of the mind which enables us to see the genus in the individual, the whole in the many, and to form a word by connecting a subject with a predicate, is the same which leads men to find God in the universe, and the universe in God."[34]

MAX MÜLLER, LANGUAGE, AND HUMAN SPIRITUAL AGENCY

Despite the pressure applied by Prichard and his allies, the position of ethnology within the BAAS remained largely unchanged through most of the 1840s. At the 1847 meeting, ESL members mounted another push to align ethnology with philology by recruiting two German scholars, Christian von Bunsen and Friedrich Max Müller, to deliver papers alongside Prichard. Bunsen, a gifted linguist and student of Niebuhr's, was serving as the Prussian ambassador to the Queen and represented something of an envoy of German philology in England; Müller, who had previously studied under Franz Bopp at Berlin and Eugène Burnouf at Paris, had become Bunsen's protégé after moving to England in 1846 to work on the East India Company's copy of the Rig-Veda.[35] At the meeting, Bunsen read a paper entitled "On the Results of the Recent Egyptian Researches in Reference to Asiatic and African Ethnology, and the Classification of Languages," which offered a broad defense of "ethnological philology" as the basis for a comprehensive science of man.[36] Müller, meanwhile, delivered an essay concerning "The Relation of the Bengali to the Arian and Aboriginal Languages of India" which trumpeted the advances of

---

[32] [William B. Carpenter], "Ethnology, or the Science of Races," *Edinburgh Review* 88 (1848): 432.

[33] [D. R. Goodwin], "The Unity of Language and of Mankind," *North American Review* 73 (1851): 173.

[34] Ibid., 175, quoting C. C. J. Bunsen, "On the Results of the Recent Egyptian Researches in Reference to Asiatic and African Ethnology, and the Classification of Languages," *Report of the Seventeenth Meeting of the British Association for the Advancement of Science; Held at Oxford in June 1847* (London, UK: John Murray, 1848), 287.

[35] See Stocking, *Victorian Anthropology*, 56–8; Richard Dorson, *The British Folklorists: A History* (Chicago, IL: U of Chicago P, 1968), 161; Lincoln, 66.

[36] Bunsen, 256.

comparative philology and outlined its potential contributions to the studies of mythography, ethnology, and archaeology.[37]

As allies of the Ethnological Society, Bunsen and Müller articulated in a bolder philosophical register (informed by Kant and German Idealism) the central thrust of Prichard's work: that religion and language together anchored humankind's special capacity for spiritual agency and cultivation. Not only did they employ comparative philology to retrace humankind's origins—like Prichard's book on the Celts, Bunsen's work on African languages sought to give a maligned race its own special branch on the Indo-European family tree—but they also insisted that the science of man had to be a linguistic science because, in Bunsen's words, it was "the expression of thought" that made human beings unique in nature.[38] Müller would make his most ambitious version of the case in a series of *Lectures on the Science of Language* that he delivered in 1861 as Oxford's Taylorian Professor of Modern European Languages. Rejecting the claims of some conjectural historians that language had developed out of early human imitations of natural sounds or emotive interjections—the so-called "bow-wow" and "pooh-pooh" theories of language—Müller maintained that all existing dialects could be traced back to a small set of phonetic roots that were themselves attached to a priori thought categories.[39] These innate "general ideas," Müller continued, could never have been derived from sensory experience, or assembled from simpler ideas over time, but must have been humankind's possession from the start.[40] In this way, Müller insisted, language constituted a "Rubicon" that "no brute will dare cross" and that no developmental theory could bridge:

[T]he first step . . . which, however small in appearance, separates man for ever from all other animals, is *the naming of a thing*, or the making a thing knowable. All naming is classification, bringing the individual under the general; and whatever we know, whether empirically or scientifically, we know it only by means of our general ideas. Other animals have sensation,

---

[37] F. Max Müller, "On the Relation of the Bengali to the Arian and Aboriginal Languages of India," *Report of the Seventeenth Meeting of the British Association for the Advancement of Science; Held at Oxford in June 1847* (London, UK: John Murray, 1848), 319–50. Müller would describe the 1847 BAAS meeting in his autobiography, recalling his awe at having his section presided over by "the famous Dr. Prichard," who defended him "most chivalrously against the somewhat frivolous objections of certain members who were not over friendly towards Prince Albert, Chevalier Bunsen, and all that was called German in scholarship." *My Autobiography: A Fragment* (New York, NY: Scribners, 1901), 211.

[38] Bunsen, 285.

[39] Müller, *Lectures on the Science of Language Delivered at the Royal Institution of Great Britain in April, May, and June, 1861. First Series* (London, UK: Longman, Green, Longman, and Roberts, 1861), 344.

[40] Ibid., 385.

perception, memory, and, in a certain sense, intellect... Man has sensation, perception, memory, intellect, and his reason is conversant with general ideas only.[41]

Linguistic diversity for Müller, like ethnic diversity for Prichard, was not the expression of different racial spirits but rather the product of deformation from a pristine source. Different languages had emerged as human beings joined various root-words together through habit or for convenience, almost inevitably obscuring their original meanings; *forti mente* became *fortment*, with *-ment* being transformed from a genuine signifier into an all-purpose adverbial suffix.[42]

In turn, Müller's major treatises on the history of religion—most notably his *Introduction to the Science of Religion* (1870) and *Lectures on the Origin and Growth of Religion* (1878)—would expand upon Prichard's claim that humankind's special linguistic capabilities revealed a unique spiritual patrimony too. Just as philology could vouch for the existence of perfectly developed conceptual categories from the beginnings of human thought, Müller argued, so did a comparative study of the world's religions point toward a "primitive intuition of God... neither monotheistic nor polytheistic" that had been with humankind since its earliest history.[43] Although Müller would revise his term for this intuition from a "faculty of faith" in 1870's *Introduction* to the more positivist-friendly "perception of the infinite" in the *Lectures*, the concept, as Marjorie Wheeler-Barclay notes, remained essentially Kantian in its insistence on the mind's capacity to actively reach out and make sense of reality.[44] Confronted with the sensible universe, the human mind works "to elaborate the finite out of the infinite, the seen out of the unseen, the natural out of the supernatural, the phaenomenal world out of the universe which is not yet phaenomenal."[45]

---

[41] Ibid., 340, 364. As Bunsen put it in his BAAS address, those who pictured a slow development of human reason out of animal savagery "have never been able to show the possibility of the first step," for "how indeed could reason spring out of a state which is destitute of reason? How can speech... develop itself, in a year or in millions of years, out of the unarticulated sounds, which express feelings of pleasure, pain and appetite?" (285).

[42] Müller, *Lectures on the Science of Language, First Series*, 45.

[43] Müller, "Semitic Monotheism" (1860), in *Chips from a German Workshop* (4 vols.; London, UK: Longmans, Green, 1867), 1: 352.

[44] Müller, *Introduction to the Science of Religion: Four Lectures Delivered at the Royal Institution in February and March 1870* (London, UK: Spottiswoode, 1870), 5; *Lectures on the Origin and Growth of Religion, as Illustrated by the Religions of India* (London, UK: Longmans, Green, 1878), 1–51. See Marjorie Wheeler-Barclay, *The Science of Religion, 1860–1915* (Charlottesville, VA: U of Virginia P, 2010), 54–7.

[45] Müller, *Origin and Growth*, 374.

For our purposes, the crucial thing about Müller's work is that it betrays a deep ambivalence within this way of thinking about language and religion. For although language, in Müller's account, represented the chief sign of humankind's spiritual nature, it did so only negatively, by covering up and indeed stymying this nature. The reason why the "primitive religious instinct" had fractured into the world's different religions, he wrote, was because language was ultimately unable to express it fully. The ancient Aryans of India had felt a powerful sense of the divine in natural phenomena, but their attempts to express such intimations of immortality had been hijacked by inflection, "appellatives," and other grammatical structures, which led them to personify natural phenomena like thunderclouds or the sun.[46] These confusions, exacerbated by centuries of linguistic diffusion, had slowly given rise to humankind's many sagas of gods and heroes.[47] For instance, the various European myths of young, dying heroes, "whether ... Baldr, or Sigurd, or Sîfrit, or Achilcs, or Mclcagcr, or Kephalos," had been "first suggested by the Sun, dying in all his youthful vigor, either at the end of a day, conquered by the powers of darkness, or at the end of the sunny season, stung by the thorn of winter."[48] More broadly, Müller attributed the differences between Indo-European and Semitic religions to the distinctive ways in which those languages had shaped and constrained religious thought. Where the highly inflective Indo-European languages tended to ascribe abstract qualities directly to personified figures, the Semitic languages, owing to reduced capacity for inflection, tended to imagine a single transcendent God who possessed various abstract qualities:

> The Semitic man would call on God in adjectives only, or in words which always conveyed a predicative meaning. Every one of his words was more or less predicative, and he was therefore restricted in his choice to such words as expressed some one or other of the abstract qualities of the Deity. The Aryan man was less fettered in his choice.... Being startled by the sound of thunder, he would at first express his impression by the single phrase, It thunders ... It would be more in accordance with the feelings and thoughts of those who first used these so-called impersonal verbs to translate them by He thunders, He rains, He snows. Afterwards, instead of the simple

---

[46] Müller, "Semitic Monotheism," 1: 359.

[47] For summaries of this process, see Dorson, 162–4; Stocking, *Victorian Anthropology*, 60–1. For primary texts, see F. Max Müller, "Comparative Mythology" (1856), in *Chips from a German Workshop*, 2: 1–143, as well as the lecture on "Jupiter, the Supreme Aryan God," in *Lectures on the Science of Language Delivered at the Royal Institution of Great Britain in February, March, April, and May, 1863. Second Series* (London, UK: Longman, Green, Longman, Roberts, and Green, 1864), 413–61.

[48] Müller, *Chips from a German Workshop*, 2: 107.

impersonal verb He thunders, another expression naturally suggested itself. The thunder came from the sky, the sky was frequently called Dyaus (the bright one), in Greek Ζεύς; and though it was not the bright sky which thundered, but the dark, yet Dyaus had already ceased to be an expressive predicate, it had become a traditional name...[49]

For this reason Müller, in what would become his most celebrated soundbite, called religious mythology a "disease of language,"[50] a corruption of humankind's noblest spiritual aspirations by the medium of the word. "Most of the Greek, the Roman, the Indian, and other heathen gods are nothing but poetical names," he wrote, "which were gradually allowed to assume a divine personality never contemplated by their original inventors."[51]

Müller's understanding of religion as a purely spiritual impulse historically corrupted by theological and ritual language arguably reflected the influence of his German Pietist mother.[52] As Wheeler-Barclay puts it, his writings on language and religion are shot through with "a pietistic sensibility very close to that of nineteenth-century evangelicalism allied with a liberal emphasis on free inquiry in theological matters."[53] In his posthumously published *Autobiography* (1901), Müller describes himself arriving at an Oxford still abuzz from the Tractarian controversy and feeling dismayed by so much hubbub over ritual and articles: "What was my surprise when I found that most of these excellent and really learned men were much more deeply interested in purely ecclesiastical questions, in the validity of Anglican orders, in the wearing of either gowns or surplices in the pulpit, in the question of candlesticks and genuflections. 'What has all this to do with true religion?'"[54] Nevertheless, Müller would eventually become a "devoted member of the English Church," whose members, he wrote, "enjoy greater freedom and more immunity from priestcraft than those of any other Church."[55] Importantly, this pietistic sensibility also gave him wider ecumenical designs for a global religious future. He hoped that "the study of Eastern religions" could become "an ally of European theological liberalism," instigating a "new reformation... in which the aims of the sixteenth-century reformers would at last be fulfilled" as Christianity would drop its final theological and ritual peculiarities and become a religion of pure spirit.[56]

---

[49] Ibid., 1: 357.   [50] Müller, *Science of Language, First Series*, 11.
[51] Ibid.   [52] Stocking, *Victorian Anthropology*, 56–7.
[53] Wheeler-Barclay, 59.   [54] Müller, *My Autobiography*, 290–1.
[55] *The Life and Letters of the Right Honourable Max Müller*, ed. Georgina Adelaide Müller (2 vols.; London, UK: Longmans, Green, 1902), 2: 391. See Eric Sharpe, *Comparative Religion: A History* (La Salle, IL: Open Court, 1986), 39.
[56] Wheeler-Barclay, 61.

By Keane's reckoning, this muted hostility toward language represents the necessary flipside of the liberal and Protestant valorization of language as the sign of humankind's unique spiritual agency. To the Protestant Reformers, he shows, the written word was valuable not in itself but because it could be seen as the most direct conduit between the human mind and the divine.[57] But if language had the virtue of being the least mediating of media, this also made it the target of what Bruno Latour calls "the work of purification," or the ongoing project of keeping words subservient to thoughts and "draw[ing] a clear line between humans and non-humans, between the world of agency and that of natural determinism."[58] Müller's work, for instance, is obsessed with the tendency of language to exceed individual human intentions. As he put it in the preface to his *Lectures*, quoting Francis Bacon: "[w]ords, as a Tartar's bow, shoot back upon the understanding of the wise, and mightily entangle and pervert the judgment."[59] Years later, in an 1879 address to the Birmingham and Midland Institute, Müller would argue that although Mill's *On Liberty* (1859) had portrayed popular groupthink as the primary enemy of individual liberty, a far more insidious influence was the one exercised by language over thought. Ostensibly language is the tool of reason, but in fact it comes to us as "the work of other people, not of ourselves, which we pick up at random," "the detritus of thoughts which were first thought, not on these isles nor in Europe, but on the shores of the Oxus, the Nile, the Euphrates, and the Indus."[60] In a series of "Literary Recollections" (1896–97), Müller mentions a "long-standing feud about poetry" between himself and fellow Oxonian Matthew Arnold. Where Arnold, according to Müller, regards poetry as a special kind of language, "a thing by itself" with a unique "force," Müller counters that the best language is that in which the meaning is straightforward.[61] Indeed, Müller tells the reader, he has struggled for all of his life against "suppressed poetry," like "suppressed gout"—a disease of language that asserts itself despite our best efforts to master it rationally.[62]

In *Language and Decadence at the Fin de Siècle* (1986), written at the height of the linguistic turn in literary studies, Linda Dowling portrayed such sentiments as a proto-deconstructive recognition of language's mischievous autonomy.[63] Indeed, while Müller's evaluation of this autonomy

---

[57] Keane, 7; see 59–82.   [58] Ibid., 7.
[59] Müller, *Science of Language, First Series*, x.
[60] Müller, "On Freedom," *Contemporary Review* 36 (1879), 386, 379.
[61] Müller, "Literary Recollections" (part 3 of 4), *Cosmopolis* 5 (1897): 651–2, 654.
[62] Müller, "Literary Recollections" (part 2 of 4), *Cosmopolis* 4 (1896): 626.
[63] Linda Dowling, *Language and Decadence in the Victorian Fin de Siècle* (Princeton, NJ: Princeton UP, 1986), 46–103. For instance, compare the final line of Müller's 1847 BAAS speech—"There is more indeed to be read in human language itself than in anything that

is never celebratory, it does lead him toward a methodological organicism that subtly undermines his overall evaluation of language as an absolute "Rubicon" between human reason and animal instinct. Prichard had always denied that either ethnicity or language developed by a set of autonomous laws. Both ethnology and philology, as he understood them, were exercises in a posteriori historical reconstruction: attempts to retrace particular historical events like vowel-shifts rather than to deduce a priori historical laws.[64] In this sense Prichard was reaffirming what Daniel Smail identifies as a central premise of both Protestant and Enlightenment historiography: the gap between human history, understood as a theater of conscious action by reflective individuals, and the "deep" history of those gradualistic processes that predate and inscribe the human.[65] As ESL mainstay Robert Gordon Latham put it, philology and ethnology were exercises in "civil history," or the study of particular actions by willful human subjects, rather than in "natural history," which investigated unconscious organic laws.[66] Müller, however, recognized that the two were much harder to separate. Rejecting the Enlightenment linguistics of Adam Smith and Dugald Stewart, which treated language as a consciously invented technology, Müller insisted that "language is not a work of human art, in the same sense in which painting, or building, or writing, or printing are," but rather changes by impersonal laws of organic development.[67] In this sense language is barely even a matter of history, for "*History* applies to the actions of free agents; *growth* to the natural unfolding of organic beings."[68] History is what kings and emperors make happen, but emperors cannot change language, which operates by a strange synergy of necessity and free will.

Perhaps most significantly, Müller's wariness toward language points toward a deeper ambivalence within the story of "progressive cultivation" that Prichard's various allies were telling. Ostensibly, Prichard and his

has been written in it" ("On the Relation" 350)—with Derrida's epigraph from Montaigne in "Structure, Sign, and Play in the Discourse of the Human Sciences" (1966): "Il y a plus affaire à interpréter les interprétations qu'à interpréter les choses . . ." *Writing and Difference* (1967), trans. Alan Bass (Chicago, IL: U of Chicago P, 1978), 278.

[64] For this reason Prichard would argue that ethnology and philology were closer to geology than to biology; for geology, he wrote, "is not an account of what Nature produces in the present day, but of what it has long ago produced. It is an investigation of the changes which the surface of our planet has undergone in ages long since past . . . the series of repeated creations which have taken place." "Of the Relations of Ethnology to Other Branches of Knowledge," *Journal of the Ethnological Society of London* 1 (1848): 303.

[65] Daniel Lord Smail, *On Deep History and the Brain* (Berkeley, CA: U of California P, 2008), 4–5; see 1–73.

[66] Robert Gordon Latham, *Man and His Migrations* (London, UK: John Van Voorst, 1851), 1–3.

[67] Müller, *Science of Language, First Series*, 31.   [68] Ibid., 65.

coalition were valorizing a Whiggish subject who had the capacity to reflect, learn, and grow with experience. Yet at the same time it was unclear whether they possessed any positive image of cultivation itself. Human nature, as these theorists pictured it, was such a pristine thing that it could not change for the better, only be distorted by historical modifications. Indeed, the only cultivation actually described by their work was a *negative* process: the local sedimentations of language, custom, religion, and external physical markings that prevented different peoples from recognizing their shared human nature.

To put this in stronger terms: the cultivation actually described by the Ethnological Society was in many ways closer to what we would call cultural determinism. Critics like Raymond Williams and Adam Kuper have demonstrated how three general senses of the word *culture*, each derived from the metaphor of cultivated growth, took shape over the long nineteenth century: (i) culture as a process of self-cultivation or *Bildung*; (ii) culture as the universal evolution of human society; and (iii) culture as the organic whole of a particular people's way of life.[69] The first two were central to the developing ideology of liberalism, with its valorization of individual self-development and civilizational uplift. The third, meanwhile, is the Romantic *Kultur* of Herder and the relativistic culture of modernist ethnography, both of which bear a family resemblance to concepts of race. Prichard and his allies, we might say, accidentally discovered this third sense of culture as a foil to the first two. The Whig-liberal self whose freedom of growth they were championing was so abstract, so static, that they had to posit something like ethnographic culture in order to account for human differences without giving them too much substance. They were attracted to culture, that is, in the same way that today we oppose culture to nature:—as a form of variation shallow enough not to challenge a vision of human commonality.

Müller's work on language and religion illustrates this "negative" discovery of anthropological culture especially clearly. While sometimes Müller will describe humankind's religiosity advancing "to a higher and more spiritual stage" over time, he more typically uses the word *higher* to designate the "higher power" that human beings have always perceived and that most historical development has, unfortunately, been away from.[70] "History never tells us of any race with whom the simple feeling of reverence for higher powers was not hidden under mythological disguises," he

---

[69] Adam Kuper, *Culture: The Anthropologists' Account* (Cambridge, MA: Harvard UP, 1999), 5–9; Raymond Williams, *Keywords: A Vocabulary of Culture and Society* (1976; New York, NY: Oxford UP, 2015), 49–54.

[70] Müller, *Science of Religion*, 29.

writes.[71] As an almost necessary consequence, Müller's work ends up developing a detailed eye for the peculiarities of different languages, customs, and mythologies. This is why Tomoko Masuzawa, in her history of comparative religion, can present Müller as a tolerant pluralist who views different religions as "incidental, contingent, and synthetic" formations.[72] Yet the fact is that this apparent relativism is only the helpmeet of a deeper universalism, one that is constantly beset by the worry that human variety will eventually cause us to forget human unity. Prichard and Müller, however, remained largely blind to this ambiguity because of their opposition to polygenesis, an opposition that would only be hardened by developments in the 1850s and 1860s.

POLYGENESIS AND THE ILLIBERAL IMAGINATION

By the 1860s, Max Müller had become a bona fide intellectual celebrity for his ability to present the formidable new Indo-European philology in a genial prose style and comforting piety.[73] Müller's lectures were attended by men of letters from Tennyson to Mill and would be cited with reverence by George Eliot and John Ruskin.[74] One newspaper, reviewing Müller's first series of lectures, noted that "it is a fact of no ordinary significance that, in the height of the London season, an enthusiastic audience of both sexes crowded the benches and endured the heat of a popular lecture-room, not to witness the brilliant experiments, or be fascinated by the revelations of a Faraday or an Owen, but to listen to a philosophical exposition of the inner mysteries of language."[75]

Indeed, Müller's voice had become increasingly relevant in the face of a re-energized polygenism that emerged in scientific circles following Prichard's death in 1848. As Catherine Hall has shown, frustrations with the colonial uprisings in India (1857) and Jamaica (1865), not to mention the specter of the American Civil War, instigated a turn from "the cultural racism of the 1830s with its liberal and progressive attachments"—the paternalistic meliorism of Prichard, the Aborigines Protection Society, and abolition—to a "more aggressive biological racism, rooted in the assumption that blacks were not brothers and sisters but a different species, born

---

[71] Ibid., 23.   [72] Masuzawa, *Invention*, 219; see 216–21.
[73] Hence Hans Aarsleff argues that Müller should be classed among John Holloway's "Victorian sages." See *From Locke to Saussure: Essays on the Study of Language and Intellectual History* (Minneapolis: U of Minnesota P. 1982), 38; Wheeler-Barclay, 53.
[74] Dowling, 72–3.   [75] Cited in Chaudhuri, 185.

to be mastered."[76] Within the Ethnological Society, this turn toward biological race was led by a new wave of members that included John Beddoe, Robert Knox, and, most importantly, James Hunt.[77] Hunt was trained as a speech therapist, and indeed it was his sense that linguistic capabilities were ultimately rooted in the body that had steered him toward the work of comparative anatomists such as Paul Broca in France.[78]

Although Hunt rose quickly through the ranks of the ESL, his views attracted considerable controversy, and he would eventually leave the Society in 1863 to found a competing organization called the Anthropological Society of London (ASL).[79] Hunt's goal for "anthropology," a term he had borrowed from Broca, was to move the human sciences away from the "theological, metaphysical, and *a priori* assumptions" of Prichard and Müller.[80] First, where the Ethnological Society had seen human beings as sharing a common nature beneath the pliable differences of color and creed, ASL members tended to agree that that there was "an extraordinary *fixity of type* which, during every period of history from its earliest dawn, has characterized the races, and even the varieties of mankind."[81] Second, Hunt's allies saw humankind's physical constitution, instead of its mental or spiritual attributes, as definitive. To understand human beings, one had to look at their bodies, and when one did so the grand distinction between human and animal dissolved into a series of finer gradations running from chimpanzee to African to Caucasian.[82] For instance, Luke Owen Pike's "On the Place of the Sciences of Mind and Language in the Science of Man" (1864) disparaged Müller's claim that language reflected a special human capacity for forming "general ideas" and took up a more empiricist account of ideas as the direct imprint of sense impressions that

[76] Catherine Hall, "Missionary Stories: Gender and Ethnicity in England in the 1830s and 1840s," in Lawrence Grossberg, Cary Nelson, Paula Treichler (eds.), *Cultural Studies* (New York, NY: Routledge, 1992), 242. Cited in Simon Gikandi, *Maps of Englishness: Writing Identity in the Culture of Colonialism* (New York, NY: Columbia UP, 1996), 59. See also Lorimer, 12–13.

[77] Stocking, *Victorian Anthropology*, 246–7.

[78] Ibid., 247–8. See James Hunt, *Stammering and Stuttering, Their Nature and Treatment* (London, UK: Longman, Green, Longman and Roberts, 1861).

[79] Stocking, *Victorian Anthropology*, 247–50; Burrow, *Evolution and Society*, 120–1. See Tim Watson, *Caribbean Culture and British Fiction in the Atlantic World, 1780–1870* (New York, NY: Cambridge UP, 2008), 160–73.

[80] Hunt, "On Physio-Anthropology: Its Aims and Methods," *Journal of the Anthropological Society* 5 (1867): ccxii. For Hunt's appropriation of the term *anthropology*, see Stocking, "What's in a Name? The Origins of the Royal Anthropological Institute," *Man* 6 (1971): 376–7.

[81] F. W. Farrar, "On Fixity of Type," *Transactions of the Ethnological Society of London* 3 (1865): 394; cited in Lorimer, 140.

[82] On the ASL's preference for comparative anatomy, see Burrow, *Evolution and Society*, 129–30.

worked the same in humans as it did in animals.[83] Other members rejected Prichard's and Müller's largely linguistic focus by turning to visual art, which they took as a less ambiguous record of the physical realities of race. Hunt praised the ancient Greek sculptors for their attentiveness to the physical markers of ethnic character, while Robert Knox would cite a set of ancient Assyrian reliefs as evidence that the races of man had been fixed and unchanging for thousands of years.[84]

More broadly, Hunt's fellow travelers advanced a very different understanding of what religion was and what role it played in human affairs. If Prichard and Müller had sought to prove that the different religions of the world represented deformations of a single spiritual impulse, a good deal of the work published in the new *Journal of the Anthropological Society* maintained that there could be no universal religiosity, only the projections of particular racial natures. Knox pointed to Ireland for evidence of the limited effects that Protestant charity could have upon a non-Anglo-Saxon people and spoke of the essential heterogeneity of "Celtic, Saxon, Sarmatian... Greek, Roman, Lutheran forms of worship."[85] Dunbar Heath, a former Cambridge Egyptologist whose heretical publications had cost him his position at that university, published a paper in 1867 "On the Great Race-Elements in Christianity," which argued that it was impossible for a Semitic religion to have taken root in Aryan Europe, and that Christianity's true origins must therefore lie somewhere in Asia.[86] Although Heath's essay did not consider the apparent counterexample provided by modern missionary work, this was also a subject very much on the minds of other ASL members, and in 1865 a series of meetings was devoted to the question of whether European religion could really have an effect among the populations of Africa and the South Pacific.[87]

---

[83] Luke Owen Pike, "On the Place of the Sciences of Mind and Language in the Science of Man," *Anthropological Review* 2 (1864): cxciii. See also Dunbar Heath, "On the Primary Anthropoid and Secondary Mute Origin of the European Races, versus the Theory of Migration from an External Source," *Journal of the Anthropological Society* 4 (1866): xxxiii–xlviii; Farrar, "Language and Ethnology," *Transactions of the Ethnological Society of London* 4 (1866): 196–203.

[84] Robert Knox, "Abstract of Observations on the Assyrian Marbles, and on their Place in History and Art," *Transactions of the Ethnological Society* 1 (1861): 146–54. See Hunt, "On Physio-Anthropology," ccl.

[85] Knox, *The Races of Men: A Fragment* (Philadelphia, PA: Lea and Blanchard, 1850), 11.

[86] Dunbar Heath, "On the Great Race-Elements in Christianity," *Journal of the Anthropological Society* 5 (1867): xx–xxi; see Kidd, 190–1.

[87] Stocking, *Victorian Anthropology*, 252. One special guest in attendance at these meetings was John William Colenso, the Bishop of Natal, who would later deliver a response paper; see "On the Efforts of Missionaries among Savages," *Journal of the Anthropological Society* 3 (1865): cclviii–cclxxxix.

This rejection of Protestant universalism was part of a contrarian political agenda within Hunt's Anthropological Society. As Stocking puts it, "the leading 'anthropologicals' were opposed to Bentham, Mill, and the Westminster philosophy, to Bright, Gladstone, and the Liberal party, to missionaries and 'social science' reformers"; where Huxley and other more agnostic members of the Ethnological Society shared many of the same values as their Dissenting peers, Hunt, Knox, and more than a few other ASL members were avowed atheists who rejected the ESL's middle-class piety.[88] One of Hunt's main goals in founding the ASL had been to influence popular opinion on issues like American slavery, colonialism, and the condition of Ireland. He charged his erstwhile companions in the ESL with "what I will call respectively the religious mania, and the rights-of-man mania," and wrote that "the age of revolution and anarchy is drawing to a close" as "men ... ask everywhere for a strong government, adequate to the suppression of aimless insurrection."[89] After Hunt, perhaps the most politically vocal member of the ASL was the Scottish surgeon Knox, whose treatise, *The Races of Men* (1855), had employed the doctrine of polygenesis to question "wild Utopian theories ... of human progress, of human civilization."[90] At an early meeting of the Society, Hunt delivered an address entitled "On the Negro's Place in Nature" (1863) that lamented "the misery which has been inflicted on the Negro race, from the prevailing ignorance of Anthropological Science, especially as regards the great question of race. By our ignorance of the wants and aspirations of the Negro, and by a mistaken theory respecting his origin, this country has been the means of inflicting a prodigious, and, at present, totally unknown amount of mischief on these people."[91] In the wake of the Morant Bay Rebellion of 1865, Governor Eyre was made an honorary member of the Anthropological Society along with Sir James Brooke, famous for his role in helping suppress the Indian Mutiny.[92]

Through all of this, Müller remained vocally skeptical. He thought that the Anthropological Society's talk of bodies and racial instincts lent a falsely empirical feel to a concept of race that was, at its root, no less metaphysical than his own "perception of the infinite." In a highly critical essay on Ernest Renan, a French Orientalist whose scholarship mixed philology with polygenesis, Müller wrote that although "the word 'instinct'

---

[88] Stocking, *Victorian Anthropology*, 251–2; see Lorimer, 158.
[89] Hunt, "President's Address," *Journal of the Anthropological Society* 5 (1867): lix; Hunt, "Race in Religion," *Anthropological Review* 4 (1866): 291. Cited in Lorimer, 153.
[90] Knox, *Races*, 10.
[91] Hunt, "On the Negro's Place in Nature," *Memoirs Read before the Anthropological Society of London, 1863–64*, (2 vols.; London, UK: Trübner and Company, 1865), 1: 52–3.
[92] J. W. Burrow, *Evolution and Society* (New York, NY: Cambridge UP, 1966), 125.

has its legitimate application in natural history, where it is used of the unconscious acts of unconscious beings," as soon as "we transfer the word to the conscious thoughts of conscious beings...we use it in order to avoid other terms which would commit us to the admission either of innate ideas or inspired truths."[93] Elsewhere he took a more stridently political tone, disparaging the fact that "in America comparative philologists have been encouraged to prove the impossibility of a common origin of languages and races, in order to justify, by scientific arguments, the unhallowed theory of slavery": "Never do I remember to have seen science more degraded than on the title-page of an American publication in which, among the profiles of the different races of man, the profile of the ape was made to look more human than that of the negro."[94] Assessing the fallout of the Indian Rebellion of 1857, meanwhile, Müller penned a series of letters to the *Times* insisting that a greater knowledge of Indian languages could have ameliorated the situation by allowing the English and the Indians to communicate better with each other and by reminding them of their joint Indo-European origins.[95]

Despite such objections from Müller, the Anthropological Society's membership expanded rapidly during the 1860s, until by 1866 "Anthropology" would appear as an official subsection of Biology at the annual BAAS meeting in Nottingham.[96] Although in many ways the ASL can be seen as tapping a reactionary vein in mid-Victorian culture, such a reading misses the way in which it nourished forms of what Frank Turner has called Victorian cultural apostasy.[97] As Burrow puts it, the ASL gained infamy as "a stamping-ground for cranks and exhibitionists of every description...men with an eye for phallic symbols, determined to prove that the Israelite Ark of the Covenant contained one; clergymen prepared to refer to the biblical account of the Creation as 'the quite baseless traditions of the former barbarous inhabitants of Syria'..."[98] Many of the ASL's members frequently met at the so-called Cannibal Club, where meetings were "gavelled to order by a mace in the form of a Negro head,"

[93] Müller, *Chips from a German Workshop*, 1: 350.

[94] Müller, *Science of Language, First Series*, 12.

[95] Chaudhuri, 182–4. These letters can be found collected in *Correspondence Relating to the Establishment of an Oriental College in London* (London, UK: Williams and Norgate, 1858), 1–6, 8–18, 20–31.

[96] Stocking, *Victorian Anthropology*, 254; see *Report of the Thirty-Sixth Meeting of the British Association for the Advancement of Science; Held at Nottingham in August 1866* (London, UK: John Murray, 1867), 93–7.

[97] See Frank Turner, *Contesting Cultural Authority: Essays in Victorian Intellectual Life* (New York, NY: Cambridge UP, 1993), 38–72.

[98] Burrow, *Evolution and Society*, 126. See Dunbar Heath, "Anniversary Address," *Journal of the Anthropological Society* 6 (1868): xci.

and members sang a special "Cannibal Catechism" composed for the occasion by sometime member Algernon Charles Swinburne.[99] Yet this brand of eccentricity also allowed for more nuanced varieties of cultural skepticism that questioned the ESL's idea that what was best for the Englishman was best for everyone. "Human nature is, or appears to be, very different in China or America," commented Edouard Villin at one meeting. "If the doubt on this point was not shared by almost everyone, would the Anthropological Society exist? Would not a Londoner be quite as good a subject for study as twenty different races, for the purpose of knowing what is and what is not human nature?"[100] Along similar lines, the explorer Richard F. Burton wrote that "[n]ations are poor judges of one another; each looks upon itself as an exemplar to the world, and vents its philanthropy by forcing its infallible system or systems upon its neighbour."[101]

Burton's case is worth dwelling upon because it suggests how the ASL's strong reading of racial difference could be parlayed into a surprising relativism. After being booted from the Indian Civil Service on suspicions of homosexual behavior, Burton would go on to make a name for himself in the 1850s and 1860s as an ethnographer and travel writer. Most notably, he became one of the first Europeans ever to make the *Hajj*, the sacred Muslim pilgrimage to Mecca while in the garb of a Pashtun doctor.[102] The great paradox of Burton is that he was a polygenist who nevertheless enjoyed courting a sympathy for the other—a curiosity about different ways of being in the world. As Dane Kennedy puts it, Burton's "understanding of race as a closed space defined by difference serves a double purpose: it supports the standard racists' contention that biology is destiny, but it also ventures the view that [different] races have their own systems of beliefs and behavior, each incommensurate with the other and implicitly standing against any universalist standard of values."[103] Sometimes this relativism comes across through a blend of polemic and satire, as when, in *A Mission to Gelele, King of Dahome* (1864), Burton

---

[99] Stocking, *Victorian Anthropology*, 252; see also Philip Henderson, *Swinburne: The Portrait of a Poet* (London, UK: Routledge and Kegan Paul, 1974), 108–9, and Dane Kennedy, *The Highly Civilized Man: Richard Burton and the Victorian World* (Cambridge, MA: Harvard UP, 2005), 168–70.

[100] Edouard Villin, "Discussion" of "On Phallic Worship," *Anthropological Review* 8 (1870): cxliii. Cited in Burrow, *Evolution and Society*, 128.

[101] Burton, *A Mission to Gelele, King of Dahome* (2 vols.; London, UK: Tinsley Brothers, 1864), 2: 207. Cited in Kennedy, 159.

[102] For Burton in the ASL, see Stocking, *Victorian Anthropology*, 253; Burrow, *Evolution and Society*, 125; Lorimer, 152–3; Kennedy, 131–63. For a good introductory biography, see Fawn M. Brodie, *The Devil Drives: A Life of Sir Richard Burton* (New York, NY: Norton, 1967).

[103] Kennedy, 156.

asks, "How long is it since popular literature has begun to confess that the British constitution is not quite fit for the whole human race...?", and invites his readers to picture a team of African explorers "marching uninvited through [an English] Squire's manor, strewing his lawn and tennis-ground with all manner of rubbish, housing their belongings in his dining [and] bedrooms... and rummaging [through] the whole mansion for curios and heirlooms interesting to the negro anthropologist."[104]

At other times, Burton's relativism approaches what Uday Mehta calls a cosmopolitanism of sentiments: an openness to the lived experience of others that ends up being more tolerant than a classical liberal "cosmo-politanism of reason," obsessed with constructing universal categories.[105] For Burton, it is the very impossibility of getting under the other's skin that makes him want to get under the other's clothing, language, and affects instead. Indeed, Burton's career may be read as one long succession of the kinds of cultural dalliance that Leela Gandhi documents in *Affective Communities* (2006), in which otherness provokes an intense personal attraction precisely because it is other.[106] For example, one of the signa-tures of Burton's ethnographic writing is the hyper-detailed script, a catalogue of behaviors whose stupendous complexity reminds the reader that no outsider could ever internalize this mode of life fully. Here, for instance, is Burton's account of how an Indian Muslim drinks water:

> [T]he performance includes no fewer than five novelties. In the first place he clutches his tumbler as though it were the throat of a foe; secondly, he ejaculates, "In the name of Allah the Compassionate, the Merciful!" before wetting his lips; thirdly, he imbibes the contents, swallowing them, not sipping them... and ending with a satisfied grunt; fourthly, before setting down the cup, he sighs forth, "Praise be to Allah"—of which you will understand the full meaning in the Desert; and, fifthly, he replies, "May Allah make it pleasant to thee!" in answer to his friend's polite "Pleasurably and health!"[107]

---

[104] Richard Burton, *Mission to Gelele*, 2: 207; Richard F. Burton and Verney Lovett Cameron, *To the Gold Coast for Gold: A Personal Narrative* (2 vols.; London, UK: Chatto and Windus, 1883), 2: 190. The latter is quoted in Jonathan Bishop, "The Identities of Sir Richard Burton: The Explorer as Actor," *Victorian Studies* 1.2 (1957): 131.

[105] Uday Singh Mehta, *Liberalism and Empire: A Study in Nineteenth-Century British Liberal Thought* (Chicago, IL: U of Chicago P, 1999), 20–2. This curiosity about difference is why Burton sometimes figures as an unlikely hero in postcolonial criticism. See, for example, Sara Suleri Goodyear's *The Rhetoric of English India* (Chicago, IL: U of Chicago P, 2012), 134.

[106] Leela Gandhi, *Affective Communities: Anticolonial Thought, Fin-de-Siècle Radialism, and the Politics of Friendship* (Durham, NC: Duke UP, 2006). See also the chapter on Burton in Jerrod Seigel's *Between Cultures: Europe and Its Others in Five Exemplary Lives* (Philadelphia, PA: U of Pennsylvania P, 2016), 13–64.

[107] Richard Burton, *Personal Narrative of a Pilgrimage to Al-Madinah and Meccah* (3 vols.; London, UK: Longman, Brown, Green, and Longman, 1855), 1: 8.

As a principle of description, this microcataloguing of actions serves to alienate what already seems alien. The closer an English observer studies the particularities of the Muslim's drinking habits, the harder it becomes to imagine actually inhabiting them. Where Clifford Geertz's "thick description," a hallmark of latter-day anthropological relativism, aims to reveal the virtual symbolic structure uniting the particulars of cultural activity, Burton's descriptions actively prevent the parts from ever quite adding up to a whole.[108] He seems to be writing a script that defeats its own enactment, a script that dramatizes the fact that one could never really learn to act this way *by* script.[109]

In all of these ways Burton inverts the paradox that we saw in Müller. If Müller showed how the ESL's valorization of linguistic agency could harbor a hidden determinism, Burton's work suggests how polygenist anti-universalism could open the door to a kind of liberality, albeit one markedly different from the Whig-progressivism of Prichard and the Ethnological Society. Perhaps the most striking difference between Burton and normal mid-Victorian liberalism is that, in his disdain for middle-class convention, he advertises himself as exceptional rather than exemplary. Instead of offering what David Wayne Thomas calls a regulative framework that says, "here is how to be," Burton's ethnographic adventures cry out, "look what I can do that the rest of you cannot."[110] At the same time, there are elements of Burton's persona that preview the anti-bourgeois aesthetic liberalism of many-sidedness that we will see Arnold and Pater develop in subsequent chapters. For one thing, Burton's literary persona is premised upon an ability to "bracket [one's] own viewpoint to a profound extent" and entertain ideas and points of view that one cannot understand.[111] This many-sidedness, however, is derived less from a Millian countenancing of opinions than from an ability to try different ways of thinking and acting in the world. Many of Burton's most celebrated performances center upon religion precisely because they emphasize the priority of embodied stances over mental states. Indeed, there is something oddly Pascalian about Burton's treatments of religion—a sense that religion begins with corporeal activity and only later enters the sphere of conviction. His description of a Muslim prayer, for instance,

---

[108] Clifford Geertz, *The Interpretation of Cultures* (New York, NY: Basic Books, 1973), 3–30.

[109] For Burton and performance, see Bishop.

[110] See David Wayne Thomas, *Cultivating Victorians: Liberal Culture and the Aesthetic* (Philadelphia, PA: U of Pennsylvania P, 2004), 14–15; see also Elaine Hadley, *Living Liberalism: Practical Citizenship in Mid-Victorian Britain* (Chicago, IL: U of Chicago P, 2010), 10.

[111] Thomas, 31.

combines a rote description of physical action with an avowedly literalistic translation:

> Then, placing our hands a little below and on the left of the waist, the palm of the right covering the back of the left, in the position of prayer, and beginning with the dexter feet, we pace slowly forwards down the line called the Muwajihat al-Sharifah, or "the Illustrious Fronting," which, divided off like an aisle, runs parallel with the Southern wall of the Mosque. On my right hand walks the Shaykh, who recites aloud the following prayer, making me repeat it after him. It is literally rendered, as, indeed, are all the formulae, and the reader is requested to excuse the barbarous fidelity of the translation. "In the Name of Allah and in the faith of Allah's Apostle! O Lord, cause me to enter the Entering of Truth, and cause me to issue forth the Issuing of Truth, and permit me to draw near to Thee, and make me a Sultan Victorious!"[112]

Although Burton pretends to apologize for it, the "barbarous fidelity" of the translation is crucial, insofar as it remains at the surface of the performance instead of trying to plumb its essential meaning. Burton was one of Victorian Britain's most accomplished translators, responsible for introducing the *Arabian Nights* and the *Kama Sutra* to English readers, yet his work is more often obsessed with the untranslatable dimensions of "Eastern" experience—those aspects that require being in a particular corporeal position, not grasping some universal idea.

EVOLUTION AND THE DIVORCE OF COMPARATIVE RELIGION FROM ANTHROPOLOGY

By the early 1860s, the Ethnological and Anthropological Societies had become caught in an intellectual deadlock that appeared to exhaust the spectrum of possible views on race and religion. On one side stood a coalition of evangelical humanitarians and liberal reformers who saw religion as the lynchpin of the spiritual interiority and potential for growth that all human beings shared, irrespective of color. On the other stood a motley crew of reactionaries who regarded religious, linguistic, and cultural differences as the expressions of insoluble racial ones. Yet in fact, as I have shown, neither position was free of ambiguities. In the case of James Prichard and Max Müller, their picture of a progressively cultivated human self was haunted by an understanding of cultivation closer in some respects to cultural determinism. In the case of Richard Burton, meanwhile, racial polygenesis opened up a curiously liberal relativism, a

---

[112] Burton, *Personal Narrative*, 2: 63–4.

sympathy toward otherness predicated not on the idea of sameness but rather on a recognition of differences. What all three figures reveal is that there were multiple possible relationships between the project of self-cultivation and deterministic accounts of embodied identity.

The central chapters of this book will trace how a group of literary liberals made good upon this ambiguity by incorporating racialized readings of religion into a vision of the many-sided self. In what remains of this chapter I want to suggest how the battle lines of the monogenesis-polygenesis standoff were perhaps definitively vexed by a new anthropological paradigm in which cultivation and determinism converged like never before: evolution. Stadial history, as we have seen, had been the dominant anthropological paradigm of the French and Scottish Enlightenments. Why it passed out of vogue among social theorists in the early nineteenth century remains a matter of some dispute,[113] but by the 1860s various forces had brought theories of social evolution back into vogue in England. These included the success of Herbert Spencer and Charles Darwin, but also a fervent new phase of imperialism. If Prichard's monogenesis had been the anthropology of abolition, and polygenesis that of the mid-century reaction to India and Jamaica, then evolution helped articulate the ideology of Britain's worldwide civilizing mission. Within the Ethnological Society, evolution was advanced as a paradigm by figures including John Lubbock, John Ferguson McLennan, and Edward Burnett Tylor. A Quaker scion much like Prichard, Tylor had first become interested in anthropological questions during an 1855 trip to Mexico; upon returning to England he soon joined both the ESL and ASL and began to express concerns about the limitations of Prichard's monogenist paradigm.[114] In a review of Carl Buschman's *Traces of the Aztec Language in Northern Mexico* (1859), delivered before the Ethnological Society in 1863, Tylor questioned whether diffusion alone could account for modern-day human diversity. Buschman's book, he wrote, supported "the commonly received theory" that the resemblances between different North American languages could be explained by "the migration of the Aztec and kindred races" in prehistoric times.[115] Yet Tylor confessed that it was "not easy to suppose" that deep-seated resemblances of grammar, mythology, and religion could "have been the result of mere

---

[113] See Burrow, *Evolution and Society*, 1–23; Stocking, *Victorian Anthropology*, 145–85.

[114] Stocking, *Victorian Anthropology*, 156–7; Burrow, *Evolution and Society*, 242. Burrow notes that in belonging to both competing societies Tylor "behaved like a professional" anthropologist long before such a thing existed (235).

[115] Tylor, "Remarks on Buschman's Researches in North American Philology," *Transactions of the Ethnological Society of London* 2 (1863): 135.

intercourse."[116] Tylor did not say what the alternative to "mere intercourse" might be, but he dropped some hints that same year in an address to the Anthropological Society on "Wild Men and Beast-Children," which proposed that only the postulate of long-term historical evolution could fully explain the chain of resemblances between animals, primitive humans, and modern subjects.[117]

Thus Tylor arrived at the model of "culture" that he would famously expound in 1871's *Primitive Culture*: "Culture, or Civilization," according to Tylor, is a "complex whole which includes knowledge, belief, art, morals, law, custom," and progresses in "uniform... stages of development or evolution" in all societies.[118] Human beings had indeed spread from a single point of origin, as Prichard had contended, but this spread was developmental rather than diffusionary. Africans and Polynesians had not fallen farther away from the original human type; rather, Europeans had advanced farther than Africans and Polynesians beyond an original condition of barbarism. Though it rode the cultural coattails of Darwinism, Tylor's revived stadial history, like the original, was very un-Darwinian in its teleological picture of a uniform evolutionary sequence through which all peoples were destined to pass.[119] Methodologically, however, that teleological narrative had the advantage of allowing one to complete the gaps in the archaeological record by drawing analogies between modern "primitives" and ancient peoples. As Tylor would put it at the 1866 meeting of the BAAS, "the study of the lower races is capable of furnishing most important knowledge about ourselves, about our own habits, customs, laws, principles, prejudices."[120]

A survey of the ethnological and anthropological papers read before the BAAS during the 1860s reveals that by the end of the decade the research agenda had very much shifted away from the question of human diversity and toward a debate about the evolutionary dynamics that could have brought it about.[121] Indeed, it was thanks partly to evolution that the Ethnological and Anthropological Societies would merge in 1871 to form a single organization called the Anthropological Institute of Great Britain

---

[116] Ibid., 134.

[117] Tylor, "Wild Men and Beast-Children," *Anthropological Review* 1 (1863): 21–32.

[118] Tylor, *Primitive Culture*, 1: 1.

[119] Bernard Lightman notes that most Victorian evolutionary theory was Spencerian rather than Darwinian in its bent. See "Darwin and the Popularization of Evolution," *Notes and Records of the Royal Society* 64.1 (2010): 5–24.

[120] Tylor, "Phenomena of the Higher Civilisation Traceable to a Rudimental Origin Among Savage Tribes," *Anthropological Review* 5 (1867): 303–4.

[121] See *Report of the Thirty-Ninth Annual Meeting of the British Association for the Advancement of Science* (London, UK: John Murray, 1870), 130–2, 137–51.

and Ireland.[122] Historians of science have shown how the politics of evolution in Victorian Britain were extraordinarily complex, and indeed Tylor's evolutionism had a range of effects when it landed among the contentious battle lines of the monogenesis-polygenesis controversy.[123] In certain respects Tylor's model was friendlier to the party of Prichard and Müller. Although we have learned to think of evolutionism as the enemy of Victorian Protestant orthodoxy, its broad assertions of human universality and meliorist politics matched up perfectly with the old Ethnological Society's moral polemic. Not only was evolution, strictly speaking, a form of monogenesis, but, as Stocking demonstrates, it was also culturally of a piece with Prichard's ethnology: Tylor, Lubbock, and McLennan came from the same liberal-Dissenting milieu as Prichard and affirmed an optimistic history of economic progress and human cultivation.[124] In its narrative of a steadily advancing human civilization, evolutionary anthropology bore a much closer resemblance to classical stadial history than to Darwin's contemporaneous model. Many polygenists therefore rejected evolution as a *deus ex machina* with no more empirical grounding than six-day special creation. The only difference between "a disciple of Darwin and a disciple of Moses," wrote Hunt, was that "one calls in natural selection with unlimited power, and the other calls in a Deity provided in the same manner."[125] Indeed, many polygenists found themselves retrenching around an Ussherian young-earth chronology in order to insist that six millennia of history was simply not enough time for all existing human forms to have diverged from one ancestor. John Crawfurd's 1868 essay "On the Plurality of the Races of Man," for example, would reject the importance of temporal development because such changes could not be documented in the historical record. "[W]hat the races of man now are," Crawfurd argued, they have evidently been "from the earliest dawn of authentic history," for "[t]he representations of Egyptians and Negroes on the monuments of Egypt, estimated to be 4,000 and

---

[122] Stocking documents the complicated institutional wrangling that led to this eventual rapprochement in *Victorian Anthropology*, 254–7.

[123] For disambiguation of different versions of Victorian evolutionary theory and their politics, see James R. Moore, "Deconstructing Darwinism: The Politics of Evolution in the 1860s," *Journal of the History of Biology* 24.3 (1991): 353–408; Adrian J. Desmond, *The Politics of Evolution* (Chicago, IL: U of Chicago P, 1989); Ronald L. Numbers and John Stenhouse, *Disseminating Darwinism* (New York, NY: Cambridge UP, 1999); and Piers J. Hale, *Political Descent: Malthus, Mutualism, and the Politics of Evolution in Victorian England* (Chicago, IL: U of Chicago P, 2014).

[124] Stocking, *Victorian Anthropology*, 250–4.

[125] Hunt, "On the Doctrine of Continuity Applied to Anthropology," *Anthropological Review* 5 (1867): 116.

5,000 years old, differ in no appreciable degree from the Egyptians and Negroes of the present day."[126]

Perhaps even more importantly, evolutionism had a sneaky way of coopting polygenesis's strongest feature, its insistence on an empiricist methodology. The most astute feature of Hunt's polygenism, and the thing that has occasionally caused historians to mistake it for a forerunner of Darwinism,[127] was the fact that it insisted on physical data for claims about human origins and constantly questioned the monogenists' desire to place the human and the animals in separate metaphysical categories. But by telling a story about humankind's "progressive cultivation" that began deep in the past and extended into increasingly civilized futures, Tylor allowed one to have the best of both worlds—to remain committed to broadly Whiggish politics while sticking largely to the data of observable material culture.[128]

At the same time, it soon became apparent that Tylor's evolutionary model of culture posed significant challenges, if not to monogenesis as such, then certainly to the larger moral narrative that Prichard and Müller had built around it. Most notably, the shared point of origin from which it derived all humankind was now indistinguishable from the animal kingdom broadly. The common ancestor in Tylorian monogenesis was not a spiritual, linguistic agent but rather a primitive creature who likely lacked the capacities for inward reflection. More importantly, Tylor's work offered a very different picture of human cultivation than Prichard had: collective rather than individual, and deterministic instead of voluntary. Where Prichard and Müller had defended a vision of human agency and spirituality so rarefied that cultivation was more its foil than its essence, Tylor imagined a human nature that had been built up by a historical process of material advancement. Instead of stressing the essential equality of individuals beyond the particular accumulations of language or custom, Tylor emphasized the story of increasing reason in which all individuals took part.[129]

One can see both implications of Tylor's model at work in C. Staniland Wake's essay on "The Aim and Scope of Anthropology" (1870), which

---

[126] John Crawfurd, "On the Plurality of the Races of Man," *Transactions of the Ethnological Society of London* 6 (1868): 49.

[127] See Burrow, *Evolution and Society*, 121.

[128] Darwin himself felt that evolution, whether his own model or Tylor's, would inevitably obviate the monogenesis-polygenesis controversy: "When the principle of evolution is generally accepted, as it surely will be before long, the dispute between the monogenists and the polygenists will die a silent and unobserved death." *The Descent of Man, and Selection in Relation to Sex* (1871; New York, NY: D. Appleton, 1878), 180.

[129] For the deterministic undertones of evolution, see Burrow, *Whigs and Liberals*, 22–3.

kicked off the first issue of the new *Journal of Anthropology*. Wake began by rejecting the notion that anthropology was merely a description of external human differences and asserted that it was more properly concerned with "discover[ing] the laws of human being, in relation to its continued activity, past, present, and future, as well as, if possible to define the nature of that being itself."[130] He agreed with Prichard that "the external differentiae of race" were "secondary" phenomena, and moreover that language should be the anthropologist's central object of study.[131] Unlike Prichard, however, Wake framed language not as an index of humankind's abstract agency but rather as the very medium through which human consciousness had evolved: "That the intellectual culture attained by mankind has been almost wholly due to the use of symbols of thought is unquestionable; and language may, therefore, be described as the special mental *instrument* of human progress."[132] He argued the same of religion, suggesting that different religions were not the deformed fragments of an original revelation but systems of value that had been integral to the growth of human civilization at all stages. "Even if...it could be established, as some writers have attempted to do, that all religions are ultimately founded on a primitive revelation," he ventured, "it would still be necessary to examine them to ascertain in what way they have affected other developments of human thought," given the great "influence which religion had among the civilised peoples of antiquity...throughout the whole range of their social life and condition."[133]

There is a tendency within Victorianist scholarship to credit evolution, whether Tylor's or Darwin's, with instigating a turn toward racial determinism in Victorian social-scientific thought. Strictly speaking, this claim represents a misunderstanding of history, for if anything race saw its heyday with Knox and Hunt in the 1850s–60s and was rendered a marginal concept by Tylor. Moreover, to levy this charge is to confuse two very different kinds of racism: the chauvinistic universalism of empire, which asserts that the colonizer has some kind of moral duty to the colonized, and the more isolationist, sometimes anti-imperialist racism of Knox, which disavowed any moral relationship between the two. Nevertheless, this conflation of Tylor with scientific racism does capture the way in which Tylor's paradigm combined elements of liberalism and determinism in a way previously unprecedented within Victorian anthropology. It pictured all human beings as sharing a single nature, but regarded that nature as more or less developed among different strata of

---

[130] C. S. Wake, "The Aim and Scope of Anthropology," *Journal of Anthropology* 1 (1870), 4.
[131] Ibid., 4.   [132] Ibid., 10.   [133] Ibid., 11.

civilization. In this sense Tylor also offered a different story of secularization: instead of placing religion prior to culture as the thing that guaranteed human equality, it assimilated religion into a wider history of
"knowledge, belief, art, morals, law, custom" that human beings had
cultivated over centuries.

For all of these reasons, Müller, despite playing a key role in arranging
Tylor's appointment as Oxford's first Professor of Anthropology, would
become a critic of evolutionism.[134] Evolution, he submitted, fudged the
essential question of where, and wherein, lay the exact transition from
animal to human. By dizzying the mind with a chronology of millions of
years, evolution could suggest a gradual, quantitative transition from
animal to human, where in fact that difference was qualitative. In a series
of "Lectures on Mr. Darwin's Philosophy of Language," published in
Fraser's in 1873, Müller contended that Tylor and Darwin alike "first
imagin[e] a continuous scale, and then poin[t] out its indivisibility,"
leaving open the question of how one actually crossed the proverbial
Rubicon posited in the *Lectures on the Science of Language*.[135] Evolution
tried to build man up out of the sum of lower developmental parts, but in
fact the a priori mental categories implied by language must have been
inherited already complete and could not be broken down into simpler
units.[136] More worrisome to Müller was the fact that evolution framed
human beings as the pawns of overriding developmental laws instead of as
agents enacting their own histories. For Müller, by contrast, all historical
growth was a secondary process that shaped, enhanced, or damaged
humanity's primal abstract agency; "[e]volution," he wrote, "can never be
more than the second act."[137]

Müller's resistance to Tylor ultimately led him into a period of methodological retrenchment. In 1868 he had been appointed Oxford's inaug-
ural Professor of Comparative Philology, but in 1875 he would begin to

---

[134] Stocking, *Victorian Anthropology*, 300.

[135] F. Max Müller, "Lectures on Mr. Darwin's Philosophy of Language" (part 2 of 3),
Fraser's Magazine 7 (1873): 668.

[136] For Darwin's relation to comparative philology, see Stephen Alter, *Darwinism and
the Linguistic Image* (Baltimore, MD: Johns Hopkins UP, 1999). In response to Müller's
original *Lectures*, Darwin wrote Müller a letter in which he diplomatically stated a difference
of competency: "As far as language is concerned . . . [h]e who is convinced, as I am, that man
is descended from some lower animal, is almost forced to believe *a priori* that articulate
language has been developed from inarticulate cries; and he is therefore hardly a fair judge of
the arguments opposed to this belief" (Chaudhuri, 257). Later the two men would sit down
to hash out their differences, with Lubbock serving as a mediating figure; Müller refused to
back down from his position that language showed man to be "a real anomaly" in the
animal kingdom, and in response Darwin warned him that he was "a dangerous man."
"Literary Recollections," part 4 of 4, *Cosmopolis* 6 (1897): 347.

[137] Müller, "Literary Recollections" (part 4 of 4), 331.

scale back his university duties and shift his focus toward editing a groundbreaking series of the *Sacred Books of the East*.[138] In so doing he would retreat from his earlier dalliances with what Smail calls "deep history"—his claim that philology studied the unconscious, organic laws behind language—in favor of a focus upon conscious historical actors and the texts they wrote.[139] In an 1884 essay called "Forgotten Bibles," a plug for the *Sacred Books* series, Müller would name these the "theoretical" and "historical" approaches to religious history.[140] When he first proposed the series back in 1875, Müller wrote, many writers, under the new spell of Tylor, had considered it unnecessary to study the great texts of Indian, Persian, or Chinese religion on the grounds that evolution had already made clear the outlines of religion's history *avant le fait*:

> When I humbly suggested that these books had a purely historical interest, and that the history of religion could be studied from no other documents, I was told that it was perfectly known how religion arose and through how many stages it had to pass in its development from fetishism to positivism, and that, whatever facts might be found in the Sacred Books of the East, they must all vanish before theories which are infallible and incontrovertible. If anything more was to be discovered about the origin and nature of religion it was not from dusty historical documents but from psycho-physiological experiments, or possibly from the creeds of living savages.[141]

Those who see religion as the product of determinate evolutionary laws, Müller proposes, not only find themselves in the position of making vast and dubious generalizations, but also downplay the importance of individual minds in the development of religious experience. In seeking a more rigorous historicism, the evolutionists write human individuals out of their own history, denying the subjective and experiential investment in religion that makes human beings want to study it in the first place.

By retrenching around a largely textual humanism, Müller would effectively split off from the history of anthropology and become the progenitor of a separate scholarly tradition: comparative religion. Ann Taves notes how religious studies in the twentieth century became divided between an ecumenical approach that focused on a core of "religious experience" supposedly looming behind different global traditions—generally privileging scripture-based religions such as Christianity, Buddhism, and Islam—and anthropological methods oriented toward "lived

---

[138] Arie L. Molendijk, *Friedrich Max Müller & the* Sacred Books of the East (New York, NY: Oxford UP, 2016), 43–4.
[139] Smail, 2.
[140] F. Max Müller, "Forgotten Bibles," *Nineteenth Century* 15 (1884): 1006.
[141] Ibid., 1005.

religion" in tribal or indigenous contexts.[142] This is, in effect, the gap
that opened up between Müller and his former ESL allies. If anthropologists would increasingly theorize religion as a determinate feature of
particular societies, comparative religion, with Müller as its presiding
spirit, tended to follow a set of essentially Prichardian assumptions: that
human beings possessed an inalienable spiritual instinct that had been
cultivated differently among different peoples and had found its best
expressions in classic scriptural texts.[143] Thus, as against anthropology's
largely material focus, comparative religion would remain text-oriented,
valorizing the insights of great spiritual geniuses and the records of their
deeds and teachings.[144] Above all, comparative religion kept alive a
transcendentalist desire not just to trace the history of human religiosity
but also to restore a vision of the primal religious instinct that modern
religious diversity, the very data of anthropology, obscured. As Louis
Henry Jordan put it in his 1905 manual of the subject, comparative
religion placed "the numerous Religions of the world side by side, in
order that, deliberately comparing and contrasting them, it may frame a
reliable estimate of their respective claims and values."[145] As such, Jordan
argued, it was not just "a useful adjunct to the study of Apologetics"
but also a preparation for the more ambitious enterprise that he called
the "Philosophy of Religion," which sought to show that there was "a
great eternal principle" that "underlies, and is answerable for, the various
divergent Religions."[146]

We have seen how this ecumenical and syncretistic project had been
present in Müller's thinking from the start. "[L]ike an old precious
medal," Müller had rhapsodized in his *Introduction to the Science of
Religion*, "the ancient religion, after the rust of ages has been removed,

---

[142] See Anne Taves, *Religious Experience Reconsidered* (Princeton, NJ: Princeton UP,
2009), 3–8.

[143] For recent accounts of this continuing disciplinary dichotomy, see Taves, 6; Masuzawa, *Invention*, 42–3.

[144] As E. E. Evans-Pritchard put it in the mid-1960s, the "data" of comparative religion
"are derived almost entirely from books—sacred texts, theological writings, exegetics,
mystical writings, and all the rest of it. But for the anthropologist or sociologist, I would
suggest, this is perhaps the least significant part of religion, especially as it is very evident
that the scholars who write books on the historical religions are sometimes uncertain what
even key words meant to the authors of the original texts." The precise grounds on which
Müller had mistrusted anthropology—the fact that it seems relatively uninterested in the
language and ideas of particular religious texts—is for Evans-Pritchard its virtue, since "[t]he
philological reconstructions and interpretations of these key words are only too often
uncertain, contradictory, and unconvincing, e.g. in the case of the word 'god.'" *Theories
of Primitive Religion* (New York, NY: Oxford UP, 1965), 119.

[145] Louis Henry Jordan, *Comparative Religion: Its Genesis and Growth* (Edinburgh, UK:
T & T Clarke, 1905), xi.

[146] Ibid., x, 20, 19.

will come out in all its purity and brightness; and the image which it discloses will be the image of the Father, the Father of all the nations upon earth; and the superscription, when we can read it again, will be, not only in Judaea, but in the languages of all the races of the world."[147] What is interesting is how such ambitions came to dominate his late work as a public intellectual. Increasingly marginal both to linguistics and to anthropology, Müller instead became a cosmopolitan grandee of interfaith dialogue within the Empire. Most famously, he delivered the keynote at the 1893 World's Parliament of Religions at the Columbian Exhibition at Chicago, calling the event an "unprecedented" happening in the history of religious syncretism and quoting the following lines from Robert Browning's "Christmas Eve": "Better pursue a pilgrimage / Through ancient and through modern times, / To many peoples, various climes, / Where I may see saint, savage, sage, / Fuse their respective creeds in one / Before the general Father's throne."[148]

The key thing about this ecumenical Müller is that, for all his talk of history over theory, his work had very little use for the actual historical materials of religion. In the *Introduction to the Science of Religion*, Müller had demanded a division of labor between "comparative theology," which studied the teachings of great religious founders as preserved in sacred texts, and "theoretic theology," which studied an invisible human faculty of faith attested to by the world's different creeds.[149] Importantly, neither "Comparative Theology" nor "Theoretic Theology," as Müller defines them, has much interest in the particulars of existing religious traditions. The first aims to reconstruct the original doctrines of bygone religious geniuses; the second extrapolates from these materials a transcendentalist yearning that they may not actually contain. This ahistoricism is, if you will, the one of which classical liberalism is often accused: its emphasis on universals over particulars, and on abstract sameness over embodied differences. What is interesting, and what the rest of this book will examine, is how approaches that stressed those more embodied, non-propositional elements of religion, whether polygenist race or Tylorian culture, could open up alternative liberal imaginaries, as they had for Burton—liberal imaginaries based not on Protestant belief, but rather on the idea of an eclectic self made up of inheritances it did not choose, and situated in a world of differences rather than commonalities.

---

[147] Müller, *Science of Religion*, 12.
[148] Quoted in Müller, "The Parliament of Religions, Chicago, 1893," *Last Essays* (London, UK: Longmans, Green, 1901), 326. For an overview of the Parliament, see Richard H. Seagar, *The World's Parliament of Religions: The East/West Encounter, Chicago, 1893* (Bloomington, IN: Indiana UP, 1995).
[149] Müller, *Science of Religion*, 6.

2

Arnoldian Secularism
Race and Political Theology from *Celtic Literature* to *Literature and Dogma*

In the last chapter I used the monogenesis-polygenesis debates to explore what was at stake, for mid-Victorian liberals, in identifying religion with belief. Those debates saw James Cowles Prichard, F. Max Müller, and other theorists defend a kind of liberal universalism by arguing that all human beings shared a common religious faculty for abstract thought and spiritual cultivation. Matthew Arnold made Müller's acquaintance at Oxford and the two would continue to share ideas via correspondence; Arnold, however, would take up the racialized constructions of religion opposed by Müller and use them to imagine a different sort of liberal subjectivity.[1] In his major essays on religion, literature, and politics—*Culture and Anarchy* (1869), *St. Paul and Protestantism* (1870), and *Literature and Dogma* (1873)—Arnold parlays the polygenist claim that humankind is comprised of multiple, incommensurate racial instincts to model a liberal self built not around abstract interiority but rather around an ethos of many-sidedness. Just as different races, in polygenist theory, cannot fully mix with one another, so (in Arnold's analogy) must the "Hebraic" genius for religion, the "Hellenic" talent for science, and the "Celtic" feeling for beauty be harmonized within the personality of the individual. Religion, for Arnoldian liberalism, is not the free spirituality that makes self-cultivation possible but rather the epitome of all those narrow, one-sided commitments that cultivation must simultaneously incorporate and subdue.

By thus reimagining religion's relationship to cultivated individuality, Arnold is waging a specific polemic against a Dissenting liberalism that he sees as wielding a destructive force upon national life. For Arnold, the traditional British liberalism of voluntary belief, laissez-faire competition, and "doing as one likes" actually narrows the self's horizons and must be

---

[1] Sadly, their letters no longer survive; see F. Max Müller, *My Autobiography: A Fragment* (New York, NY: Scribners, 1901), 282–3.

combated by a program of "culture" that teaches us to see religion in its proper place alongside art, science, and "the best which has been thought and said in the world."[2] The general outlines of this argument are well known, but I would like to suggest here that Arnoldian culture ends up having a more ambivalent relation to religion than this brisk summary suggests. For in fact Arnold posits several relationships between culture and religion, a fact that ultimately reflects the contradictory goals of the former term. On one level, Arnoldian culture is defined by religion as the whole is defined by the part. Religion represents one of many incomplete value systems that culture can balance against one another. At the same time, culture does not simply incorporate religion but also requires the supplement of religion's "fire and strength" in order to carry normative force itself (5:178). More vexingly still, the fact that religion, as Arnold portrays it, tends to reject the very spirit of many-sidedness hints that culture may conceal an exclusionary logic of its own. Religion, in other words, comes to stand for Arnoldian culture's ideal subject, its intransigent opponent, and its secret ingredient; it is the thing that culture must prove itself broader than, something without which culture is incomplete, and an image of what culture may need to become despite its best intentions. At stake in all of this, I argue, is Arnold's hope that culture might serve as a new, secular value system—a neutral framework for incorporating and tempering narrow commitments inherited from the past—with the constant fear being that culture will prove illiberal in its own right.

One immediate goal of this chapter is thus to consider anew what Arnold can tell us about the secular. Arnold cuts a familiar figure in narratives of Victorian secularization, where he tends to play one of two roles. In some studies, we meet him as a melancholy humanist who laments the loss of a no-longer-tenable faith but feels powerless to produce alternatives—"Wandering," in a famous couplet, "between two worlds, one dead, / The other powerless to be born."[3] Other critics, meanwhile, cast Arnold as a cautionary example of aggressive counter-secularization, a liberal whose "sacralization of art," in Steven Marcus's phrase, becomes as absolutist as the religion it is designed to supplant.[4] What both accounts

[2] *The Complete Prose Works of Matthew Arnold*, ed. R. H. Super (11 vols.; Ann Arbor, MI: U of Michigan P, 1960–77), 5: 115, 5: 233. All subsequent citations from Super's editions will be given parenthetically by volume and page number.

[3] Matthew Arnold, "Stanzas from the Grand Chartreuse," *The Poems of Matthew Arnold* (Oxford, UK: Oxford UP, 1950), 299–306, lines 85–6. For classic accounts of religion in Arnold's oeuvre, see J. Hillis Miller, *The Disappearance of God: Five Nineteenth-Century Writers* (1963; New York, NY: Schocken, 1965), 212–69; Ruth Roberts, *Arnold and God* (Berkeley, CA: U of California P, 1983).

[4] Steven Marcus, "Culture and Anarchy Today," in *Culture and Anarchy*, ed. Samuel Lipman (New Haven, CT: Yale UP, 1994), 169. See also Raymond Williams, *Culture and*

tend to assume, however, is that Arnold is attempting to fill a gap vacated by religion with a secular substitute. In reality, Arnold's brand of secularism is engaged in a messier project of defining religion, its boundaries, and its relation to the modern. For example, when Arnold writes in his late manifesto, "The Study of Poetry" (1888), that as history advances "most of what now passes with us for religion and philosophy will be replaced by poetry," he does not mean that Milton or Pope present readers with rites and practices that make for salvation (9:161–2). Rather, his claim is that these poets offer sources of emotional energy that more truly deserve the name of religion: "More and more," he explains, "mankind will discover that we have to turn to poetry to interpret life for us, to console us, to sustain us" (9:161). Instead of replacing religion with poetry, Arnold back-projects "religion" as a generic term for the moral and emotional coherence that modern individuals are increasingly tasked with making for themselves, by literary or other means.

More broadly, I want to reassess why Arnold's essays on culture should command our attention now that the culture wars of the 1980s and 1990s are some decades behind us. During those years, Arnold was typically read as a defender of the great books of the European canon against the fragmenting effects of mass media and democracy.[5] This Arnold has seen his stock decline considerably within the field. Yet it was never a terribly accurate portrait of Arnold to begin with, for the truth is that *Culture and Anarchy* is designed largely as a critique of organic, insular value systems. The book's project is not to defend a holistic common culture against outside intrusions but rather to use the free play of cosmopolitan literature to disrupt the stultifying atmosphere of bourgeois Protestant religiosity. For this reason, it finds a better contemporary analogue in the problem of political theology—that is, the question of how secular visions of political authority relate to the theological antecedents they often define themselves against.[6] As Arnold sees it, culture is

---

Society, 1780–1950 (New York, NY: Columbia UP, 1958), 125–6, and Gauri Visawanathan, "Secularism in the Framework of Heterodoxy," *PMLA* 123.2 (2008): 466–76.

[5] See Gerald Graff, "Arnold, Reason, and Common Culture," in Lipman, 186–201; Nancy Armstrong, "Contemporary Culturism: How Victorian Is It?", in John Kucich and Diane Sadoff (eds.), *Victorian Afterlife: Postmodern Culture Rewrites the Nineteenth Century* (Minneapolis, MN: U of Minnesota P, 2000), 311–26. On the American right's appropriations of Arnold, see Eugene Goodheart, "Arnold Among the Neoconservatives," *Clio* 25.4 (1996): 455–8. On the uses and abuses of Arnold in British debates about English literary curriculum, see Bill Bell, "The Function of Arnold at the Present Time," *Essays in Criticism* 47.3 (1997): 203–19.

[6] The term "political theology" is taken from the title of Carl Schmitt's 1922 volume and has become a blanket term for the interrelated problematics of secularism and sovereignty. For an overview, see Hent de Vries, "Introduction" to de Vries and Lawrence

a secularist ethos that can gather up older, illiberal principles like religion and harmonize them in their ideal relations. The ongoing burden of his argument is therefore to demonstrate that culture is a qualitatively different ideal than those it incorporates, one that can implement its values without excluding anything, saying no to anything, or silencing anyone. In this sense Arnold's diatribe against English "Hebraism" needs to be situated, not just among Victorian discourses on Judaism, but also within a wider debate among nineteenth-century historians over the relationship between Western pluralism and Abrahamic monotheism. For Ernest Renan and other scholars on whom Arnold drew, the theology of Moses and Mohammed represents at once the opposite of secular pluralism and its mirror. It is a universalism that attempts to impose a single set of values on the entire world, as against a universalism that would try to sum up a world of contending values within one framework. The fact that it also represents a key historical ingredient of the latter reminds the liberal intellectual that there are at least two different roads to universalism that intersect in frequently vexing ways.

THE BROAD CHURCH, AESTHETIC LIBERALISM, AND THE USES OF POLYGENESIS

The past two decades have seen a number of scholars address the role of race in Matthew Arnold's social criticism. Such work is often driven by a plot of gothic revelation in which Arnold's seemingly non-controversial humanism turns out to be built over a dungeon full of sinister and discredited racial theories, thus rendering us, his disciplinary descendants, complicit in their wicked logic.[7] In fact, Arnold's use of racial anthropology is quite overt, something he advertises up front as giving his

---

E. Sullivan (eds.), *Political Theologies: Public Religions in a Post-Secular World* (New York, NY: Fordham UP, 2006), 25–47.

[7] For recent treatments of race in Arnold, see Robert J. C. Young, *Colonial Desire: Hybridity in Theory, Culture, and Race* (New York, NY: Routledge, 1995), 55–89 (a chapter entitled "The Complicity of Culture"); Vincent Pecora, *Secularization and Cultural Criticism: Religion, Nation, and Modernity* (Chicago, IL: U of Chicago P, 2006), 131–56; Daniel G. Williams, *Ethnicity and Cultural Authority: From Arnold to DuBois* (Edinburgh, UK: Edinburgh UP, 2006), 33–71. These accounts build upon the work done half a century ago by Frederic E. Faverty in *Matthew Arnold the Ethnologist* (Evanston, IL: Northwestern UP, 1951). For more focused analyses of Arnold's relationship to Judaism, see Michael Ragussis, *Figures of Conversion: "The Jewish Question" and English National Identity* (Durham, NC: Duke UP, 1995), 211–33; Lionel Gossman, "Philhellenism and Antisemitism: Matthew Arnold and His German Models," *Comparative Literature* 46.1 (1994): 1–39; Brian Cheyette, *Constructions of "The Jew" in English Literature and Society: Racial Representations, 1875–1945* (New York, NY: Cambridge UP, 1993), 13–23.

humanistic polemics an edge of modern scientificity. "Science has now made visible to everybody the great and pregnant elements of difference which lie in race," Arnold announces in *Culture and Anarchy*, much as a public intellectual writing today might borrow the prestige of cognitive science or evolutionary psychology (5:173). In this spirit, Arnold drew freely and unsystematically upon the two competing lines of race theory that we traced in the last chapter: on the one hand, comparative philology, which read human progress as the collaborative project of different racial families, and, on the other hand, the polygenist anthropology of Robert Knox and James Hunt. Arnold's main exposure to philology came through his father, Thomas, who had picked it up from Max Müller's old mentor, Christian von Bunsen. Thomas Arnold first met Bunsen during an 1828 visit to Rome, where the latter was acting as secretary for Barthold Niebuhr, Prussian envoy to the Pope and unofficial dean of German historiography. Bunsen, himself an accomplished scholar of Arabic, Persian, and Hebrew, gave Thomas a copy of Niebuhr's *Roman History* (1827–32) and encouraged his own *History of Rome* (1838–42).[8] More importantly, he introduced the future Rugby headmaster to a certain German approach to incorporating Romantic race-concepts into liberal historiography. As Wilhelm Friedrich Schlegel described it in his *Philosophy of History* (1829), humankind shared a common origin but had been divided millennia ago "into a multitude of nations, races, and languages," which meant that the four basic faculties of Understanding, Will, Reason, and Imagination were now distributed among "the peculiar character[s] of particular ages or nations."[9]

The idea that historical progress was the joint endeavor of different nations and races, each making its own limited contribution during an appointed period of ascendancy, appealed to liberal Anglicans writing in the wake of the Napoleonic Wars in that it allowed one to affirm a basic faith in progress while distancing oneself from the more militant or deterministic versions of that narrative.[10] As such, it became a key tool

---

[8] Eugene L. Williamson, *The Liberalism of Thomas Arnold: A Study of His Religious and Political Writings* (Tuscaloosa, AL: U of Alabama P, 1964), 62–6; Ralph Albert Owen, *Christian Bunsen and Liberal English Theology* (Montpelier, VT: Capital City P, 1924), 15–73; Robert Preyer, "Bunsen and the Anglo-American Literary Community in Rome," *Der Gelehrte Diplomat: zum Wirken Christian Carl Josias Bunsens*, ed. Erich Geldbach (Leiden, the Netherlands: Brill, 1980), 35–64; Susanne Stark, *"Behind Inverted Commas": Translation and Anglo-German Cultural Relations in the Nineteenth Century* (Clevedon, UK: Multilingual Matters, 1999).

[9] W. F. Schlegel, *The Philosophy of History in a Course of Lectures, Delivered at Vienna* (1829), trans. James Burton Robertson (London, UK: Henry G. Bohn, 1852), 162–3.

[10] Duncan Forbes, *The Liberal Anglican Idea of History* (New York, NY: Cambridge UP, 1952), 15–16, 67–70. See also Richard K. Barksdale, "Thomas Arnold's Attitude Toward Race," *The Phylon Quarterly* 18.2 (1957): 174–80.

in the rhetorical arsenal of the Broad Church party that Thomas Arnold joined upon his appointment as Regius Professor of Modern History in 1841. The Broad Church, whose other members included Connop Thirlwall, Julius Hare, Richard Whately, and Renn Dickson Hampden, were contemporaries of the Oxford Movement and shared the Tractarians' fear that the 1832 Reform Parliament might further roll back the Anglican Church's power in Ireland and at home, especially in light of the growing political power of Dissent.[11] The Broad Church writers parted ways with the Tractarians, however, in blaming the Church's troubles upon its own reluctance to modernize, and thus eagerly brought new currents of continental thought to bear upon Anglican institutions and teachings. Some Broad Church members contributed to *Essays and Reviews*, the notorious 1860 volume that reappraised the Thirty-Nine Articles in light of the Higher Criticism and geology, while Thomas Arnold himself published *An Essay on the Right Interpretation and Understanding of the Scriptures* (1831) which proposed that no biblical passage could be rightly interpreted without fully comprehending the social and political conditions surrounding its composition.[12] More locally, Arnold looked to the established Church as a mixing institution that had the potential to stimulate a new sense of the common good. He hoped that one day multiple forms of worship might be accommodated within the Church, advocated the admission of Dissenters to Oxford, and, drawing again upon Niebuhr, developed a relativistic reading of Christian history that justified different historical practices and institutions as tools in a divine education of humankind.[13]

Many of these same commitments—to pluralism within national institutions; to a historicist reading of the Bible—would animate the work of Matthew Arnold. Even more than his father, Matthew was an aesthetic liberal who saw the goal of human life as being the development of all sides of the human character into "a complete and consistent whole."[14] In his early lectures as Oxford Professor of Poetry, a mostly ceremonial appointment that he received in 1857, Arnold sought to defend the role of such

[11] Lionel Trilling, *Matthew Arnold* (1939; New York, NY: Columbia UP, 1949), 46–7. For a wider survey, see Tod E. Jones, *The Broad Church: A Biography of a Movement* (Lanham, MD: Lexington Books, 2003).

[12] Jones, 80–3.

[13] Trilling, 47–62. See also J. P. Parry, *Democracy and Religion: Gladstone and the Liberal Party, 1867–1875* (New York, NY: Cambridge UP, 1986), 57–104.

[14] Wilhelm Von Humboldt, *The Sphere and Duties of Government*, trans. Joseph Coulthard (London, UK: John Chapman, 1854), 11. For Arnold's German reading, see David DeLaura, *Hebrew and Hellene in Victorian England* (Austin, TX: U of Texas P, 1969), 181–91 and Kenneth Allott, "Matthew Arnold's Reading-Lists in Three Early Diaries," *Victorian Studies* 2.3 (1959): 254–66.

activity within an English modernity deeply shaped by industrialization and utilitarianism. "The Function of Criticism at the Present Time" (1864), for example, insists that England cannot make "spiritual progress" (3:282) until it has embraced the process of disinterested, many-sided reflection that he calls criticism: "keeping aloof from what is called 'the practical view of things'" and allowing "a free play of the mind . . . to know the best that is known and thought in the world" (3:270). "[T]he criticism which alone can much help us for the future," he writes, asks England and other European nations to look beyond themselves and to develop "a knowledge of Greek, Roman, and Eastern antiquity, and of one another" (3:284). The essay derides Macaulay's claim that "the literature now extant in the English language is of far greater value than all the literature which three hundred years ago was extant in all the languages of the world together" by calling "all mere glorification by ourselves of ourselves or our literature . . . both vulgar, and, besides being vulgar, retarding" (3:257). In another early lecture entitled "The Modern Element in Literature" (1857), Arnold argued that England could no longer produce great poetry because, unlike France or Germany, its intellectuals had not committed themselves to reappraising that "immense system of institutions, established facts, accredited dogmas, customs, rules" inherited "from times not modern" (3:109). The chief job of poetry, according to Arnold, was to make sense of the intellectual currents of an age, but Victorian writers, thanks to the reactionary mindset inspired by the French Revolution and the Napoleonic Wars, had shirked this duty and retrenched around an insular nationalism.

But perhaps the most striking feature of Arnold's early aesthetic liberalism is the way in which it models the play of different national characters upon a polygenist understanding of race. In this Arnold was drawing upon the work of the French scholar Ernest Renan, whom he first met in Paris in 1859. Trained as a philologist of the Semitic languages, Renan would become best known to British readers through his historicist *Vie de Jésus* (1863), but also published numerous other works that interpreted religious and literary history through the lens both of philology and of polygenist race theory. Taking his cue from Renan's "Sur la poésie des races celtiques" (1854), Arnold published his own lectures *On the Study of Celtic Literature* (1867), which asserted that science had shown humankind to be comprised of different races with radically irreconcilable natures.[15] By way of evidence, he cited W. F. Edwards's *Des Caractères Physiologiques des Races Humaines* (1839), which argued upon the basis of

[15] See Lewis F. Mott, "Renan and Matthew Arnold," *Modern Language Notes* 33.2 (1918): 65–73; Faverty, 167–70; Young, 68–72.

anatomical data that the Saxon conquest of the Angles and the subsequent Norman conquest of the Anglo-Saxons had bestowed upon England a surprisingly heterogeneous character:

> How little the triumph of the conqueror's laws, manners, and language, proves the extinction of the old race, we may see by looking at France; Gaul was Latinised in language, manners, and laws, and yet her people remained essentially Celtic. The Germanisation of Britain went far deeper than the Latinisation of France, and not only laws, manners, and language, but the main current of the blood became Germanic; but how, without some process of radical extirpation, of which, as I say, there is no evidence, can there have failed to subsist in Britain, as in Gaul, a Celtic current too? (3:338)

Unlike a typical polygenist, however, Arnold takes from this claim not a vision of inevitable racial strife but rather the idea that England needs to abandon any myth of its own purity. As against the notion that the Irish are "aliens in speech, in religion, in blood," Arnold maintains that England remains animated by separate racial energies—a German industrial and scientific temperament, a Celtic penchant for stylish melancholy, a Norman talent for rhetoric—that work best when they are balanced (3:300). As a result, Arnold's lectures very nearly invert the strategy of Prichard's *Eastern Origin of the Celtic Nations* (1831). For Prichard, the English were obliged to sympathize with the Celts because they were essentially the same beneath the superficial variations of language and physiognomy; for Arnold, by contrast, it is because the Celts, the Saxons, and the Normans are irreconcilably different that they must instead be played off against each other as aesthetic elements within English civilization.

To this end, Arnold offers literary criticism as a moral adjunct to polygenist science. Just "[a]s there are for physiology physical marks, such as the square head of the German, the round head of the Gael, the oval head of the Cymri, which determine the type of a people, so for criticism there are spiritual marks which determine the type, and make us speak of the Greek genius, the Teutonic genius, the Celtic genius, and so on" (3:340). By turning this literary lens upon race, he ventures, the English can bring these energies into a free play where they will enhance rather than stymie each other:

> So long as we are blindly and ignorantly rolled about by the forces of our nature, their contradiction baffles us and lames us; so soon as we have clearly discerned what they are, and begun to apply to them a law of measure, control, and guidance, they may be made to work for our good and to carry us forward. Then we may have the good of our German part, the good of our Latin part, the good of our Celtic part; and instead of one part clashing with the other, we may bring it in to continue and perfect the other, when the other has given us all the good it can yield, and by being pressed further, could

only give us its faulty excess. Then we may use the German faithfulness to
Nature to give us science, and to free us from insolence and self-will; we may
use the Celtic quickness of perception to give us delicacy, and to free us from
hardness and Philistinism; we may use the Latin decisiveness to give us
strenuous clear method, and to free us from fumbling and idling.   (3:383)

Lionel Trilling deemed it contradictory for Arnold to prescribe traits that
he also defined as predetermined, but in many ways this objection misses
the point.[16] For Arnold, attaching desirable qualities to fixed racial characters is attractive precisely because it necessitates an aesthetic solution to
political and social problems. England's Saxons and its Celts may war, and
they may miscegenate, but they will never be able to eliminate one
another's distinctive traits from the English population, which means
that the English must try to cultivate an eclectic relationship between
them. The narrative that emerges is much like that of Walter Scott's
Waverley (1814), which imagines the defeated Highlander society as a
collection of artifacts, styles, and sensibilities that can be absorbed into
modern Great Britain as aesthetic, if not as political, realities.[17]

In *The Powers of Distance* (2001), Amanda Anderson argues that Arnold
uses the idea of race to temper cosmopolitanism by grounding it in
particular "cultivated stances" where objective and subjective, global and
local, meet.[18] By orienting her reading of Arnold around these poles,
however, Anderson avoids the peculiar problem of plurality, or minority,
that Arnold opens up in a text like *Celtic Literature*. This is because Arnold
is using race not just to mitigate liberal abstraction but also, as Vincent
Pecora points out, to construct something like our own multiculturalist
theory, which celebrates "the cross-fertilization enabled by transnational
flows of ideas" and "the discursively (rather than racially) hybrid character
of cultures around the globe."[19] Thus the real burden of Arnold's argument is to imagine how pluralism might be sustained by internalizing
principles that, in and of themselves, contradict any ideals of harmony or
many-sidedness. What Arnold finds attractive in the Celtic character is the
fact that it necessitates pluralism by embodying qualities that are at some
level irreconcilable—impracticality, sentimentality, the willingness "*to
react against the despotism of fact*" (3:344):

> If his rebellion against fact has thus lamed the Celt even in spiritual work,
> how much more must it have lamed him in the world of business and

---

[16] Trilling, 236.
[17] See James Buzard, *Disorienting Fiction: The Autoethnographic Work of Nineteenth-
Century British Novels* (Princeton, NJ: Princeton UP, 2005), 63–104.
[18] Amanda Anderson, *The Powers of Distance: Cosmopolitanism and the Cultivation of
Detachment* (Princeton, NJ: Princeton UP, 2001), 96.
[19] Pecora, 151; see 150–3.

politics! The skilful and resolute appliance of means to ends which is needed both to make progress in material civilisation, and also to form powerful states, is just what the Celt has least turn for ... And as in material civilisation he has been ineffectual, so has the Celt been ineffectual in politics. This colossal, impetuous, adventurous wanderer, the Titan of the early world, who in primitive times fills so large a place on earth's scene, dwindles and dwindles as history goes on, and at last is shrunk to what we now see him. For ages and ages the world has been constantly slipping, ever more and more, out of the Celt's grasp. "They went forth to the war," Ossian says most truly, "*but they always fell.*" (3:345–6)

These traits are at once a difficulty to overcome and the very thing that keeps many-sidedness *many*. Hence Arnold arrives at a series of dilemmas that will bedevil much of his subsequent thinking. When are specific values opposed to the greater universalisms that seek to incorporate them? But also: when is wholeness or totality itself a parochial quality? For in fact the Saxons play a surprisingly dual role in Arnold's essay. Sometimes Arnold uses them to epitomize modern virtues of progress and universalism, but at other times he presents them as just another race whose virtues are striking but also incomplete. Anglo-Saxon civilization, for Arnold, is limited precisely because of its universal aspirations, which in the settler context threaten to unleash an aggressive homogenization upon the world. Until we harness the best of our Celtic and other non-Saxon parts, Arnold writes,

> we ride one force of our nature to death; we will be nothing but Anglo-Saxons in the Old World or in the New; and when our race has built Bold Street, Liverpool, and pronounced it very good, it hurries across the Atlantic, and builds Nashville, and Jacksonville, and Milledgeville, and thinks it is fulfilling the designs of Providence in an incomparable manner. (3:383)

Likewise, when Arnold's essay nods to the ongoing Governor Eyre controversy in Jamaica, his worry is not the supposed savagery of the West Indian slaves (as it was for Knox and Hunt) but rather the destructive power of the English. "At this moment," he observes, recent events in Jamaica are seeing "the narrow Philistinism, which has long had things its own way in England ... sho[w] its natural fruits" (3:385–6). What one might think of as modern civilization may be just another racial nature that refuses to recognize itself as such.

HEBRAISM, HELLENISM, AND CULTURE

In 1867, the same year in which *Celtic Literature* was published, the passage of the Second Reform Act provoked Arnold to turn his full attention toward combating this "narrow Philistinism" with a series of essays subsequently collected as *Culture and Anarchy* (1869).[20] Like "The Function of Criticism" and the lectures on Celtic literature before it, *Culture and Anarchy* theorizes modern civilization as a multifaceted project within which different human energies find their ideal equilibrium. Yet now it is English bourgeois civilization that represents a problematic parochialism in need of reconciliation to some larger complex of values. Specifically, Arnold coins the term "Hebraism" to refer to a middle-class ethic of "duty, self-control and work," driven by the simple imperatives of biblical religion (5:163), that must be tempered by a more disinterested intellectual curiosity called "Hellenism":

> [W]hile Hebraism seizes upon certain plain, capital intimations of the universal order and rivets itself, one may say, with unequalled grandeur of earnestness and intensity on the study and observance of them, the bent of Hellenism is to follow, with flexible activity, the whole play of the universal order, to be apprehensive of missing any part of it, of sacrificing one part to another ... (5:165)

Arnold has, of course, borrowed these two terms from the comparative philology of Müller, which contrasted the strict religiosity of the Semitic imagination with the more playful love of art and beauty supposedly displayed by the Indians, the Greeks, and other Indo-European peoples.[21] In turning from racial polygenesis to Indo-European philology as his scholarly source material, Arnold continues his practice of using racial difference to imagine the necessary internal heterogeneity of modern many-sidedness, but also attempts an account of many-sidedness that is more rigorously dialectical. Hebraism and Hellenism, as Arnold constructs them, stand for centripetal and centrifugal approaches to human life: each aims for "man's perfection or salvation" (5:164), but if Hebraism maintains that it is possible to find a single principle for regulating human existence, "a rule telling [us] the *unum necessarium*, or one thing needful," Hellenism insists that perfection can only be attained through a knowledge of the many and of the whole (5:180). Most crucially, Hebraism is associated with "the religious side in man" (5:252), which Arnold defines as a kind of "intense and convinced energy" (5:255), an "earnestness in going manfully with the best light we have, as one force" (5:163). Arnold develops this understanding of religion at greater length in *St. Paul and*

---

[20] For the context surrounding *Culture and Anarchy*'s composition, see Trilling, 243–51.

[21] Arnold seems to have taken this concept most directly from the German-Jewish poet Heinrich Heine; see Gossman, 15–18.

Protestantism and *Literature and Dogma*, where he writes that "the true meaning of religion" is "*morality touched by emotion*" (6:176), "a powerful attachment [that] will give a man spirits and confidence which he could by no means call up or command of himself" (6:39).

Although Hellenism itself certainly does sound a lot like "criticism," a comprehensive many-sidedness that contextualizes racial impulses such as Hebraism, Arnold's decision to poise it rhetorically against Hebraism suggests that it is less than this. Hebraism and Hellenism, as he puts it, represent limited ethics that "ought to be . . . evenly and happily balanced" against each other (5:164). Hebraism by itself "strikes too exclusively upon one string in us" (6:125), while Hellenism's "scientific passion for pure knowledge" needs to be energized with Hebraism's "moral and social passion for doing good" (5:91) if it is not to dissipate into mere "cultivated inaction" (5:191). Each stands for a distinctly limited vision of modernity: on the one hand, a Weberian modernity of middle-class materialism, Protestant religion, and laissez-faire capitalism, and on the other hand an aesthetic modernity of intellectual curiosity and free play. At the same time, it is unquestionably Hebraism, with its drive for "perfection in one part of our nature and not in all" (5:185), that Arnold sees lying at the root of most of Victorian England's problems. Two centuries of unchecked dominance by the conviction that "strictness of conscience" is our "one thing needful," he argues, has encouraged an aggressive individualism among the middle classes that now undermines any sense of social authority or community (5:179). Not only this, but Hebraism has also inspired forms of disruptive moral idealism on the far left: "Jacobinism loves a Rabbi" (5:111), according to Arnold, because the nineteenth-century revolutionist and the biblical fundamentalist share a "fierceness" and an "addiction to an abstract system" (5:109). In all cases, Hebraism becomes a nexus of several kinds of narrowness: right and left, Jacobin and Puritan, smug English provincialism and "the moral ideal of the individual passionately dedicated to a single overriding imperative."[22] The radically authoritarian God of biblical monotheism has bred both a middle-class Philistine with an attic full of "stock notions and habits" (5:190) and an urban anarchist who considers it perfectly desirable for everyone "to march where he likes, meet where he likes, enter where he likes, hoot as he likes, threaten as he likes, smash as he likes" (5:119).

---

[22] Gossman, 25. On the links between Hebraism and older constructions of Jewish minority status, see Aamir Mufti, *Enlightenment in the Colony: The Jewish Question and the Crisis of Postcolonial Culture* (Princeton, NJ: Princeton UP, 2007), 37–126; Brian Cheyette, *Constructions of "The Jew" in English Literature and Society: Racial Representations, 1875–1945* (New York, NY: Cambridge UP, 1993), 13–54; Ragussis, 174–233.

"Culture," in turn, is Arnold's new neologism (replacing criticism) for the many-sided ethos that can bring Hebraism, Hellenism, and all the other energies of the modern world back into their proper places. By familiarizing ourselves with "the best which has been thought and said in the world" (5:233), Arnold writes, we not only pursue "*harmonious* perfection, developing all sides of our humanity" (5:235) but also turn "a stream of fresh and free thought upon our stock notions and habits" (5:134), limiting our attachment to any single source of values and establishing a sense of social "authority," "controlling individual wills in the name of an interest wider than that of individuals" (5:117).

The fact that Arnold intends culture to counteract "anarchy" led many commentators during the American culture wars to associate it with the Romantic concept of *a* culture, or the set of shared principles that binds a people together. Gerald Graff, for example, portrays Arnold as a Victorian George Will who valorizes the Western canon as "the common culture that is the nation's social cement."[23] In fact, *Culture and Anarchy* pushes the much weirder notion that such traditional sites of authority ultimately beget social fragmentation, while true consensus can only be restored by the free play of disinterested knowledge. By momentarily taking leave of our parochial commitments, Arnold suggests, we can find a better grounding for social consensus in a vision of "all sides of our humanity" (5:235) held in their proper places. Arnoldian culture may be old, insofar as it includes both Homer and the *Bhagavad Gita*, but it is not traditional, since its force comes from its power to disturb our prior expectations.[24] If the 1980s culture warriors tended to locate the canon's authority in its commonality—the fact that everyone has supposedly already read it— Arnold instead points toward great literature's capacity to defamiliarize our stock ideas: "Far more of our mistakes," he writes, "come from want of

---

[23] The phrase is Will's and is cited in Graff, 188. Graff's essay is an excellent example of this misreading, a brilliant takedown of Reagan-era culture warriors that displays a curiously loose sense of Arnold's own argument. His claim is that it is disingenuous to enjoin others to celebrate a "common culture" because the force of such a culture is supposed to be that it exists prior to choice (192–3). Once you need to prescribe "emotional loyalty to common traditions" (189), they have already lost their potency. And he is right, but the whole point of Arnoldian culture is that it is *not* common: it is what the English middle class does not already know, and actually bears some resemblance to the multicultural literature that commentators like Will mistrust. For Arnold, encountering "the best that has been thought and said in the world" involves reading the marginalized Irish and Welsh, the mistrusted French and Germans, and even the *Bhagavad Gita*. Arnold's writings on education thus upbraid English secondary schools for, unlike their French counterparts, ignoring Indian and Japanese literatures as well as the religions of Asia (4:137). See Park Honan, *Matthew Arnold: A Life* (New York, NY: McGraw-Hill, 1981), 291, 313–14.

[24] As Gossman points out, Arnold's concept is neohumanist rather than Romantic-organicist in its genealogy (21).

fresh knowledge than from want of correct reasoning" (6:168), for "the notion of possessing, even in the most precious words or standards, the one thing needful, of having in them, once for all, a full and sufficient measure of light to guide us," inevitably leads to "strange distortions and perversions" (5:183–4). Indeed, Arnold's core claim is that immersing oneself in the internal logic of any single tradition impairs one's ability to grasp it adequately. The Protestant literalist who regards the biblical texts as an "all-sufficient" guide to life is "apt to make of them something quite different from what they really are" (6:7), and in particular to "mis-attribut[e] to the Bible—the Book of *conduct* . . . a science and an abstruse metaphysic which is not there" (6:408). In contrast, the reader who is familiar with the world's various literatures will be able to "feel what the Bible writers are about," "to read between the lines," and "discern where he ought to rest his whole weight, and where he ought to pass lightly" (6:152).

Arnold's counterintuitive claim that mental free play will restore social authority mirrors his wider assertion that a strong, centralized state, rather than a laissez-faire marketplace of ideas, can create a space within which the different sides of human nature may interact. In this sense, Arnoldian culture functions like a conflation of liberal self-culture and Tylor's "Culture, or Civilization": it makes the play of the many-sided personality an image for larger types of human association both national and global.[25] It also comes very close to the nineteenth-century liberal model of the nation described by Eric Hobsbawm, which rejected the idea of nationality as "an expression of language, or common history" and instead envisioned the nation as an intermediate stage in the historical expansion of social bodies:

> [T]he building of nations was seen inevitably as a process of expansion . . .
> [I]t was accepted in theory that social evolution expanded the scale of human social units from family and tribe to county and canton, from the local to the regional, the national and eventually the global. Nations were therefore, as it were, in tune with historical evolution only insofar as they extended the scale of human society.[26]

---

[25] For the complex relationship between Arnoldian culture and various anthropological senses of the term, see George Stocking, "Matthew Arnold, E. B. Tylor, and the Uses of Invention" (1968), in *Race, Culture, and Evolution: Essays in the History of Anthropology* (Chicago, IL: U of Chicago P, 1982), 69–90.

[26] E. J. Hobsbawm, *Nations and Nationalism since 1780: Programme, Myth, Reality* (New York, NY: Cambridge UP, 1990), 32–3. For Arnold's place on the spectrum of Victorian statisms, see David Lloyd and Paul Thomas, *Culture and the State* (New York, NY: Routledge, 1998); Lauren M. E. Goodlad, *Victorian Literature and the Victorian State: Character and Governance in a Liberal Society* (Baltimore, MD: Johns Hopkins UP, 2003);

Thus *Culture and Anarchy* defends the Church of England against both liberals and Dissenters on the grounds that "a Church which is historical as the State itself is historical, and whose order, ceremonies, and monuments reach, like those of the State, far beyond any fancies and devisings of ours" obliges its members to confront a diverse range of religious sensibilities and to distinguish what is "essential" in religion from "what is not essential" (5:239).[27] While Arnold is sympathetic to the plight of Dissenters, his solution to sectarian conflict is not further disestablishment but rather the Prussian and French practice of allowing multiple Christian bodies to practice their peculiar forms of worship within the state church.[28] In the case of the Church of England, he writes, granting a limited autonomy to the Presbyterians and other groups would "unite the main bodies of Protestants who are now separatists" and "bring Nonconformists into contact again, as their greater fathers were, with the main stream of national life" (5:250, 5:249). He calls for Parliament to open the universities to Nonconformists without severing their ties to the Church—for "to cure the evil of the Nonconformists' provincialism, the right way can hardly be to provincialise us all around" (5:240)—and advises the government to initiate relations with the Irish Catholic Church on the grounds that the old policy of leaving Irish Catholicism "an entirely private concern of the persons attached to it" has meant that "in no country, probably, is Roman Catholicism so crude, blind, and unreasoning as in Ireland" (7:102). Indeed, although Arnold never floated the idea of a nationalized Jewish synagogue, he would celebrate the ennoblement of Sir Nathaniel Rothschild, Parliament's first Jewish peer, in 1885, with a similar rhetoric of recuperating otherwise wasted "forces" for "the main stream of national life": "I feel really proud ... and happy for the British public to have, by this peerage, signally marked the abandonment of its old policy of exclusion ... What have we not learned and gained from the people who we have been excluding all these years!"[29]

Daniel S. Malachuk, *Perfection, the State, and Victorian Liberalism* (New York, NY: Palgrave Macmillan, 2005). Arnold's view of the state finds precedent in the work of Humboldt and Mill, yet Arnold also goes further than they do in imagining how political "machinery" might play the main role in facilitating a free play of ideas. For example, where Mill sought to protect education from state control by placing it in private hands, Arnold feared that privatizing education would transform it into an expression of sectarian differences. See Edward Alexander, *Matthew Arnold and John Stuart Mill* (New York, NY: Columbia UP, 1965), 220–9, and Stefan Collini, *Arnold* (New York, NY: Oxford UP, 1988), 71–2.

[27] For Arnold on the church as a means to create a national community through education, see Joshua King, *Imagined Spiritual Communities in Britain's Age of Print* (Columbus, OH: Ohio State UP, 2015), 96–126.

[28] See "Disestablishment in Wales" (1888), especially 11: 337.

[29] Quoted in Cheyette, 18. See 16–18, as well as Gossman, 33–4.

Finally, Arnold contends that England's class antagonisms will best be ameliorated, not by abolishing class itself, but by using state institutions to place the present classes into more open communion with each other. In a late essay entitled "Equality" (1878), Arnold argues that France's aggressive redistribution of wealth has brought its lower classes closer in spirit to its middle and upper classes. *Culture and Anarchy* imagines this sort of meliorism in more abstract terms by constructing a three-part schema of Barbarians (aristocrats, with their penchant for field sports and physical display), Philistines (middle class), and Populace (working class), and then venturing that "in each class there are born a certain number of natures with a curiosity about their best self," with a "heaven-bestowed" "bent for seeing things as they are . . . for the pursuit, in a word, of perfection" (5:145). These "*aliens*," as Arnold calls them, "emerge in all classes" and can therefore serve as mediators between different class interests (5:145–6). As in *Celtic Literature*, the fixities of different human constitutions necessitate a model of dialogic difference. Trilling long ago noted how strange this claim looks—for if class is "a category whose very essence is interest," how could different classes possibly remain separate once their antagonistic interests have been removed?[30] Yet the seeming redundancy of interest-less classes perfectly captures *Culture and Anarchy*'s sense that the only truly liberal solutions will be composite and piecemeal. Making everyone the same would be the Hebraistic move, the Jacobin move, while the truly many-sided state will cultivate forms of productive difference that produce free play instead of antagonism.

The paradoxical argument of *Culture and Anarchy*, in which mental free play leads to social cohesion and a centralized state counteracts insular nationalism, finds a parallel in several rhetorical paradoxes that animate the essay. Like Carlyle, Ruskin, and other so-called Victorian sages, Arnold is telling a story of reversal that sees "the marginal position of the alienated intellectual [become] the very centre of society" while the great English middle class is refigured as one of several minority interests that need to be balanced.[31] Unlike Carlyle or Ruskin, however, Arnold uses this rhetoric of inversion not to find some new counter-system of values but rather to relativize all particular positions. Hence the distinctive way in which Arnold employs redefinition, neologism, and caricature. Carlyle's satirical coinages ("quackery," "machinery") aim to discredit singular bourgeois fetishes, but Arnold's frequently come in twos or threes— Hebraism and Hellenism; Barbarians, Philistines, and Populace—and work

---

[30] Trilling, 253.   [31] Young, 58.

to map out systems of hierarchy or equilibrium from which nothing is excluded.[32]

Most importantly, Arnold employs such wordplay to pigeonhole his opponents as Dickensian or Thackerayan grotesques who have fallen victim to their own parochialism. Although Arnold is seldom treated as a comic writer, Raymond Williams observed (not sympathetically) that his social criticism often wields "a kind of witty and malicious observation better suited to minor fiction."[33] Indeed, before his experiment with prophetic invective in *Culture and Anarchy*, Arnold levied many of the same critiques in a series of fictional epistles entitled *Friendship's Garland* (1867). Much as *Culture and Anarchy* would opportunistically seize upon such actual names as Bazley and Blewitt and Blowzitt, the Rev. W. Cattle and the Prophet Joe Smith, so does *Friendship's Garland* see Arnold concoct Viscount Lumpington, Bottles Esquire, and the Reverend Esau Hittal.[34] Here is the *nouveau riche* industrialist Bottles displaying a Philistine's admiration for the scientist Silverpump:

> Original man, Silverpump! . . . Fine mind! Fine system! None of your antiquated rubbish—all practical work—latest discoveries in science—mind constantly kept excited—lots of interesting experiments—lights of all colours—fizz! fizz! bang! bang!   (5:71)

The rub in all of this, of course, is that Arnold winds up using stock notions to combat stock notions and classist condescension to combat class parochialism. His typologies and caricatures, designed to offer a critical survey of the social landscape, turn out to depend upon a certain smug familiarity, especially where middle-class religiosity is concerned. Cosmopolitan many-sidedness, in other words, easily becomes its own variety of parochialism, and it is to the consequences of that irony that we now turn.

RELIGION AND THE VEXATIONS
OF UNIVERSALISM

Of all the curious features of *Culture and Anarchy*, few are more striking than the book's overdetermination of the relationship between religion and culture. In theory, the essay regards Hebraism, or "the religious side of man," as one of several human energies that need to be held in balance by culture. It is the side with which the English tend to get the most carried

---

[32] For a detailed examination of such strategies, see John Holloway, *The Victorian Sage: Studies in Argument* (London, UK: Archon, 1962), 220–7.
[33] R. Williams, 116.   [34] See Holloway, 323–33.

away, but in principle it is no more problematic than the drive for scientific knowledge or for sentimental beauty. At the same time, Hebraism tends to assume a more troublesome role as culture's primary competitor. Religious energy becomes the driving force behind English national life since the seventeenth century, and culture's main task becomes that of either containing religion or of providing some alternative to it. In this section I explore how Arnold's concepts of religion and culture circle each other as he poses a number of overlapping relationships between them—sometimes competitive, sometimes assimilative, and still other times involving a logic of inheritance. What is at stake, I argue, is the question of whether culture itself is capable of remaining a disinterested framework that transcends religion or whether, in order to stymie Hebraism, it must become an antagonistic counter-religion of its own. Is *Culture and Anarchy* the story of secularism versus religion, the story of two competing religions, or, as Pecora ventures, a contest between two equal and opposite visions of modernity: "the 'worlding' or translation of Judeo-Christian tradition, in which the modern machinery of utilitarian reform and democratic enfranchisement. . . . could be described as the intemperate, oppositional consequence of religiously derived enthusiasms, laws, and obedience," and "a purely rational and enlightened construction of human ideas and institutions guided by attenuated Aristotelian notions of virtue and right reason"?[35]

Arnold's typical position on the relationship between culture and religion is that they differ in kind and are therefore compatible with each other. Culture is a bigger, more complex ideal than religion—an ideal of having multiple ideals—and for this reason can incorporate religion within itself. In one passage, for instance, Arnold writes that culture differs from "the religious side of man" (5:252) in refusing to "sacrific[e] one part" of human nature "to another" (5:165), even those parts that, like religion, demand sacrifice themselves (see 5:238). Culture does not engage religion as a "rival fetish" (5:235) but instead embraces it among the necessary spheres of human activity, "the great works by which, not only in literature, art, and science, generally, but in religion itself, the human spirit has manifested its approach to totality and to a full, harmonious perfection" (5:237). And again:

> Culture, disinterestedly seeking in its aim at perfection to see things as they really are, shows us how worthy and divine a thing is the religious side in man, though it is not the whole of man. . . . Therefore to the worth and

---

[35] Pecora, 132.

grandeur of the religious side in man, culture is rejoiced and willing to pay any tribute, except the tribute of man's totality.   (5:252)

Defined thus, culture is a version of what William Connolly calls academic secularism, a secularism that goes back to Kant and "model[s] public life upon an organization of university life," with its neat divisions between different kinds of knowledge.[36] Rhetorically, however, culture in this passage does not just balance religion against other spheres of activity but also assumes for itself the privilege of deciding what is "divine" and what is not, just as elsewhere Arnold evidently hands culture the keys to the kingdom: " . . . falling short of harmonious perfection," he writes, the Dissenters and other opponents of culture "fail to follow the true way of salvation" (5:236).

Thus emerges a second imagined relationship in which culture and religion are fundamentally the same in kind and therefore engaged in direct competition with each other. "Hebraism" now represents not the entire "religious side in man" (5:91) but a particularly restrictive form of religion that Arnold associates with English Dissent, while culture stands for a broader and more generous religion that locates "reason and the will of God" in the pursuit of our "total perfection" (5:233). In *Literature and Dogma*, Arnold goes so far as to picture two different gods, a god of "righteousness" and a god of the "total man," one of whom is positively dismayed by the things that satisfy the other:

> [I]n this wider sense God is displeased and disserved by many things which cannot be said. . . . to displease and disserve him as the God of righteousness. He is displeased and disserved by men uttering such doggerel hymns as: *Sing glory, glory, glory to the great God Triune!*   (6:409–10)

Hence those moments in *Culture and Anarchy* where Arnold seems to make the state itself a "sacred" fetish instead of a mere tool for encouraging perfection. If the volume's preface insists that inward perfection "alone" is "sacred and binding for man" (5:251), and government "machinery" only a means to this end (5:117), elsewhere Arnold seems far more willing to insist that "the very framework and exterior order of the State, whoever may administer the State, is sacred" (5:223). Raymond Williams saw this

---

[36] William Connolly, *Why I Am Not a Secularist* (Minneapolis, MN: U of Minnesota P, 1999), 19–20. Arnold's insistence that the different spheres of human inquiry must remain differentiated if they are to fulfill their proper functions recalls not only Kant's *Contest of the Faculties* (1798) but also John Henry Newman's *Idea of a University* (1852, 1858). David DeLaura notes the impact of Newman's *Idea* on Arnold's conception of many-sidedness, arguing that Newman offered Arnold an inverted image of his own position: humanistic culture in the service of Anglo-Catholic religion, rather than an established Church encouraging many-sidedness (xii–xiii).

as an ironic but predictable consequence of Arnold's attempt to ground culture not in any historical tradition but only in its own negative, critical stance. "Burke rested on an existing society, and on a faith. Coleridge drew nourishment, in a period of transition, from the values known from the old kind of society, and again from a faith."[37] Arnold, by contrast, denies culture such a basis and thus obliges it to become self-authorizing.

Finally, Arnold posits a third relationship in which culture is neither a neutral framework above religion, nor a competing creed itself, but rather is dialectically bound up with religious energies that it must both internalize and subdue. Instead of simply including religion among other human drives, here Arnold asserts that culture itself needs to draw upon religion's "fire and strength," its "intense and convinced energy" (5:93), if it is to make perfection "*prevail*" (5:238), even if these things ostensibly contradict culture's ideals. For example, toward the end of *Culture and Anarchy* Arnold increasingly insists that the principles of culture cannot be disseminated until there is already some degree of consensus established through the muscular force of Hebraism. "[F]or resisting anarchy the lovers of culture may prize and employ fire and strength," he writes, even as they insist "that it is not at this moment true... that the world wants fire and strength more than sweetness and light" (5:224). Culture is no longer religion by other means, but rather draws upon religion toward different ends.

This overdetermining of religion vis-à-vis culture is important because it reflects Arnold's own ambivalence as to what manner of social ideal culture itself might be. Religion becomes the narrow ethos that tests culture's broad ethos by resisting the latter's attempts to incorporate it, and the shifting relationship between these two terms within the argument points back toward tensions among the different goals that Arnold has set for culture. For instance, the clear friction between Arnold's claim that culture is a qualitatively larger ideal than religion and his impulse to tout it as a nobler form of religion suggests that culture may not be able to become an all-inclusive framework without also developing a certain quality of exclusivity. As Lionel Gossman puts it, the notion that Hebraism could be incorporated into culture if only it would first lose its "intransigent transcendentalism" forgets that intransigence *is* Hebraism's best aspect, the "special force... that underlies its capacity to generate the most radical and uncompromising criticism of worldly institutions."[38] Trilling, as we have seen, detects the same problem within Arnold's take

---

[37] R. Williams, 127. Anderson (96–7) notes the slippage between Arnoldian culture as a character-stance and as a social process facilitated by institutions.

[38] Gossman, 29.

on class-reconciliation when he notes that voiding the different classes of their interests would not just make them more tolerant of each other but also abolish their *raisons d'être*.[39] Either way, what at first looks like a simple matter of fitting a positive doctrine into an accommodating framework turns out to involve a conflict between the positive doctrine of "one thing needful" and the positive doctrine of many-sidedness.

This particular tension within Arnold's work echoes a now popular complaint among conservative legal critics regarding Anglo-American liberalism's treatment of religion. Stephen L. Carter and others have frequently maintained that liberalism's supposedly neutral strictures for religious tolerance end up constituting what American theologian Harvey Cox once called "a new closed world view" that rejects certain forms of religious practice and expression.[40] What Arnold's work suggests is that this intolerant streak within liberal governance stems not from disingenuous motives but rather from the subtle ways that toleration must alter its subjects to render them tolerable. In order for particular allegiances to be assimilated into a wider state framework, that is, they must sometimes be asked to change their self-conceptions to accord with the tenets of that framework. Arnold details this process in his treatment of Anglican history in *St. Paul and Protestantism*, which traces the struggle of the "negative Protestantism of the Church of England" to accommodate the "positive Protestantism of Puritanism" during the sixteenth and seventeenth centuries (6:13). The problem with the Puritans, writes Arnold, was that they regarded their idiosyncratic reading of Christ's Atonement as the *unum necessarium* both for salvation and for church membership. This attitude could have been softened by their inclusion within a national church, but the Puritans consistently rejected any institutional formulas broad enough to bring them into a diverse religious body in the first place (see 6:75). Thus ensued a series of cases in which the Anglican establishment drafted rubrics that included Calvinist formulas, only to cast out the Calvinists themselves for insisting too strongly that the rest of the document be brought into line with their own theology. The Lambeth Articles of 1595, for instance, were "recalled and suppressed" because they were too strictly Puritan, while the Savoy Conference of 1661, convened after the Restoration to reconstruct the *Book of Common Prayer* along lines that both Puritans and High Churchmen could accept, ultimately broke down when the Puritans refused to let their formulas be included only piecemeal (see 6:77). This refusal led to a reactionary period during which

---

[39] Trilling, 253.
[40] Harvey Cox, *The Secular City* (1965; New York, NY: Macmillan, 1966), 18. See Stephen L. Carter, *The Culture of Disbelief* (New York, NY: Anchor, 1994), 3–22.

documents such as the Act of Uniformity pushed many individuals out into Dissenting congregations. Nevertheless, insists Arnold, while "the Church undoubtedly said and did to Puritanism after the Restoration much that was harsh and bitter" (6:81), historians who portray "the Puritans as the religious party favorable to civil liberty" (6:77) miss the necessary paradox that the post-Restoration squashing of Dissent resulted less from "the lust of haughty ecclesiastics for dominion" than from "a real sense that [the Anglican] formularies were made so large and open, and the sense put upon subscription to them was so indulgent, that any reasonable man could honestly conform" (6:82). In this passage Arnold's use of the word "reasonable" echoes John Rawls's when he writes that "[t]he problem of political liberalism is to work out a conception of political justice for a constitutional democratic regime that the plurality of reasonable doctrines ... might endorse," while "unreasonable and irrational, and even mad, comprehensive doctrines" must be kept from "undermin[ing] the unity and justice of society."[41] Arnold too is trying to imagine a kind of overlapping consensus between positive doctrines—an ideal sphere within which various human values and projects intersect in their "best aspects"—and in both cases we might well wonder: what is this quality of reasonableness that defines the difference between a tolerable "comprehensive doctrine" and an intolerable one? For Rawls, the difference seems to be that a reasonable doctrine can acknowledge its own status as one possible position among many; it can, as Saba Mahmood puts it, "recognize itself, and articulate this self-recognition, within the terms of liberal national discourse."[42] But this then gives the state more coercive force than either Rawls or Arnold really wants it to have, namely the power to judge the contents of different doctrines and to force some to change in accordance with its judgment.[43]

A more subtle tension between religion and culture emerges when we juxtapose Arnold's claim that culture's normative force emanates from the totality of its internal parts with his suggestion that it comes from a "fire and strength" specifically derived from Hebraism. For while the first position portrays culture as reproducing the effects of religion by more benign means, the second suggests that culture's capacity to create

---

[41] John Rawls, *Political Liberalism* (New York, NY: Columbia UP, 1993), xviii, xvi–xvii.

[42] Saba Mahmood, "Secularism, Hermeneutics, and Empire: The Politics of Islamic Reformation," *Public Culture* 18.2 (2006): 328n.

[43] See Stephen Macedo, *Diversity and Distrust: Civic Education in a Multicultural Democracy* (Cambridge, MA: Harvard UP, 2000), and, for a useful overview, Ronald Beiner, *Liberalism, Nationalism, Citizenship: Essays on the Problem of Political Community* (Vancouver, Canada: U of British Columbia P, 2003).

authority depends largely upon its channeling of an energy that, in isolation, contradicts the project of "total perfection." In this way Arnold comes to anticipate the political philosopher Carl Schmitt's notorious claim, in *Political Theology* (1922), that the secular state inevitably relies upon theological models of sovereignty that it purports to have eclipsed.[44] But he also locates himself within a wider debate among nineteenth-century historians and philologists regarding Western modernity's vexed kinship to Abrahamic monotheism. For many nineteenth-century intellectuals, Near Eastern monotheism represented an aporia at the heart of Western universalism—a worldview that opposed European art and science yet was also one of their core foundations. For instance, Ernest Renan began his *Études d'Histoire Religieuse* (1857) by drawing the customary dichotomy between the Semitic genius for religion and the Indo-European genius for civilization: "To the Indo-European race pertain nearly all the great military, political, and intellectual movements in the history of the world; to the Semitic race the religious movements."[45] In Renan's estimation, the logical consequence of the ancient Semites' exclusive religiosity was an attitude of "intolerance" that prevented them from advancing in the scale of culture.[46] "A race, incomplete by its very simplicity, having neither plastic arts, nor rational science, nor philosophy, nor political life, nor military organization" could never attain "civilisation in the sense we attach to that word."[47] Yet Semitic intolerance did introduce one idea that would prove central to great civilizational projects: the notion that what is good for one should be good for all. Ancient Israel, "exclusively possessed by its religious idea," remained mired in parochialism, but the Indo-European tribes that assimilated Semitic morality through the Bible were able to use it to transform their instinct for plurality into a desire to make the many one.[48] "[B]efore their conversion to Semitic ideas," Renan writes, the Indo-Europeans remained "strangers to intolerance or proselytism," and only by internalizing monotheism did they eventually learn to proclaim ideals like "freedom of thought" as a good *for others*.[49] "No doubt Indo-European tolerance springs from a loftier sentiment of human destiny, and from a greater breadth of mind; but who shall dare to say that by revealing the divine Unity, and definitely

---

[44] Carl Schmitt, *Political Theology: Four Chapters on the Concept of Sovereignty* (1922), trans. George Schwabb (Cambridge, MA: MIT P, 1985). See also Kevin McLaughlin, "Culture and Messianism: Disinterestedness in Arnold," *Victorian Studies* 50.4 (2008): 615–39.

[45] Ernest Renan, *Studies in Religious History* (1857), trans. William M. Thomson (London, UK: Mathieson, 1893), 61.

[46] Ibid., 63.   [47] Ibid., 64.   [48] Ibid., 85.   [49] Ibid., 63.

suppressing local religions, the Semitic race has not laid the foundation stone of the unity and progress of humanity?"[50]

In short, the strange duality of cosmopolitanism and parochialism that Amanda Anderson has identified in Victorian portraits of Judaism is for Renan Judaism's vital contribution to Western modernity.[51] This means, among other things, that in his mind there persists an occult resemblance between nineteenth-century liberalism and premodern authoritarian societies. The ancient Hebrews, for instance, represent for him an inverted image of universalism: they "aspir[ed] to realize a cult independent of provinces and countries," not because they sought to establish a universal creed, but simply because they "declare[d] all religions different from their own to be bad."[52] Similarly, when Renan writes of "the cosmopolitan habits of the Jewish people," he is referring to their supposed talent for diffusing themselves throughout the globe without intermixing: "We see Abraham, Isaac and Jacob . . . in possession of pure and simple ideas, passing through the different civilisations, without confounding themselves with them, and without accepting anything from them."[53] The Islamic empires, meanwhile, become for Renan emblems of the parochialism hidden within any project of universal civilization. Where the Hebrews ultimately took the doctrine of One God to imply separatism and isolationism, Christianity and Islam both gleaned from it a project of global expansion; yet while Christianity interpreted the concept of divine unity as a warrant for synthesizing the different local traditions it absorbed, Islam amplified Abrahamic intolerance and projected it onto as wide a political field as possible. Islam thus parallels Christianity as an alternative road to modernity, or even a parody-modernity, markedly illiberal in its principles yet able to produce certain "civilizing" effects. For instance, Renan argues, in the hands of medieval Arab scribes Mohammed's life "remained a biography like another, without prodigies, without exaggerations," not because these scribes had attained nineteenth-century historicism, but rather because their austere monotheism "was completely wanting in the element which engenders mysticism and mythology."[54]

This image of a fanatically religious Semite who contributes a key element to a modern civilization that he also opposes is in many ways the figure of the Middle Eastern extremist still haunting Euro-American political discourse today—a character whose absolute faith in his one big idea tests how strong "our" pluralism can be in response.[55] Within

---

[50] Ibid., 63–4.   [51] See Anderson, 126–8.   [52] Renan, 63.
[53] Ibid., 91, 65.   [54] Ibid., 119, 121.
[55] See, for instance, Bernard Lewis, *What Went Wrong?* (New York, NY: Oxford UP, 2002).

mid-Victorian writing, as Tomoko Masuzawa has shown, it would eclipse the indolent "Mussulman" who had played the foil to Enlightenment progress and articulate new fear, borne out of a half-century of European political upheaval, that even the most progressive political projects contained deeply illiberal elements.[56] For many writers, drawing grand contrasts between Judaism, Islam, and Christianity—as well as other Indo-European religions such as Buddhism—became a way to explore the slippery relationship between different versions of universalism.[57] For example, in *The Religions of the World and their Relation to Christianity* (1847) Broad Church luminary F. D. Maurice argued that Islam was a parochial ideology that eerily mirrored civilization in its goals. "The Mahometan claims to be a universal religion; to set up a universal society," he wrote; "[t]he gospel does so too," yet where Christianity placed its universal society under the rule of an "Unseen King," Islam has missed the "vital, historical, progressive character" of revelation and remains wedded to an Old-Testament project of establishing a "visible, mortal man to reign over the Universal Family," much as the "Jewish king reigned . . . over a particular nation."[58] Islam's universal society, in other words, was little more than a national theocracy expanded through military might. For Maurice, this is ultimately a false vision of civilization—yet it has also, he concedes, given Islam the capacity to build large, imperial bodies in a way that the West has found attractive. Islam's stark message that "God is" has proven "capable of exercising a mastery over the rudest of tribes, of giving them an order, of making them victorious over all the civilisation and all the religion which has not this principle for its basis."[59] Maurice insists, however, that this "theological transcendent principle" represents only a prelude to civilization, a moment of stripping away that renders future progress possible.[60] Mohammed "was right that there is something in the world which we are not to tolerate, which we are sent into it to exterminate," but by itself this principle of sacrifice can lead only to stasis.[61] "In the seventh century after Christ," he concludes, "Mahomet taught that the world was to begin its history again; but to begin it with no hope of a progress. That principle, which had been the mere starting-point of Jewish faith, the ground of what it was learning for nineteen hundred years, was to be the one, all-sufficing maxim of Mahometan life."[62]

---

[56] Tomoko Masuzawa, *The Invention of World Religions* (Chicago, IL: U of Chicago P, 2007), 170.

[57] See Masuzawa, 107–206; Brent Nongbri, *Before Religion: A History of a Modern Concept* (New Haven, CT: Yale UP, 2013), 124–49.

[58] Frederick Denison Maurice, *The Religions of the World and Their Relations to Christianity* (1847; London, UK: Macmillan, 1877), 145, 157, 152, 157.

[59] Ibid., 24.   [60] Ibid., 25.   [61] Ibid., 33.   [62] Ibid., 151.

The German theologian Otto Pfleiderer would tell much the same story in his widely read *Religion and Historic Faiths* (1906), which argued that Islam's combination of expansionist ambitions and parochial mindset explained how it could simultaneously "discipline raw peoples" while also retarding the broader progress of "free human civilization":

> Islam, the religion of Mohammed, is the latest among the historical religions, a late after-impulse of the religion-forming power of the Semitic race. Founded by the prophet Mohammed under Jewish and Christian influences among the half-barbaric Arabic people in the seventh century, Islamism shares the monotheistic, rigidly theocratic and legalistic character of Judaism, without its national limitation; with Christianity, it shares the claim and propagating impulse of world-religion, but without the wealth of religious thought and motives and without the mobility and the capacity for development which belongs to a world religion. It might be maintained, probably, that Islamism is the Jewish idea of theocracy carried out on a larger scale by the youthful national vigor of the Arabians, well calculated to discipline raw barbaric peoples, but a brake on the progress of free human civilization.[63]

Along similar lines, the Dutch scholar Abraham Kuenen (whom Arnold would cite in *Literature and Dogma*[64]) proposed in *National Religions and Universal Religions* (1882) that the radical moral tradition exemplified by the Hebrew prophets contained intimations of a genuine universalism that would only blossom under the care of Christianity. Judaism itself had a "rigidly national and exclusive character to it," yet contained "the internal leaven of universalism."[65] Contrasting Christianity with Buddhism, both of which preach a doctrine of universal love, he argued that what distinguished the former over the latter was its continuous reliance upon a specifically Semitic element of intolerance that paradoxically made its universalism more effective. "Buddhism," he writes, "misses the aggressive Character which Christianity has always displayed" toward "unbelievers."[66] This is because "the Christian's God was Israel's Yaweh ... 'a jealous God,' who will endure 'no other gods before his face'"—and it is "the belief in the triumph of Yaweh over everything that opposes him," Kuenen concludes, that has ultimately given Christianity its success on the global stage.[67]

I have surveyed these wider variations upon Arnold's theme because, taken together, they illustrate how a certain vision of liberal pluralism

---

[63] Otto Pfleiderer, *Religion and Historic Faiths* (1906), trans. Daniel A. Heubsch (New York, NY: B. W. Heubsch, 1907), 274. Cited in Masuzawa, 199.

[64] See Arnold, 6: 372–3.

[65] Abraham Kuenen, *National Religions and Universal Religions* (London, UK: Macmillan, 1882), 169. Cited in Masuzawa, 193.

[66] Ibid., 289–90.   [67] Ibid., 290, 291.

freights the idea of religion with contradictory baggage. For modern writers who advocate openness to the heterogeneity of human experience and to multiple points of view, religion, understood as "the strong holding of beliefs" (in Michael Warner's phrase) stands at once for the opposite of liberal pluralism ("the weak holding of beliefs"), for pluralism's main competitor on the world stage, and for something that pluralism must learn to internalize.[68] Viewed thus, liberalism's debts to religion become simultaneously necessary and a deep scandal. Recent theorists of the postsecular, for instance, imagine an ironic dialectic in which Western secularism must keep affirming its religious sources in order to function. As Jürgen Habermas puts it, the historical fact that "modern forms of consciousness encompassing abstract right, modern science, and autonomous art" developed under the influence of "the organizational forms of Hellenized Christianity and the Roman Catholic Church" means that

> Philosophy, even in its postmetaphysical form, will be able neither to replace nor to repress religion as long as religious language is the bearer of a semantic content that is inspiring and even indispensable, for this content eludes . . . the explanatory force of philosophical language and continues to resist translation into reasoning discourses.[69]

The problem with this way of thinking is that it actually remystifies religion in attempting to reclaim it for secular civilization. Conceived as a blind, opaque energy that "resist[s] translation into reasoning discourses," religion becomes something that by definition cannot influence the Enlightenment tradition without compromising the latter's self-image as a space of universally perspicuous norms. A groundless and objectless conviction that signifies nothing but itself, religion cannot simply be another element of Western liberalism's genealogy, like Roman jurisprudence or Saxon folkmoots. Instead, it is either a curse that universalism cannot shake—the dirty secret at the heart of the modern—or a talisman that intellectuals must keep reaffirming if liberalism is not to lose its mysterious power.

What is more, this overdetermination of religion is what allows it to function like race within Arnold's thinking. For if religion is a strong belief that is detachable from particular objects, then it becomes in many ways interchangeable with ethnic inheritance as the epitome of those one-sided

---

[68] See Michael Warner, "Is Liberalism a Religion?", in *Religion: Beyond a Concept*, ed. Hent de Vries (New York, NY: Fordham UP, 2008), 610–17.

[69] Jürgen Habermas, *Religion and Rationality*, ed. Eduardo Mendieta (Cambridge, MA: Polity P, 2002), 147, 162. The second quote is cited from Habermas, *Postmetaphysical Thinking: Philosophical Essays*, trans. Fred Lawrence (Cambridge, MA: Polity, 1992), 51.

commitments that liberal pluralism is defined against. As the political philosopher Sheldon Wolin argued years ago, classical liberalism, while valorizing religion as the ur-site of private conscience, also associates conscience with interest as much as with reason.[70] The liberal relegation of religion to the domain of belief, in other words, ambiguously identifies belief both as that which *can* be privatized and as that which *needs* to be privatized, depoliticizing religion as a species of reasonable, self-bracketing opinion while also stigmatizing it as a form of subjective conviction that is scarcely more transparent than ancestral prejudice.[71] For example, Renan's claim that the ancient Israelites practiced "the purest religious form which humanity has known" follows from the fact that, as he sees it, Semitic religiosity emerged from a set of "fixed and determinate views" that could not be cultivated, curbed, or questioned.[72] For Renan, the Semites became the most religious race because they were in some sense the most "racial" race, the race least able to complement its innate instincts with ideas assimilated from others:

> When and how did the Semitic race arrive at that conception of the divine unity which the world has received upon the faith of its preaching? I believe that it was by a primitive intuition, and that from its earliest times. Monotheism was not invented; India, which has thought with so much originality and profundity, did not arrive at it in one day; all the force of the Greek spirit was not sufficient to lead humanity to this without the co-operation of the Semitic races. We can likewise avouch that they never would have conquered the dogma of the divine Unity if they had not found it in the most exalted instincts of their mind and heart . . . The Semitic race . . . manifestly arrived without any effort at the notion of the Supreme God. This great conquest was not, for them, the effect of progress and philosophical reflection; it was a matter of first perceptions.[73]

In this passage, racial instinct—mysterious, static, "arrived" at "without any effort" and "without reflection or reasoning"—joins religious dogma as a figure for the kind of singlemindedness that is opaque to reason. The positive assertions of divine revelation and the arbitrary customs of the tribe become alternating terms for that which resists critical reflection.

---

[70] Sheldon Wolin, *Politics and Vision: Continuity and Innovation in Western Political Thought* (Boston, MA: Little, Brown, 1960), 297–307. See Wendy Brown, *Regulating Aversion: Tolerance in the Age of Identity and Empire* (Princeton, NJ: Princeton UP, 2006), 217.
[71] As Asad observes, Lockean pluralism is guaranteed by linking religion to belief, not because belief is a function of free individual choice, but rather because belief, in Locke's psychology, cannot be willed and thus is not something the state could reasonably compel one to change. See "Comment on Conversion," in Peter van der Veer (ed.), *Conversion to Modernities: The Globalization of Christianity* (New York, NY: Routledge, 1996), 269.
[72] Renan, 61–2.   [73] Ibid., 62–3.

This same equation of raciality and religiosity animates *Culture and Anarchy* as well. Vincent Pecora argues that Arnold uses race as a safe proxy that lets him criticize Christianity in seemingly secular terms.[74] In fact, as we have seen, "Hebraism" is not just another narrow instinct figured by race (Celtic sentimentality, Saxon materialism) but also becomes paired with race as a privileged term for narrow commitment itself. Racial "temperaments" (3:359), with their "great force" (3:127), and religion's "fire and strength" stand alongside one another within the essay as figures for part-ness as such—for the ethos of having only one driving principle, yet being all the more forceful for it.

This special relationship between religion and race in Arnold's aesthetic liberalism is ultimately responsible for one of the oddest features of *Culture and Anarchy*: the apparent redundancy of "Hellenism" as a concept apart from culture. As we have noticed, the two terms can seem like synonyms: "Essential in Hellenism is the impulse to the development of the whole man, to connecting and harmonizing all parts of him, perfecting all, leaving none to take their chance" (5:184). The truth is, however, that Arnold takes pains to distinguish Hellenism from culture inasmuch as identifying the two would reduce culture, at least rhetorically, from a meta-ideal that can incorporate all different sides of the human character to a single people's instinctive habits of thought. Hence a recurring rhetorical shuffle in which Arnold lays down a definition of culture, fears that it comes too close to identifying culture with a particular European tradition going back to the Greeks, and thus pulls back hastily to qualify it:

> The best art and poetry of the Greeks, in which religion and poetry are one, in which the idea of beauty and of a human nature perfect on all sides adds to itself a religious and devout energy, and works in the strength of that, is on this account of such surpassing interest and instructiveness for us, though it was,—as, having regard to the human race in general, and, indeed, having regard to the Greeks themselves, we must own,—a premature attempt, an attempt which for success needed the moral and religious fibre in humanity to be more braced and developed than it had yet been. But Greece did not err in having the idea of beauty, harmony, and complete human perfection, so present and paramount; it is impossible to have this idea too present and paramount; only the moral fibre must be braced too. (5:100)

Here Arnold begins by holding up "the Greeks" as exemplars of "a human nature perfect on all sides." But then, as if to correct himself, he cuts this achievement down to size by adding that their attempt was "premature,"

---

[74] Pecora, 134–5, 153.

needing "the moral and religious fibre in humanity to be more braced and developed." In the next sentence he qualifies himself yet again by noting that, while the Greeks may not have attained many-sided human perfection *in fact*, they at least "did not err in having the idea of beauty, harmony, and complete human perfection." Did the Greeks realize an ideal balance of Hellenism and Hebraism, or did they remain mere Hellenists? The fact that Arnold cannot decide suggests a simultaneous desire to give culture the authoritative force of historical precedent and to valorize it as a principle that eclipses all partial instantiations. In the end, it seems as though the best way to imagine culture's almost utopian comprehensiveness is to keep displacing it to a space beyond historical realization, where it cannot ossify into one more provincial vision of the good.

LATE ARNOLD: REAPPRAISING HOMOGENEITY

This chapter has sought to correct two of the most influential portraits of Arnold to emerge from postwar criticism. One is a 1960s Arnold who hopes that literature might provide an adequate substitute for a diminished Christianity. The other is a 1980s Arnold who is defending a particular vision of English literary culture as the basis for national identity. In many ways these portraits reinforce one another, since both frame Arnold as a primarily centripetal thinker in search of new bastions of cultural authority. My argument, in turn, has been that Arnold's thought has a more peculiar arc than this. His concept of culture proposes that you can achieve centripetal ends by centrifugal means, constructing new sites of authority, not by fetishizing one thing to the exclusion of others, but rather by bringing different principles into play and allowing their ideal relation to emerge. This is why Pecora has identified Arnold as a "practitioner" of what Edward Said called secular criticism: critical activity that hopes to be "reducible neither to a doctrine nor to a political position" but rather to encourage a "suspicion of totalizing concepts" and "discontent with reified objects."[75]

Yet we can also see that those who mistook Arnoldian culture for "national culture" or for a substitute religion were noticing its very real tendency to mirror the forms of religious and racial absolutism that it is designed to curb. Culture begins as an attempt to balance the different energies within human life, only to discover that the idea of balance itself is a distinct vision of the good that positively conflicts with many that it

---

[75] Pecora, 132, 4, citing Edward Said, *The World, the Text, and the Critic* (Cambridge, MA: Harvard UP, 1983), 29.

would absorb. In what remains of this chapter I want to suggest how the 1880s saw Arnold's literary criticism become more comfortable with affirming positive or homogeneous sources of value. If, as Williams argues, many of the vexations of *Culture and Anarchy* come from Arnold's attempt to ground culture's authority in *itself*, then these later essays seem to come to terms with drawing upon the "fire and strength" of culture's chosen objects. As a consequence, Arnoldian criticism becomes the thing it is so often accused of being: a secular theology based upon the worship of great texts.

For example, in "A Deptford Poet," an unsigned 1875 review of the Irish poet Charles P. O'Connor's *Songs of a Life* (1875), Arnold describes poetry in terms that recall "The Function of Criticism" but also echo his subsequent concepts of Celticism and of Hebraism:

> The right function of poetry is to animate, to console, to rejoice—in one word, to *strengthen*. This function modern poetry seldom fulfills. It has thought, fancy, ingenuity; it often makes us admire its author's powers, sometimes interests us, sometimes instructs us, occasionally puzzles us; but it in general leaves our poor humanity as rueful and broken-backed, to say the very least, as it found it.   (8:1)

In this passage the virtues of Celtic poetry ("fancy, ingenuity"), which formerly had to be defended against middle-class Philistinism, merge with those of Protestant Dissent ("to animate.... to *strengthen*"), making the latter no less than the former a site of emotional consolation. Arnold does much the same thing in "The Study of Poetry," an introduction to T. H. Ward's anthology, *The English Poets* (1880):

> The future of poetry is immense, because in poetry, where it is worthy of its high destinies, our race, as time goes on, will find an ever surer and surer stay. There is not a creed which is not shaken, not an accredited dogma which is not shown to be questionable, not a received tradition which does not threaten to dissolve. Our religion has materialised itself in the fact, in the supposed fact; it has attached its emotion to the fact, and now the fact is failing it. But for poetry the idea is everything; the rest is a world of illusion, of divine illusion. Poetry attaches its emotion to the idea; the idea *is* the fact. The strongest part of our religion to-day is its unconscious poetry.   (9:161–2)

Poetry, like Hebraism, is a centripetal, focusing energy, as it was in "Function." Now, however, the job of the critic is not to defamiliarize it but rather to tap into its strength. Instead of many-sidedness, the ideal is appreciation, and the way to get the most out of poetry is to internalize it via repetition and memorization:

> Indeed there can be no more useful help for discovering what poetry belongs to the class of the truly excellent, and can therefore do us most good, than to have always in one's mind lines and expressions of the great masters, and to

apply them as a touchstone to other poetry. Of course we are not to require this other poetry to resemble them; it may be very dissimilar. But if we have any tact we shall find them, when we have lodged them well in our minds, an infallible touchstone for detecting the presence or absence of high poetic quality, and also the degree of this quality, in all other poetry which we may place beside them.   (9:168)

Part of the virtue of this method, and what makes it warrant Arnold's trust, is the very fact that it does not involve abstract definition and judgment. The standard here is prereflective and the method circular. By reading great literature, the reader will learn to recognize greatness through an instinct that almost works like parochial inheritance: "If we are thoroughly penetrated by their power," Arnold writes, "we shall find that we have acquired a sense enabling us, whatever poetry may be laid before us, to feel the degree in which a high poetical quality is present or wanting there" (9:170–1).[76]

Herbert Tucker argues that this collapse of culture into the very objects it is supposed to scrutinize represents an inevitable consequence of the pedagogical institutionalization of literary criticism that Arnold would pioneer toward the end of his career. Institutionalizing disinterestedness meant eliminating its open, playful character, denying us a set of principles and replacing them with a cult of personality called the canon, or rather, "the *idea* of a canon."[77] Crucially, it does see Arnold revise what he means by "the best" in literature. In "The Function of Criticism at the Present Time" and *Culture and Anarchy*, the term *best* was implicitly centrifugal: the opposite of "the best which has been thought and said in the world" was not the worst but rather the parochial, or the best that had been thought and said within the confines of middle-class fundamentalism. In "The Study of Poetry," by contrast, "the best" becomes a criterion of ranking and exclusion:

[I]n poetry the distinction between excellent and inferior, sound and unsound or only half-sound, true and untrue or only half-true, is of para- mount importance. It is of paramount importance because of the high destinies of poetry. In poetry, as a criticism of life under the conditions fixed for such a criticism by the laws of poetic truth and poetic beauty, the spirit of our race will find, we have said, as time goes on and as other helps

---

[76] Graff conflates this passage with *Culture and Anarchy* in order to illustrate his misreading of the latter text as a polemic for "common culture" (196–201). In "The Study of Poetry," however, Graff's critique finds its proper object as Arnold himself advocates something whose force is supposed to be prereflective and unconscious.

[77] Herbert Tucker, "Arnold and the Authorization of Criticism," in Suzy Anger (ed.), *Knowing the Past: Victorian Literature and Culture* (Ithaca, NY: Cornell UP, 2001), 120.

fail, its consolation and stay. But the consolation and stay will be of power in proportion to the power of the criticism of life. And the criticism of life will be of power in proportion as the poetry conveying it is excellent rather than inferior, sound rather than unsound or half-sound, true rather than untrue or half-true.   (9:162–3)

Since the goal of criticism is now to tap into a prereflective force, our job is consequently to read less rather than more—to eschew the heterogeneity of world literature and focus only on the "sound" and the "true." Where "Heinrich Heine" (1863) had defined the challenge of the nineteenth century as being that of sorting through the "immense system of institutions, established facts, accredited dogmas, customs, rules, which have come to [us] from times not modern" (3:109) through a practice of intellectual expansion, "The Study of Poetry" proposes that we cope with this situation through selection, concentration, and isolation. Culture becomes a canonization process in both the theological and critical senses, which is why it should come as no surprise that the pieces in *Essays in Criticism: Second Series* (1888) originated as introductions to anthologies.

Arnold's writings on religion and culture find a curious coda in his 1883–84 lecture tour of the United States. In 1883 Arnold was introduced to Andrew Carnegie, a Philistine if ever there was one, yet a Philistine who also sought to acquire for himself and his adopted country the kind of cultural capital with which Arnold was associated. Carnegie proposed that Arnold try his hand at the lucrative American lecture circuit, and the perpetually cash-strapped school inspector could not refuse.[78] In the run-up to his trip, Arnold reflected in the *Nineteenth Century* that, so far as he knew—and he conceded that his primary source was Henry James's *Roderick Hudson* (1875)—America was an almost entirely Philistine society in which bourgeois Protestantism had neither an organized working class nor a landed aristocracy to counterbalance it. "That which in England we call the middle class," he wrote, "is in America virtually the nation"; America "is generally industrious and religious," he continued, and

[i]ts religion is even less invaded, I believe, by the modern spirit than the religion of our middle class. An American of reputation as a man of science tells me that he lives in a town of a hundred and fifty thousand people, of whom there are not fifty who do not imagine the first chapters of Genesis to be exact history.   (10:10–1)

Yet after his tour, which took Arnold up and down the northeast corridor and as far afield as Quebec and Chicago, he amended such skepticism, and

---

[78] Honan, 393–4; Trilling, 392.

with it the very theory of culture. In an essay entitled "A Word More About America" (1884), he admitted that until he had visited the United States he "had never seen a people with institutions which seemed expressly and thoroughly suited to it" (10:196). Indeed, he continued, "[a]s one watches the play of their institutions, the image suggests itself to one's mind of a man in a suit of clothes which fits him to perfection, leaving all his movements unimpeded and easy. It is loose where it ought to be loose, and sits close where its sitting close is an advantage" (10:197). As the Carlylean metaphor suggests, what Arnold really discovered in America was the value of homogeneity. "How homogeneous American society is," he marvels; "how smoothly and naturally the institutions of the United States work, how clearly, in some most important respects, the Americans see, how straight they think" (10:216). If the paradoxical thesis of *Culture and Anarchy* was that the pursuit of "one thing needful" bred fragmentation and "a stream of fresh and free thought" could restore order, "A Word About America" seems to admit that things may not be so complicated after all.

3

History's Second-Hand Bookshop
Self-Cultivation and Scripturality in George Eliot's
Daniel Deronda and *The Spanish Gypsy*

In a letter to Harriet Beecher Stowe, George Eliot explained her reasons
for writing *Daniel Deronda* (1876) by describing her alarm at learning that
"men educated at Rugby suppos[e] that Christ spoke Greek"; "They
hardly know that Christ was a Jew."[1] Although we cannot be sure that
Eliot had Matthew Arnold specifically in mind, critics have often taken
this remark as grounds for contrasting the two writers: Eliot the philo-
Semite, prophesying the emergence of a modern Jewish nation state in
Deronda, and Arnold the arch-Hellenist, warning England about the
excessive "Hebraism" in its religion and politics. Yet the fact is that both
writers were intensely attracted to Judaism as an entity whose refusal to
adhere to the liberal bifurcation of chosen beliefs and unconscious heritage
allowed them to rethink the relationship between religion, self-cultivation,
and the ethnic past. In Arnold's essays, Hebraism epitomizes all those
narrow sources of value, from opaque theological beliefs to reflexive racial
instincts, that a many-sided self needs to internalize, even as they reject its
values from within. Along similar lines, *Deronda* pictures Judaism as an
intense, parochial attachment that can give the modern self a certain
multidimensionality that abstract cosmopolitanism cannot. The novel
tells the story of a wealthy orphan who discovers that he is of Jewish
descent and takes up the charge issued by the consumptive prophet
Mordecai to aid the Zionist cause in Palestine. By rooting Daniel in
loyalties that lack the transparency of universal reason, the novel suggests,
Judaism enables him to develop a more complex form of modern subjectivity, one that is intensely aware of its involvement in a world of competing
differences.

---

[1] *The George Eliot Letters*, ed. Gordon S. Haight (9 vols.; New Haven, CT: Yale UP,
1954–5), 6: 302. Quoted in Michael Ragussis, *Figures of Conversion: "The Jewish Question"
and English National Identity* (Durham, NC: Duke UP, 1995), 265.

This reading of *Deronda* is by now a familiar one, thanks to the work of Amanda Anderson and others.[2] In this chapter I argue that Eliot's post-conventional recuperation of Judaism differs from Arnold's in focusing special attention upon what *reading* means for this kind of secular subjectivity. On one level, Eliot's narrative foregrounds reading as the activity that transforms racial inheritance into a semi-conscious resource for the modern self. To draw this out, I juxtapose *Daniel Deronda* with a work that in many ways serves as its forerunner within the Eliot corpus: her 1868 verse drama, *The Spanish Gypsy*. Both texts follow the life of an orphaned child who discovers that he or she belongs to a dispossessed race and elects to help this people find a homeland. The crucial difference is that Eliot's Gypsies are a race that lacks a scriptural tradition through which individuals can mediate their relationships to the past. The power of Gypsy identity is purely that of racial affect, which paradoxically becomes as narrowing and monomaniacal as the individual will to power. By contrast, the fact that Deronda becomes acquainted with his ethnic heritage by way of texts allows him to gain a personal handle on the tradition and thus leverage some interpretive space between himself and his Zionist mentor, a freedom that is not available to Eliot's Gypsy protagonist, Fedalma. Religion, in other words, becomes a special category for Eliot precisely because it represents the site at which textuality and blood-heritage intersect. As an ethnic inheritance, religion can never be a fully detached object of mental reflection, but as a scriptural tradition it demands the development of a hermeneutic consciousness that can bring the inheritances of the past into free play.

At the same time, Eliot worries that valorizing critical reading in this way can engender a new kind of one-sidedness. Like Arnold, Eliot was an early enthusiast of the historicist Bible criticism being developed on the continent, and, also like Arnold, she perceived a distinct ethical payoff in this new hermeneutic. For Eliot, the reader who can canvas a broad range of cultural materials and grasp their historical relationships will develop a many-sided identity that avoids the egotism encouraged by English Dissent and its rubric of *sola scriptura*. Eliot, however, also worries that

---

[2] For versions of this reading, see Philip J. Fisher, *Making Up Society: The Novels of George Eliot* (Pittsburgh, PA: U of Pittsburgh P, 1981); Suzanne Graver, *George Eliot and Community: A Study in Social Theory and Fictional Form* (Berkeley, CA: U of California P, 1984); Bernard Semmel, *George Eliot and the Politics of National Inheritance* (New York, NY: Oxford UP, 1994); Amanda Anderson, *The Powers of Distance: Cosmopolitanism and the Cultivation of Detachment* (Princeton, NJ: Princeton UP, 2001), 119–46 and "George Eliot and the Jewish Question," *Yale Journal of Criticism* 10.1 (1997): 39–61; and Thomas Albrecht, " 'The Balance of Separateness and Communication': Cosmopolitan Ethics in George Eliot's *Daniel Deronda*," *ELH* 79.2 (2012): 389–416.

this many-sided reading program may lead one into some of the same pitfalls as Protestant scripturalism. Specifically, she suspects that the disinterested survey of cultural history encouraged by many-sidedness can itself become a way of withdrawing the self from cosmopolitan involvements. Her response, in turn, is to envision a style of reading that approaches texts not as repositories of content but rather as heirlooms of historical and social relationships. By having Daniel encounter his racial heritage in the specific form of old books—first the neglected volumes of London's used book shops, and then the chest of mystic writings that Daniel inherits from his grandfather—Eliot suggests that a reader who can relate to texts as metonyms of different histories will develop a many-sidedness that a reader who simply looks to the Bible as fodder for private interpretation will not. Somewhere between the myopic Protestant hermeneut and the disengaged cosmopolite, Eliot's many-sided reader inhabits the fraught position of a used-bookstore browser who takes up these relics of the past through risky personal encounters.

Eliot's interest in nineteenth-century biblical scholarship is, of course, a familiar subject.[3] What I will argue here is that tracing her efforts to imagine a liberal reader who circumvents the pitfalls of *sola scriptura* illuminates a common set of concerns linking Victorian aesthetic liberalism to current projects of surface or distant reading in literary studies: a shared desire to picture a secularism beyond Protestantism. In recent years, a number of literary scholars have put forward critical programs that reject "the heroic myth—whether Protestant, liberal, New Critical, or New Historicist"—of private interpretation as "the source of interiority, authenticity, and selfhood" for a mode of reading that is more attentive to the empirical details or material data of texts.[4] Their work joins that of postcolonial anthropologists who have explored how Protestant practices of private reading have historically produced a certain vision of the secular subject, "a sovereign subject who reconciles the claims of scripture against those of reason, wherein reason is defined in accord with protocols of empiricist historiography."[5] What these scholars share with Eliot and Arnold is a desire to imagine a secular self that is still ethically defined in

[3] See, for example, Suzy Anger, *Victorian Interpretation* (Ithaca, NY: Cornell UP, 2005), 95–130; Mary Wilson Carpenter, "The Apocalypse of the Old Testament: Daniel Deronda and the Interpretation of Interpretation," *PMLA* 99.1 (1984): 56–71; E. S. Shaffer, *"Kubla Khan" and The Fall of Jerusalem: The Mythological School in Biblical Criticism and Secular Literature, 1770–1880* (New York, NY: Cambridge UP, 1975), 225–91.

[4] Leah Price, *How to Do Things with Books in Victorian Britain* (Princeton, NJ: Princeton UP, 2013), 16.

[5] Saba Mahmood, "Secularism, Hermeneutics, and Empire: The Politics of Islamic Reformation," *Public Culture* 18.2 (2006): 339.

terms of reading, but not via metaphors of depth. They all worry that there may be something quite *il*liberal about interpretive analysis, something that confirms our own provincial biases instead of pushing us toward fresh encounters with difference. Their response, however, is not to abandon reading as the core activity of modern subjectivity but rather to postulate an alternative reading practice that encourages breadth over than depth—a willingness to attend to multiple, unexpected objects out there in the world and to implicate ourselves in their contingent histories.

ELIOT, RELIGION, AND THE ANTHROPOLOGICAL TURN

George Eliot owed much of her intellectual radicalization to two families of freethinking intellectuals, the Brays and the Hennells, whom she met as a teenager in Warwickshire.[6] Most notably, it was by reading Charles Hennell's *An Inquiry Concerning the Origin of Christianity* (1838) that Eliot experienced a spiritual crisis and broke with the evangelical religion of her youth.[7] By the same token, Hennell's study sparked in the young Eliot a hope that philosophy and anthropology might salvage some common humanistic essence from the world's different religions. Already a promising student of languages, Eliot immersed herself in many of the recent social-scientific revaluations of religion, from the philosophy of Auguste Comte to the work of German biblical critics such as David Friedrich Strauss. Indeed, her connections to the Hennell-Bray coterie eventually won her the privilege of translating the first English version of Strauss's *Das Leben Jesu* (1835), published as *The Life of Jesus, Critically Examined* in 1846. Eliot's edition of Strauss attracted much notoriety; Charles Kingsley called Strauss, and by implication Eliot, "a vile aristocrat robbing the poor man of his savior."[8] But it also won Eliot the admiration of her publisher, John Chapman, who invited Eliot to move to London upon the death of her father in 1849 and co-edit the *Westminster Review*

[6] For overviews of Eliot's early intellectual development, see Avrom Fleishman, *George Eliot's Intellectual Life* (New York, NY: Cambridge UP, 2010), 1–92; Simon Dentith, *George Eliot* (Sussex, UK: Harvester, 1986), 9–29; Ruby V. Redinger, *George Eliot: The Emergent Self* (New York, NY: Knopf, 1975), 27–159; Gordon Haight, *George Eliot: A Biography* (New York, NY: Oxford UP, 1968), 1–95.

[7] On Eliot's break with evangelical religion, see Redinger, 117–19; Haight, *George Eliot*, 32–67.

[8] Sheila Rosenberg, "The 'Wicked Westminster': John Chapman, His Contributors and Promises Fulfilled," *Victorian Periodicals Review* 33.3 (2000), 227.

with him. Chapman's offices at 142 Strand were rapidly becoming a hub
of radical thought in the metropolis, and as Chapman's protégé Eliot
would meet such liberal luminaries as Harriet and James Martineau,
E. B. Tylor, the secularist George Jacob Holyoake, and her own future
partner, the philosopher and science-writer George Henry Lewes.[9]

What Eliot learned from the Hennells and the *Westminster Review*
crowd was a radically historicist mode of reading that insisted upon
situating texts within the limitations of their particular societies. Strauss
was a practitioner of the so-called higher criticism, which employed the
latest tools of historical scholarship to frame the Bible, not as the carrier of
a timeless message, but rather as a typical instantiation of ancient Near
Eastern theological conceptions and literary genres.[10] In this respect, his
work resonated with the revived stadial history that came back into vogue
among English radicals during the 1860s and (as we saw in Chapter 1)
portrayed different global religions as the projections of different levels of
civilizational development. As Eliot explained in an 1856 review of James
Heywood's *Introduction to Genesis* (1855), a translation of the German
scholar Peter Von Bohlen's *Die Genesis, historisch-kritisch erläutert* (1835),
modern research

> holds no conviction that removes the Hebrew scriptures from the common
> category of early national records, which are a combination of myth and
> legend, gradually clarifying at their later stages into genuine history.... [It]
> finds in them no evidence of anything exceptionally divine, but sees in them
> simply the history and literature of a barbarous tribe that gradually rose from
> fetichism to a ferocious polytheism, offering human sacrifices, and ultim-
> ately, through the guidance of their best men, and contacts with more
> civilized nations, to Jehovistic monotheism.[11]

---

[9] For Eliot's place in the milieu of English radicalism, see Graver; Simon During,
"George Eliot and Secularism," *A Companion to George Eliot*, ed. Amanda Anderson and
Harry E. Shaw (Oxford, UK: Wiley-Blackwell, 2013), 428–41; Ian Duncan, "George Eliot
and the Science of the Human," in Anderson and Shaw, 471–85; Gordon Haight, *George
Eliot and John Chapman* (New Haven, CT: Yale UP, 1969); Martha S. Vogeler, "George
Eliot and the Positivists," *Nineteenth Century Fiction* 35.3 (1980): 406–31.

[10] See Anger, 100–10; Hans Frei, *The Eclipse of Biblical Narrative: A Study in Eighteenth
and Nineteenth Century Hermeneutics* (New Haven, CT: Yale UP, 1974), 233–44.

[11] George Eliot, "Introduction to Genesis," in Thomas Pinney, *Essays of George Eliot*
(New York, NY: Columbia UP, 1963), 257–8. See also Eliot's review of Robert William
Mackay's *The Progress of the Intellect, as Exemplified in the Religious Development of the Greeks
and Hebrews* (1850), which anticipates Tylor's *Primitive Culture* (1871) in arguing that "we
are in bondage to terms and conceptions which, having had their root in conditions of
thought no longer existing, have ceased to possess any vitality," and that the virtue of social
science was to point out such survivals and thus pave the way for their elimination from
human culture. "Mackay's Progress of the Intellect," *Westminster Review* 54 (1851): 353.

As such, Eliot continues, work like Van Bohlen's refutes both "extreme orthodox" hermeneutics and an "accommodationist" theology that regards the scientifically outlandish or morally repugnant elements of the Old Testament as concessions made by the divine author to the childish minds of its original audience.[12] In a similar spirit, Eliot would dismiss allegorical apologetics on the grounds that they did scant justice to the full reality that religious symbols held for the people who invented them. It was a "mistake," she wrote, to "suppose[e] that the conscious allegorizing of a modern can be a correct reproduction of what they acknowledge to be unconscious allegorizing in the ancients."[13]

What Eliot is ultimately seeking in these early reviews is a way to affirm the Bible's historical limitations while simultaneously distilling from it something of value to the modern reader. She would find such a combination of distancing and sympathy in the work of the Hegelian philosopher Ludwig Feuerbach, whose *Das Wesen des Christenthums* (1841) she translated as *The Essence of Christianity* in 1854. Feuerbach, in effect, reinterpreted Christianity as a misplaced symbolic veneration of ordinary human life. "The true or anthropological essence of religion," he wrote, was a set of perennial moral imperatives such as mercy, justice, and love that the writers of the Bible had expressed through narrative figures: Jesus suffering on the cross, or breaking bread with his disciples.[14] But because readers in a historicist and scientific age increasingly understood these figures literally, their meanings needed to be restored through a process of demystification that would point out their origins in the immanent world around us. Much as Strauss had called the Bible "not properly a theology, but a homily," and much as Marx would later identify religion itself as a mystification of real historical wants, so did Feuerbach argue that the water of Christian baptism, for example, was a symbol "of our origin from Nature," while the bread and wine of the Eucharist reminded man that he was a product of cultivation as well as of nature.[15]

At the same time, Eliot recognized in Feuerbach's work a crucial paradox: to understand Christianity, you had to abstract its moral essence from its narrative particulars, but what you discovered in so doing was that Christianity's true meaning, *qua* religion, was particular instead of

---

[12] Eliot, "Introduction to Genesis," 256.
[13] Eliot, "Progress of the Intellect," 362.
[14] Ludwig Feuerbach, *The Essence of Christianity*, trans. Marian Evans (London, UK: John Chapman, 1854), 32.
[15] David Friedrich Strauss, *The Life of Jesus, Critically Examined*, trans. George Eliot (3 vols.; London: Chapman, 1846), 3: 440; Feuerbach, 273. See U. C. Knoepflmacher, *Religious Humanism and the Victorian Novel: George Eliot, Walter Pater, and Samuel Butler* (Princeton, NJ: Princeton UP, 1965), 52–6.

abstract. The Bible's real religious message had to be separated from its literal characters and stories, but at the same time biblical religion had no significance apart from a world of embodied human persons, affects, and physical sensations. What was needed in order to preserve the essence of religion, Feuerbach implied, was not a demystification so much as a retranslation that would embed the Bible's moral meaning in a new set of narrative specifics more impactful for modern readers.[16] This insight would become central to Eliot's work as her focus shifted from editing and reviewing to fiction-writing, since it implied that realist fiction might itself have this power to pour biblical wine into new wineskins. In *Adam Bede* (1859), for instance, Bartle Massey the schoolmaster visits Adam on the eve of Hetty Sorrel's trial and consoles him with what one might call an impromptu Eucharist:

> "And now," [Bartle] said, rising again, "I must see to your having a bit of the loaf, and some of that wine Mr. Irwine sent this morning. He'll be angry with me if you don't have it. Come, now," he went on, bringing forward the bottle and the loaf and pouring some wine into a cup, "I must have a bit and a sup myself. Drink a drop with me, my lad—drink with me.... Take a bit, then, and another sup, Adam, for the love of me. See, I must stop and eat a morsel. Now, you take some."
>
> Nerved by an active resolution, Adam took a morsel of bread and drank some wine. He was haggard and unshaven, as he had been yesterday, but he stood upright again, and looked more like the Adam Bede of former days.[17]

In this passage Eliot follows through on Feuerbach's claim that the Eucharist was designed to "typify to us the truth that Man is the true God and Saviour of man" by detaching it from the familiar figure of Jesus and reinscribing it as an act of sympathetic sharing between mortals.[18] Elsewhere in the novel, Eliot reflects upon the embeddedness of religious symbols within mundane life:

> What a glad world this looks like, as one drives or rides along the valleys and over the hills! I have often thought so when, in foreign countries, where the fields and woods have looked to me like our English Loamshire—the rich land tilled with just as much care, the woods rolling down the gentle slopes to the green meadows—I have come on something by the roadside which

---

[16] For Eliot's thoughts on translation as a moral activity, see Susan E. Hill, "Translating Feuerbach, Constructing Morality: The Theological and Literary Significance of Translation for George Eliot," *Journal of the American Academy of Religion* 65.3 (1997): 635–53.

[17] Eliot, *Adam Bede*, ed. Valentine Cunningham (1859; New York, NY: Oxford UP, 1996), 426–9.

[18] Feuerbach, 274. For a further reading of *Adam Bede*'s Eucharistic scenes, see Knoepflmacher, 56–9.

has reminded me that I am not in Loamshire: an image of a great agony—the agony of the Cross. It has stood perhaps by the clustering apple-blossoms, or in the broad sunshine by the cornfield, or at a turning by the wood where a clear brook was gurgling below; and surely, if there came a traveler to this world who knew nothing of the story of man's life upon it, this image of agony would seem to him strangely out of place in the midst of this joyous nature. He would not know that hidden behind the apple-blossoms, or among the golden corn, or under the shrouding boughs of the wood, there might be a human heart beating heavily with anguish—perhaps a young blooming girl, not knowing where to turn for refuge from swift-advancing shame, understanding no more of this life of ours than a foolish lost lamb wandering farther and farther in the nightfall on the lonely heath, yet tasting the bitterest of life's bitterness. . . . No wonder man's religion has much sorrow in it: no wonder he needs a suffering God.[19]

Here the contrast between the grim crucifix and the sunny pastoral world around it bespeaks the power of religion to articulate what is most urgent, but also most hidden, in human life. The cross, with its overtones of suffering and sacrifice, may seem incongruous among these "gentle slopes" and "green meadows," but the agony that it typifies is one that is being played out in a thousand ways all around it. Eliot's narrator compounds this disorientation by comparing it to the perplexity that we feel upon discovering that a foreign country looks a lot like home. The large cross reminds one that one is in a Catholic land, but in fact what it signifies is something that may be found back in England as well.

Ultimately, by teaching Eliot a spiritual rationale for literary realism, Feuerbach also gave her an idiosyncratic vision of many-sidedness as the transhistorical essence of religion. Eliot is more often associated with the word *sympathy* than with many-sidedness, but in general for Eliot sympathy involves less a Smithian abstraction of ourselves into the other's point of view than a capacity to attend to as many features of human life as possible.[20] For the Eliot of *Adam Bede*, and eventually of *Middlemarch* (1871–2), a modern subject who embodies the true spirit of religion will be one who can remain sympathetically attuned to multiple sites of moral obligation, multiple centers of consciousness, and multiple ways of being or thinking.[21] As Catherine Gallagher puts it, Eliot's fiction creates a

---

[19] Eliot, *Adam Bede*, 363–4.   [20] See Anger, 114–16.
[21] As described in Eliot's *Essence of Christianity*, sympathy is the structure of feeling that links divine love to the particular sensations of embodied life: "Feeling is sympathy; feeling arises only in the love of man to man. Sensations man has in isolation; feelings only in community. Only in sympathy does sensation rise into feeling" (277). Thus, by picturing "a real sympathy of the divine being in his sufferings and wants," the religious believer is able to validate the day-to-day experiences of ordinary human beings (68).

specific structure of desire whereby literary characters strike us not because they instantiate generic types but because they deviate from them.[22] We grow interested in *Middlemarch*'s Dorothea Brooke because she fails to become another St. Theresa and ends up as something more idiosyncratic instead. By such means, Gallagher argues, Eliot effects "a massive redirection of longing away from disembodied transcendence and toward embodied immanence"—"away from a desire for salvation conceived of as spiritual or ideational transcendence and toward a longing to attain a state of immanent existence that escapes the requirement of 'meaning.'"[23]

Like Arnold, Eliot contrasts this religion of many-sidedness with evangelical Protestantism's emphasis upon mental beliefs and doctrinal propositions. What repels her particularly about this tradition is its habit of approaching the Bible in search of a single truth that will alleviate the reader's Calvinist self-worry rather than using it to direct the reader's attention outward toward new knowledge or wider duties. In her 1855 review essay on the Scottish evangelical writer John Cumming, for example, Eliot condemns Cumming's apocalyptic version of Christianity for being too "forensic" and "theoretic" in its decoding of Bible prophecy.[24] This false scholasticism, she writes, masks a desperate egotism that wants only to be assured of the self's salvation and thus "unmans the nature ... allow[ing] no thorough, calm thinking, no truly noble, disinterested feeling."[25] It also encourages an "unscrupulous" use of text that is designed "not to give the deepest solutions of the difficulties in question, but to furnish Scripture Readers, City Missionaries, and Sunday School Teachers, with a 'ready reply' to sceptical arguments," a little "change in their pocket ... a little ready argument which they can employ, and therewith answer a fool according to his folly."[26] Cumming's liquidation of the Bible into petty polemical currency is the opposite of Feuerbach's or Strauss's hermeneutics in that it functions primarily to defend the self instead of expanding its view.

Yet Eliot also took a second lesson from Feuerbach—that a sympathetic many-sidedness could be developed, not just by attending to the lives of those around us, but also by paying close attention to the fine-grained

---

[22] Catherine Gallagher, "George Eliot: Immanent Victorian," *Representations* 90.1 (2005): 61–74. For more on Eliot's ethics of immanent particularity, see also Daniel S. Malachuk, "George Eliot's Liberalism," in Anderson and Shaw, 370–84.

[23] Gallagher, 72, 61. In this sense Eliot's sympathy leads toward the embrace of what Charles Taylor calls the "immanent frame"—a social imaginary in which embodied reality, without any transcendent significance behind it, constitutes our primary ground of meaning. See *A Secular Age* (Cambridge, MA: Harvard UP, 2007), 539–93.

[24] Eliot, "Evangelical Teaching: Dr. Cumming," *Westminster Review* 64 (1855): 437.

[25] Ibid., 443.   [26] Ibid., 444.

details of entire human societies. What Rae Greiner calls sympathetic realism, that is, could be complemented by an ethnographic realism that honored traditional ways of life through careful scientific study.[27] This notion finds its most striking formulation in Eliot's "The Natural History of German Life" (1856), a review of the sociologist Wilhelm Heinrich von Riehl's *Die burgerliche Gesellschaft* (1851) and *Land und Leute* (1853). In most European peasant cultures, Eliot quotes Riehl, "*Custom... holds the place of sentiment, of theory, and in many cases of affection,*" and the individual behaves "more as one of a group."[28] Such societies need to be brought into the progressive mainstream of modern civilization, Eliot continues, but not so quickly that their traditions are uprooted wholesale. Instead, someone "of sufficient moral and intellectual breadth, whose observations would not be vitiated by a foregone conclusion" must "devote himself to studying the[ir] natural history" and "give us the result of his observations in a book well-nourished with specific facts."[29] In exhibiting such qualities, Eliot argues, Riehl's work displays a healthy "*social-political-conservatism*" that is "able and willing to do justice to the elements of fact and reason in every shade of opinion and every form of effort."[30] In a veritable interdisciplinary hat trick, Riehl becomes at once an exemplary anthropologist, a paragon of many-sided sympathy, and a model of literary realism—for "the greatest benefit we owe to the artist," Eliot writes, "is the extension of our sympathies. Appeals founded on generalizations and statistics require a sympathy ready-made... but a picture of human life such as a great artist can give, surprises even the trivial and the selfish into that attention to what is apart from themselves, which may be called the raw material of moral sentiment."[31]

This ethos of ethnographic many-sidedness, with its "large-minded" conservatism, had a complex influence upon Eliot's literary output. In *Adam Bede* it creates a nostalgic portrait of rural England on the brink of industrialization. In *Felix Holt: The Radical* (1866), written in response to the debates leading up to the Second Reform Act, it yields a Burkean mistrust of all attempts to tinker deliberately with the social organism.[32]

---

[27] See Rae Greiner, *Sympthetic Realism in Nineteenth-Century British Fiction* (Baltimore, MD: Johns Hopkins UP, 2012), 1–14. Sarah Winter has shown that British liberal interest in ethnographic realism extends as far back as John Locke; see "Mental Culture: Liberal Pedagogy and the Emergence of Ethnographic Knowledge," *Victorian Studies* 41.3 (1998): 427–54.
[28] Eliot, "The Natural History of German Life," *Westminster Review* 66 (1856): 34, 32.
[29] Ibid., 31.   [30] Ibid., 38, 44.   [31] Ibid., 30.
[32] See Evan Horowitz, "George Eliot: The Conservative," *Victorian Studies* 49.1 (2006): 7–32.

Finally, it would lead Eliot to experiment with the idea that many-sidedness, and therefore the essence of religion itself, might be derived from a self-conscious recuperation of one's *own* historical inheritances. Although this notion receives its best-known treatment in *Daniel Deronda*, its most explicit articulation comes in "The Modern Hep! Hep! Hep!", the final essay in the *Impressions of Theophrastus Such* (1879), which defends the Jews' continuing sense of ethnic separateness as a political virtue:

> The eminence, the nobleness of a people depends on its capability of being stirred by memories, and of striving for what we call spiritual ends . . . It is this living force of sentiment in common which makes a national consciousness. Nations so moved will resist conquest with the very breasts of their women, will pay their millions and their blood to abolish slavery, will share privation in famine and all calamity, will produce poets to sing "some great story of a man," and thinkers whose theories will bear the test of action. An individual man, to be harmoniously great, must belong to a nation of this order, if not in actual existence yet existing in the past, in memory, as a departed, invisible, beloved ideal, once a reality, and perhaps to be restored. A common humanity is not yet enough to feed the rich blood of various activity which makes a complete man.[33]

In effect, Eliot's persona, Theophrastus, attributes three overlapping virtues to ethnic self-consciousness. Not only does a shared stock of "sentiment in common" create a sense of group solidarity, and make the individual feel like part of "something great, admirable, pregnant with high possibilities, worthy of sacrifice," but it also gives the self an internal heterogeneity that could be never be derived from cosmopolitanism. Here the language of eighteenth-century aesthetic liberalism—"harmony," "various activity"; terms one might find in Humboldt or Schiller—is re-purposed as a rationale for embracing racialized religion. To be sure, Eliot is not envisioning a self comprised of several incommensurate identities, as Matthew Arnold was in *The Study of Celtic Literature* (1867). But she is speculating that the tension between those parts of our identities that we have deliberately chosen and those that have (in effect) chosen us might yield a productive play. One could even say that Eliot is reworking Mill's claim in *On Liberty* (1859) that individuals are enriched by their encounters with diverse points of view by way of Edmund Burke's "choice of inheritance": it is only by coming to terms with the historical heterogeneity within ourselves, she suggests, that we might develop a lively sense of the multiple differences operating in realms beyond it.[34]

---

[33] Eliot, *Impressions of Theophrastus Such*, ed. Nancy Henry (1879; London, UK: William Pickering, 1994), 147. For Eliot's shifting views on Judaism, see Ragussis, 260–90.
[34] See Eliot, *Impressions*, 164.

RACE AND THE MEDIATION OF SCRIPTURE

So far this chapter has explored how George Eliot's early work, under the influence of Feuerbach and others, came to imagine that a close attention to the particulars of social life could encourage the development of a many-sided personality. We have also seen how Eliot frequently framed this line of thought as a revision of what religion meant—a turn away from a Protestant concern with individual salvation and private belief toward an attunement to the sacred duties immanent in the social worlds around us, past and present. That said, one might justifiably wonder whether the term *religion* retains much salience here. For isn't Eliot actually redefining religion as an epiphenomenon of loyalty to the *Volk*? What I want to suggest now is that, if we read *Daniel Deronda* alongside *The Spanish Gypsy*, we get a better sense of why religion, as a category, had a continuing importance to Eliot: because of its focus on texts. Whereas Eliot's early novels offer portraits of rural English society on the brink of the Industrial Revolution, her works of the 1860s are interested in the different possible relationships between recuperated heritage and culti-vated individuality and in the key role that sacred texts might play in inflecting them.

The Spanish Gypsy tells the story of Fedalma, a woman living at the height of the Inquisition who is engaged to Don Silva, Duke of Bedmar. Silva's uncle, the priest Isidor, objects to the marriage because he suspects Fedalma to be a secret pagan, and in fact Isidor's suspicions prove prescient: one day in the marketplace Fedalma meets the imprisoned Gypsy chieftain Zarca, to whom she feels an immediate attraction. Zarca reveals to Fedalma that he is her father and that she was kidnapped by Spanish soldiers at the age of three. He then tells her of his plan to become a Gypsy Moses by leading his people to a homeland in North Africa, "Where they shall plant and sow and reap their own / . . . and call our Holy Place / The hearth that binds us in one family."[35] Within the plot, Silva and Zarca represent alternate possible futures for Fedalma, with Silva offering a path of individual self-fulfillment through romantic love and Zarca a turn to ethnic solidarity. Silva champions love as a cosmo-politan antidote to the prejudices of caste and country, announcing that "love comes to cancel all ancestral hate, / Subdues all heritage, proves that in mankind / Union is deeper than division," while Zarca condemns such notions as fickleness and sings the praises of filial duty, boasting that his

---

[35] Eliot, *Poems: Together with Brother Jacob and The Lifted Veil* (New York, NY: Harper & Brothers, 1885), 163.

Gypsies are bound by "the fidelity / of men whose pulses leap with kindred fire" and share a "heritage inevitable as birth."[36]

Perhaps the most striking thing about *The Spanish Gypsy*, when read alongside *Daniel Deronda* and *Theophrastus Such*, is the way in which it sees race fail to inform any workable version of many-sidedness. Rather than assume a complementary relationship, race and individuality prove mutually antagonistic and equally ineffectual. On the one hand, personal desire turns out to be powerless next to the inextricable pull of racial bonds. Zarca convinces Fedalma that her primary loyalty is to her Gypsy heritage, persuading her to give up her planned marriage to Silva and join his quest. When Silva hears this, he follows Fedalma back to the Gypsy camp and declares that he will become a Gypsy himself and fight the Spanish with Zarca so as to keep the woman he loves. Zarca accepts Silva's offer but doubts whether such a "conversion" is really possible—and, indeed, upon seeing the blood of his former companions on the ground, Silva curses his decision and kills his father-in-law. On the other hand, racial vocation itself proves strangely ineffectual as the basis for political loyalty. The poem's finale finds Fedalma preparing to leave for Africa as the new leader of her father's people; yet Eliot's narrator also prophesies that this incipient nation will "wither and die" within a couple of generations—"break[ing] in small and scattered bands / That, living on scant prey, would still disperse / And propagate forgetfulness."[37] The problem, the poem suggests, is that the bonds of blood consist merely of blind affect and can only receive coherence from the shaping force of a tyrannical personality. Indeed, this is the poem's great irony: not only do egotism and racialism prove equally ineffective as political principles, but they also become deeply co-implicated within Eliot's plot. Much as twentieth-century *völkisch* nationalisms would depend upon the magnetic performances of single individuals, so is the Gypsies' sense of collective identity largely a projection of Zarca's own will to power. Describing her first encounter with Zarca to Silva, Fedalma recalls how his look

> found me there –
> Seemed to have traveled far to find me there
> And grasp me—claim this festal life of mine
> As heritage of sorrow, chill my blood
> With the cold iron of some unknown bonds.
> The gladness hurrying full within my veins
> Was sudden frozen, and I danced no more.[38]

[36] Ibid., 219, 162.   [37] Ibid., 249.   [38] Ibid., 142.

This sense of duty, whose immediacy Fedalma here dramatizes by switching momentarily from the past into the present tense, resonates with Zarca's own description of ethnicity as an affective energy. The Gypsies, he tells his daughter, are "men whose pulses leap with kindred fire, / Who in the flash of eyes, the clasp of hands" feel the "mystic stirring of a common life."[39] Nevertheless, this heat dissipates as soon as Zarca himself disappears at the end of the drama. As the narrator puts it,

> The Gypsy hearts were not unfaithful . . .
> But soon their natures missed the constant stress
> Of his command, that, while it fired, restrained
> By urgency supreme, and left no play
> To fickle impulse scattering desire.

Now, however,

> That great force which knit them into one,
> The invisible passion of her father's soul,
> That wrought them visibly into his will,
> And would have bound their lives with permanence,
> Was gone.[40]

In effect, the gravitational force of the ethnic chieftain's personality is both enabling and limiting. It gives a desultory collective new coherence by "le[aving] no play / To fickle impulse scattering desire"—yet the play that it shuts down, one suspects, is something that might have continued in Zarca's absence. Hence the peculiar way in which Zarca's power is described as alternately hot and cold. In retrospect, it is recalled as a "constant stress," a "great force which knit them into one," while in its presence Fedalma calls it a "heritage of sorrow" that "chills" her with "the cold iron of some unknown bonds," leaving her "frozen" and unable to dance.

  In this way *The Spanish Gypsy* offers something like an inverse image of the synthesis later realized in *Daniel Deronda*. Where the latter text pictures a complementary relationship between liberal individualism and ethnic inheritance, the former has these two forces mirror each other's inadequacies. Just as Arnold's "Hebraism" combines the extremes of anarchic individualism and provincial bigotry, so do Zarca's Romantic nationalism and Silva's liberal individualism start to resemble twin projections of the same egotism. And the element that seems to be missing—the secret ingredient that would bring these forces into productive harmony—is religion, or more precisely scripture, a shared collection of historical texts toward which individuals can develop their own interpretive

---

[39] Ibid., 162.   [40] Ibid., 249.

relationships. In the absence of such a tradition, Zarca's outsized personality moves into the vacuum and hijacks shared blood-affects through
sheer force of will. Zarca is in fact something of a scholar of comparative
religion, telling his daughter that he has "caught / Lore from the Hebrew,
deftness from the Moor / Known the rich heritage, the milder life, / Of
nations fathered by a mighty Past," and swears to her that

> Because our race has no great memories,
> I will so live, it shall remember me
> For deeds of such divine beneficence
> As rivers have, that teach men what is good
> By blessing them.[41]

The Jews and the Arabs, Fedalma admits upon reflection, were themselves
"slaves, lost, wandering, sunk beneath a curse, / Till Moses, Christ and
Mahomet were born / Till beings lonely in their greatness lived, / And
lived to save their people."[42] Yet all three of these figures were interpreters
of an older tradition, while Zarca endeavors to create one out of thin
air. For this reason his ambitions ultimately exceed the scholarly and
approach the Satanic as he aspires to become something of a deity himself.
The Gypsies, he declares, "shall be justified / By my high purpose, by the
clear-seen good / That grew into my vision as I grew"; "The Zincali have
no god / Who speaks to them and calls them his, unless / I, Zarca, carry
living in my frame / The power divine that chooses them and saves."[43]

   With *The Spanish Gypsy* in the background, we might say that what
Daniel Deronda tries to picture is how the supplement of scriptural religion can transform race into a resource for individualism along the lines
imagined by "The Modern Hep! Hep! Hep!" As Mary Wilson Carpenter
has shown, Mordecai is associated with a literalistic reading of scripture and
regards Judaism as something that he can inscribe directly onto the souls of
others.[44] Like Zarca, he tends to turn the tradition he champions into an
extension of his own will to dominate. Before Mordecai meets Daniel,
for instance, we see him attempting to pass his mission along to the Cohens'
son Jacob by cornering the boy and "repeat[ing] a Hebrew poem of his
own, into which years before he had poured his first youthful ardors."[45]
"The boy will get [my words] engraved within him," Mordecai thinks; "it is
a way of printing." Approaching Daniel later in the novel, Mordecai makes
a similar offer to pour his soul into his young protégé after death: "I desire
the body that I gave my thought to pass away as this fleshly body will pass;

---

[41] Ibid., 161.   [42] Ibid., 163.   [43] Ibid., 234.   [44] Carpenter, 63–4.
[45] Eliot, *Daniel Deronda*, ed. Graham Handley (1876; New York, NY: Oxford UP,
1986), 408. All subsequent citations from this edition will be noted parenthetically.

but let the thought be born again from our fuller soul which shall be called yours" (643). Daniel, however, insists that before he can adopt Mordecai's vocation he "must be convinced first of special reasons for it in the writings themselves"—referring to a trunk of mystical texts that he has inherited from his grandfather, Daniel Charisi—for "that blent transmission must go on without any choice of ours; but what we can't hinder must not make our rule for what we ought to choose" (643).[46] "I shall call myself a Jew," he announces, "but I will not say that I shall profess to believe exactly as my fathers have believed" (620). Race that is merely felt in the blood either stifles individuality or gives egotism an unholy medium to perform in; but race that comes to the individual by way of sacred texts can be internalized in ways that render the self eclectic and open to cosmopolitan explorations.[47]

ELIOT'S ETHNOGRAPHIES OF READING

On one level, of course, it should surprise no one to see Eliot, who began her career by translating radical Bible scholarship, frame reading as the activity by which we make the past our own. (Generically it is also unsurprising, since this contrast between Deronda, who can forge an idiosyncratic relationship to his heritage, and Fedalma, who is inexorably doomed by hers, parallels the familiar Bakhtinian distinction between novel and epic.[48]) Yet the curious thing is that such activity is only minimally represented in the novel itself. Unlike other Victorian fictions that dramatize the creation of a modern religiosity—James Anthony Froude's *The Nemesis of Faith* (1849) or Mary Arnold Ward's *Robert Elsmere* (1888)—*Deronda* contains no dramatic portrayal of its protagonist's attempts to come to terms with sacred texts; no parallel to the battle that the young Marian Evans waged to reconcile her attachment to the Gospels with the historical criticism of Strauss. Instead, the novel's main scenes of reading take place offstage in the one-on-one tutoring that Daniel receives from Mordecai as the novel's action concludes. But one

---

[46] For Daniel's trunk as the embodiment of historical heritage transformed into an assemblage of personal heirlooms and styles, see Fisher, 213–14.

[47] For more on text as the site at which Eliot imagines heritage becoming a resource for individuality, see Hao Li, *Memory and History in George Eliot* (London, UK: Macmillan, 2000), 164–5, 171–5.

[48] As Herbert Tucker observes, *The Spanish Gypsy*'s plot is cross-hatched by patterns of doom and destiny that "contravene the laws of bourgeois realism" and allow for "no more ethical freeplay." *Epic: Britain's Heroic Muse, 1790–1910* (New York, NY: Oxford UP, 2008), 417, 415.

can see why this happens: because Eliot has already, in her portraits of Cumming and other evangelical readers, erected individual interpretation as a figure for the self-absorption that her vision of many-sidedness rejects. The novel's most conspicuous statement of modernist interpretive liberty, for example, comes from the otherwise dubious philosopher Gideon, who would "[p]rune [Judaism] of a few useless rites and literal interpretations" until what remains is "the simplest of all religions" (455). Even the more nuanced historical-critical assessment of Judaism that we are told Daniel undertakes carries risks, since it would seem to imply a historical distance that foregoes sympathetic engagement.

This ambivalence toward reading can also be detected in the novel's handling of Quixotism—that is, moments in which characters confuse the contents of books with reality. Sometimes Quixotism stands for the ultimate form of egotistical reading, as it does when Gwendolen's selfish desire for Grandcourt sees her cast the two of them in a silver fork novel: "I wonder what sort of behavior a delightful young man would have!... I know he would have hunters and racers, and a London house and two country-houses—one with battlements and another with a veranda" (80). Like Dr. Cumming and his self-validating salvation history, Gwendolen becomes one-sided in her inability to deal with reality outside the narrative framework that her desires have selected. In Daniel's case, however, Eliot suggests that it is precisely his penchant for taking fantastic fictions seriously that allows him to assimilate unfamiliar elements into his developing sense of identity. Early on, Eliot's narrator calls Daniel "a boy of active perceptions" who "easily forgot his own existence in that of Robert Bruce" (143); and, when Daniel first learns of his true parentage, the event is portrayed not as a shattering of Romantic illusions but instead as a realization of events that usually only happen in books. While reading Sismondi's *History of the Italian Republics* (1807–18), Daniel quite innocently asks his tutor why it was that the medieval Popes had so many nephews, only to discover that the seamy answer indirectly implicates him:

Having read Shakespeare as well as a great deal of history, he could have talked with the wisdom of a bookish child about men who were born out of wedlock and were held unfortunate in consequence, being under disadvantages which required them to be a sort of heroes [sic] if they were to work themselves up to an equal standing with their legally born brothers. But he had never brought such knowledge into any association with his own lot, which had been too easy for him ever to think about it—until this moment when there had darted into his mind with the magic of quick comparison, the possibility that here was the secret of his own birth, and that the man whom he called uncle was really his father... The ardor which he had given to the imaginary world in his books suddenly rushed toward his own history

and spent its pictorial energy there, explaining what he knew, representing
the unknown... The terrible sense of collision between a strong rush of
feeling and the dread of its betrayal, found relief at length in big slow tears,
which fell without restraint until the voice of Mr. Fraser was heard saying:
"Daniel, do you see that you are sitting on the bent pages of your book?"
(141–2)

As the comic image of Daniel accidentally squashing his own book
implies, he is not projecting himself *into* the history it contains so much
as discovering, in the most awkward way possible, that its antiquarian
contents form a part of his world too. This epiphany teaches Daniel that
life holds stranger possibilities than we expect, a recognition that eventually allows him to grant Mirah's and Mordecai's "romance" of lost siblings
the respect that it deserves. "To Deronda," we are told, "this event of
finding Mirah was as heart-stirring as anything that befell Orestes or
Rinaldo"— for

> To say that Deronda was romantic would be to misrepresent him; but under
> his calm and somewhat self-repressed exterior there was a fervor which made
> him easily find poetry and romance among the events of every-day life. And
> perhaps poetry and romance are as plentiful as ever in the world except for
> those phlegmatic natures who, I suspect, would in any age have regarded
> them as a dull form of erroneous thinking. They exist very easily in the same
> room with the microscope and even in railway carriages: what banishes them
> is the vacuum in gentlemen and lady passengers. How should all the
> apparatus of heaven and earth, from the farthest firmament to the tender
> bosom of the mother who nourished us, make poetry for a mind that had no
> movements of awe and tenderness, no sense of fellowship which thrills from
> the near to the distant, and back again from the distant to the near? (175)

In an intriguing reversal, here the chief threat to many-sided sympathy
comes not from Quixotic fantasizing but rather from those familiar
bywords for literary realism, the scientist's microscope and the railway
passenger. Feuerbachian homiletics, meanwhile, are transvalued from a
warrant for realism into a defense of romance, as the very mental habits
that once prevented Gwendolen from seeing the world around her clearly
now permit Daniel a vision of the "poetry and romance" hidden in "everyday life."[49]

Even more than Arnold, then, Eliot is caught between a traditional
liberal impulse to imagine reading as a key site for cultivating complex
sympathies and an aesthetic wariness toward private interpretation as an

[49] For more on Quixotism as a possible avenue of sympathy in *Deronda*, see Debra
Gettelman, "Reading Ahead in George Eliot," *Novel: A Forum on Fiction* 39.1 (2005):
25–47.

egotistical feedback loop. Thirty years ago this fact inspired deconstructive critics to explore how she stages failures of interpretation within her novels.[50] In the current moment, it gives her work a subtle resonance with that of critics such as Leah Price or Sharon Marcus, who seek to envision readerly stances that avoid the myopia of hermeneutic suspicion.[51] Like Eliot, these critics articulate a discomfort with the narratives of heroic individualism that we attach to critical reading: plumbing the depths of texts, Orpheus-like, to bring forth some hidden truth or insight that then overturns or eclipses the text. Also like Eliot, however, they remain deeply, not to say professionally, attached to the idea of books as sites of self-development, and for this reason have tried to model readerly postures that can better "account for the variation and complexity of life, as well as for its richness and depth."[52] If Protestant modes of critical analysis have yielded "an ethical problematic of subject-formation... oriented to freedom and autonomous agency against the background of a modern social imaginary," Michael Warner wonders, might there not be other ways "to suture textual practice with reflection, reason, and a normative discipline of subjectivity"?[53] Thus Heather Love takes up sociological "thin" description as an alternative to hermeneutic spelunking, while Marcus attempts a mode of close reading that entails modesty and humility toward the literary text, and Price looks to Victorian novels for portrayals of books as socially significant objects rather than as interpretive heterocosms. For his own part, Warner points toward the work of Saba Mahmood, an anthropologist whose research has traced the different possible relationships between liberal subjectivity, Koranic interpretation, and feminist agency in contemporary Egypt.[54]

Eliot's work, I would argue, resonates with a number of these critical projects—especially ones that look toward the social sciences for models. "The Natural History of German Life," for example, echoes Love's work when it claims that faithful sociological description can "surprise[e]

---

[50] See, for example, J. Hillis Miller, "Optic and Semiotic in *Middlemarch*," in Jerome Hamilton Buckley (ed.), *The Worlds of Victorian Fiction* (Cambridge, MA: Harvard UP, 1975), 125–48, as well as Anger, 96–7 for an overview.

[51] Key manifestos include Stephen Best and Sharon Marcus, "Surface Reading: An Introduction," *Representations* 108.1 (2009): 1–21; Heather Love, "Close but not Deep: Literary Ethics and the Descriptive Turn," *New Literary History* 41 (2010): 371–91; Price, 1–18. For an overview, see Rachel Buurma and Laura Heffernan, "Interpretation, 1980 and 1880," *Victorian Studies* 55.4 (2013): 615–28.

[52] S. Pearl Brilmyer, "'The Natural History of My Inward Self': Sensing Character in George Eliot's *Impressions of Theophrastus Such*," *PMLA* 129.1 (2014): 36.

[53] Michael Warner, "Uncritical Reading," *Polemic: Critical or Uncritical*, ed. Jane Gallop (New York, NY: Routledge, 2004), 19, 16.

[54] Warner, 18–119 and Mahmood, *Politics of Piety: The Islamic Revival and the Feminist Subject* (Princeton, NJ: Princeton UP, 2005).

even . . . the selfish into [an] attention to what is apart from themselves."[55] Eliot's novels, meanwhile, anticipate Price by staging scenes in which books are valuable more for their social charges than for the meanings they contain. Take, for example, this passage from *Adam Bede* (1859):

> The book Adam most often read on a Sunday morning was his large pictured Bible, and this morning it lay open before him on the round white deal table in the kitchen; for he sat there in spite of the fire, because he knew his mother liked to have him with her, and it was the only day in the week when he could indulge her in that way . . . He never opened it on a weekday, and so he came to it as a holiday book, serving him for history, biography, and poetry. He held one hand thrust between his waistcoat buttons, and the other ready to turn the pages, and in the course of the morning you would have seen many changes in his face. Sometimes his lips moved in semi-articulation—it was when he came to a speech that he could fancy himself uttering, such as Samuel's dying speech to the people; then his eyebrows would be raised, and the corners of his mouth would quiver a little with sad sympathy . . . [56]

Adam's Bible is not a heterocosm that absorbs the mind but rather one social object among many, bound to his various duties and relationships. Just as Adam reads the Bible on Sunday for filial and not theological reasons, so does he interpret the book physically instead of conceptually, projecting himself into the plights of characters by mouthing their words. Similarly, the fervently evangelical Dinah is redeemed by the fact that her seemingly solipsistic reading of Scripture is closely cued to a sense of the text's physicality:

> There was light enough for her, if she opened her Bible, to discern the text sufficiently to know what it would say to her. She knew the physiognomy of every page, and could tell on what book she opened, sometimes on what chapter, without seeing title or number. It was a small thick Bible, worn quite round at the edges. Dinah laid it sideways on the window ledge, where the light was strongest, and then opened it with her forefinger. The first words she looked at were those at the top of the left-hand page: "And they all wept sore, and fell on Paul's neck and kissed him." That was enough for Dinah; she had opened on that memorable parting at Ephesus, when Paul had felt bound to open his heart in a last exhortation and warning. She hesitated no longer, but, opening her own door gently, went and tapped on Hetty's.[57]

As described here, Dinah's stereotypically evangelical habit of opening her Bible to a random page and looking for a personal message evinces not

---

[55] Eliot, "Natural History," 30.   [56] Eliot, *Adam Bede*, 497–8.
[57] Ibid., 158–9.

egotism so much as an outward attentiveness to others. In lieu of abstracting a message, Dinah knows the "physiognomy" of each page. Moreover,
by linking the physical light that falls upon this Bible to the figurative
"light" of inspiration so often sought by evangelical readers, Eliot's narrator implies that we may need nothing so spiritual in order to read well.
Ultimately Dinah is a good reader for Eliot because she can relate this text
to the plight of others around her.

Deronda, for its own part, tends to feature books as concrete metonyms
for the social histories in which characters find themselves, and thus to
some degree as indices of how characters relate to those histories.[58]
Gwendolen, for example, reveals her selfishness to us through her penchant for quotation, which liquidates books into social capital that she can
use to her own advantage. Gwendolen's original sin in the novel is to pawn
a family heirloom for gambling chips, and in the same spirit she tends to
treat books as repositories of quotations that can buy her credibility in the
eyes of others. "You are fond of books as well as of music, riding, and
archery, I hear," Mrs. Arrowpoint says to Gwendolen, who responds
by quoting Goethe ("die Kraft ist swach, allein die Lust ist gross") and
who later remarks that "imagination is often truer than fact," even
though "she could no more have explained these glib words than if
they had been Coptic or Etruscan" (36–7). As different as this might
seem from the millenarian hysterics of Dr. Cumming, it turns upon the
same strategy of hijacking others' words for one's own ends while
ignoring their contexts. Where Cumming had treated biblical texts as
polemical small change to be used against village atheists, Gwendolen
coopts the cultural capital of literary passages in order to disguise her
own intellectual and spiritual poverty.

Daniel, conversely, shows his respect for the heterogeneity of human
life through his fondness for old and neglected volumes. These include his
grandfather's chest of mystical writings, or the wares of the used book shop
in London's Jewish ghetto, where he first meets the consumptive prophet:

> One of the shop-windows he paused before was that of a second-hand book-
> shop, where, on a narrow table outside, the literature of the ages was
> represented in judicious mixture, from the immortal verse of Homer to the
> mortal prose of the railway novel . . . Mr. Ram [the bookseller] dealt ably in
> books, in the same way that he would have dealt in tins of meat and other
> commodities—without knowledge or responsibility as to the proportion of
> rottenness or nourishment they might contain.   (325–6)

[58] For more on Eliot, heirlooms, and the question of inheritance, see Catherine
Dunagan Osborne, "Inherited Emotions: George Eliot and the Politics of Heirlooms,"
Nineteenth-Century Literature 64.4 (2010): 465–93.

In Mr. Ram's shop, books stand for the jumbled detritus of a history that requires a modern reader to give it unity. Without Daniel's uptake they remain mere commodities, which is why this passage is dogged by the derogatory image of the Jew as opportunistic junk dealer. Critics have sometimes exhibited surprise at the presence of such a trope within this notoriously philo-Semitic novel, yet in many ways Eliot's commercial Jew forms a clear, if unfortunate, foil to her patrimonial Jew. Like Ezra Cohen, whose face betrays the "vulgarity...of a prosperous pink-and-white huckster of the purest English lineage" (331), Ram is a Hebrew who has fallen into the condition of a mere Hebraist, an English Philistine who can see only commercial value in social relics that Daniel will recover for a nobler purpose.

In some respects the secular ethos that emerges from *Deronda* resembles the one set forth by Franco Moretti in his distant-reading manifesto, "The Slaughterhouse of Literature" (2000). Like Moretti, Eliot pictures history as a "great unread" whose voices are too numerous for any one reader to process, yet which we also have some duty to recognize.[59] Responsible modern subjectivity involves acknowledging the complexity of this history and making some effort to assess it, instead of reading only those few books we already want to read. Yet comparing Eliot's protagonist to Moretti's distant reader reminds us of how unlike this figure he actually behaves. Daniel does not survey the great unread from an impersonal, statistical distance, or even from the disinterested perspective of Arnold's "alien." Instead, he acts like the used-bookshop browser whom Katie Trumpener describes in her own critique of Moretti—a reader who pursues particular voices as they strike her fancy, rather than trying to take in all voices at once.[60] The mode of readerly engagement pictured by the novel involves, to borrow Trumpener's words, "[b]rowsing in addition to quantification" and "incessant rather than distant reading."[61] Indeed, we might even say that Daniel becomes the seduced reader whom David Kurnick finds in several Eliot novels. As Kurnick sees it, there is "a rush of erotic energy" in the way that Daniel is attracted to books, or to Mordecai, or even to race itself.[62] It is a mode of attraction that operates somewhere between the tyrannical weight of inheritance (think of Zarca's charge to Fedalma)

[59] Franco Moretti, *Distant Reading* (London, UK: Verso, 2013), 45, 63.
[60] Katie Trumpener, "Paratext and Genre System: A Response to Franco Moretti," *Critical Inquiry* 36.1 (2009): 159–71.
[61] Ibid., 171.
[62] David Kurnick, "An Erotics of Detachment: *Middlemarch* and Novel-Reading as Critical Practice," *ELH* 74.3 (2007): 600.

and the vicissitudes of mere choice through a "cohabitation of credulity and skepticism, feverish, 'feminine' surrender and critical, 'masculine' detachment."[63] For Daniel, the inheritance of race is like the mystery of personal attraction, or the serendipity by which old objects strike our fancy—not something he chooses, but something that he must work at to make his own.

MANY-SIDEDNESS, THE *BILDUNGSROMAN*, AND THE PREDICAMENT OF GENDER

But why always Daniel? What I would like to propose by way of closing is that in many respects it is Gwendolen who emerges as the novel's representative figure of secular reading: the character whose interaction with books most models a many-sided relationship to social life mediated through readerly activity. For if reading, in *Daniel Deronda*, is sometimes the thing that gets you stuck in your head and sometimes the thing that gets you out of it, then the same might be said of many-sidedness itself. Over the course of the novel, many-sidedness features alternately as the problem in need of solving and the condition that needs to be attained. Indeed, the novel very nearly diverges into two very different "plots" of many-sidedness that ultimately appraise Daniel's moral development, and the role of reading itself, very differently. In one plot, Daniel's Arnoldian predisposition toward distanced, contrarian thinking is what opens him up to Mordecai's seemingly outlandish claims about race and destiny. A man of practical action, we are told, might have dismissed Mordecai's religious nationalism as anachronistic, but Daniel's diffusive curiosity refuses to reject it out of hand:

> Deronda did not speak. He felt himself strangely wrought upon. The first-prompted suspicion that Mordecai might be liable to hallucinations of thought—might have become a monomaniac on some subject which had given too severe a strain to his diseased organism—gave way to a more submissive expectancy. His nature was too large, too ready to conceive regions beyond his own experience, to rest at once in the easy explanation, "madness," whenever a consciousness showed some fullness and conviction where his own was blank. It accorded with his habitual disposition that he should meet rather than resist any claim on him in the shape of another's need; and this claim brought with it a sense of solemnity which seemed a radiation from Mordecai, as utterly nullifying his outward poverty and lifting him into authority as if he had been that preternatural guide seen in the

---

[63] Ibid.

universal legend, who suddenly drops his mean disguise and stands a manifest Power.   (423–4)

What in other contexts might look like aloofness here enables what Eliot calls a "submissive expectancy"—a willingness to "meet rather than resist" the claims of others and to take seriously what one does not immediately understand. Daniel's Quixotic relationship to books allows him to see a shabby figure like Mordecai as the "disguise" worn by a character from "universal legend" and to elect to take part in his saga. In the other plot of many-sidedness, however, Daniel's "too-diffusive sympathy" and "activity of imagination on behalf of others" are precisely what a turn to Jewish identity will help him overcome:

> It happened that the very vividness of his impressions had often made him the more enigmatic to his friends, and had contributed to an apparent indefiniteness in his sentiments. His early-wakened sensibility and reflectiveness had developed into a many-sided sympathy, which threatened to hinder any persistent course of action: as soon as he took up any antagonism, though only in thought, he seemed to himself like the Sabine warriors in the memorable story—with nothing to meet his spear but flesh of his flesh, and objects that he loved. His imagination had so wrought itself to the habit of seeing things as they probably appeared to others, that a strong partisanship, unless it were against an immediate oppression, had become an insincerity for him. His plenteous, flexible sympathy had ended by falling into one current with that reflective analysis which tends to neutralize sympathy.   (307)

Here the very words that one would usually associate with many-sidedness (impressions, sensibility, reflectiveness) stymie moral engagement in that they prevent Daniel from locating himself specifically within the world that he contemplates. Sympathizing with others too broadly ironically "neutralize[s] sympathy" by discouraging Daniel from electing one "persistent course of action."

Importantly, this second plot frames Daniel's discovery of his textual patrimony as the thing that saves him from many-sidedness by giving him a world-historical vocation in the form of what Amanda Anderson calls "a reflective return to a kind of *prereflective* cultural embeddedness."[64] In turn, it is Gwendolen who is left behind to live out the paradoxes of many-sidedness and to forge a solution through a species of secular reading. Gwendolen, not unlike Daniel, begins the novel in a position of "bad" many-sidedness, but is rescued by no *deus ex machina* of destiny and instead must deal with the ramifications of that position fully. Early on

---

[64] Anderson, *Powers of Distance*, 137.

she is said to consist of "a little of everything and not much of anything" (40) and to possess an "iridescence of . . . character—[a] play of various, nay, contrary tendencies" (33). She announces to Rex Gascoigne that "my plan is to do what pleases me" (56) and lists among her intentions to "go to the North Pole, or ride steeplechases, or go to be queen in the East like Lady Hester Stanhope" (57). She also, crucially, reserves the right to choose only the husband who perfectly suits her desires (110–11). But as soon as Gwendolen receives the very offer she had been hoping for— from the wealthy Grandcourt—she freezes, because suddenly choosing looks like a loss of freedom:

> On the whole she wished to marry him; he suited her purpose; her prevail-ing, deliberate intention was, to accept him. But was she going to fulfill her deliberate intention? She began to be afraid of herself, and to find out a certain difficulty in doing as she liked. (116)

Gwendolen, who at first desired a life of boundless possible actions, discovers that actually acting requires eliminating possibilities and slowly ensnaring herself in a web of necessity. This is why her response to Grand-court's proposal is to run away and embrace a "new phase of indifference" that preserves, if only superficially, the nebulous freedom that she possesses at the novel's outset (132). Her plot does not see her exchange personal liberty for epic vocation but instead learn the hard way that being an agent means giving up certain choices and setting off patterns of contingency that may impede her down the road. This is many-sidedness as a sobering, pragmatic reality more than as an egotistical fantasy of having it all ways at once.

Commentators have often described *Deronda*'s Gwendolen and Daniel plots as realistic and Romantic, respectively.[65] In this context, we might note that they also resemble what some have called the English and continental versions of the *Bildungsroman*—one version, exemplified by Carlyle's *Sartor Resartus* (1836), in which a diffusive self discovers a focusing social vocation, and another in which the self's complexities are never fully reconciled to the world around it.[66] Daniel's plot ultimately becomes a kind of English *Bildungsroman* in which the self integrates with

[65] The foundation of such reading is arguably Jerome Beaty's "*Daniel Deronda* and the Question of Unity in Fiction," *Victorian Newsletter* 15 (1959): 16–20; see Sarah Gates, "'A Difference of Native Language': Gender, Genre, and Realism in *Daniel Deronda*," *ELH* 68.3 (2001): 699.

[66] For versions of this distinction, see G. B. Tennyson, "The *Bildungsroman* in Nineteenth-Century English Literature," *Medieval Epic to the "Epic Theater" of Brecht: Essays in Comparative Literature* (Los Angeles, CA: USC, 1968), 141–5; Franco Moretti, *The Way of the World: The* Bildungsroman *in European Culture* (1987; London, UK: Verso, 2000), 5–6; Barry V. Qualls, *The Secular Pilgrims of Victorian Fiction* (New York, NY:

the social through the discovery of a Calvinist vocation that subordinates the unruly energies of individualism to the growing good of the world. In Gwendolen's plot, by contrast, the self reaches an ambivalent standoff with the social world, a productive but never resolved suspension of the boundless energies of individualism against the necessities of tradition and social life. As Carolyn Lesjack puts it, Gwendolen "remains as a glimpse of another possibility, the existence of chaotic desires, of a *dis*continuous sense of self, of the *internal* splits and ruptures that disrupt or refuse the production of a coherent, cohesive national identification" (36). What is more, within Gwendolen's plot many-sidedness itself takes on a distinctly female cast to the extent that it becomes a virtue available to those who have been specifically denied grand vocations. Many-sidedness is often assumed to be an ethos that encodes cosmopolitan male privilege; for Eliot, however, it offers a way for individuals who do not have grand vocational paths laid out before them to discover some sense of purpose within circumscribed options. Like Dorothea Brooke in *Middlemarch*, Gwendolen is described in terms of an epic potentiality that she never fulfills, but in this respect she becomes more resonant as a paradigm for all those who are forced to make do with imperfect circumstances.[67] If Eliot ultimately seems to have mixed feelings regarding many-sidedness, then this is because it is a virtue made from necessity and an ethos invented to deal with limited possibilities.

For this reason it is also Gwendolen who emerges as the character who is most tasked with sorting out the world through readerly activity. Daniel is led to Judaism by recovering its textual detritus, but soon passes into a world of epic action where he will not need to read because the characters of history have come to life. His male-heroic privilege of a religious vocation takes him out of the sphere of modern moral complexity figured by reading and its various pitfalls. Gwendolen, by contrast, does not enjoy the luxury of such an exit and remains enmeshed in a mundane realm where interpretive thinking must happen. Indeed, we might claim (following Daniel Cottom) that Gwendolen makes sense of her own predicament by "translating" the epic actions of Daniel's plot into prosaic terms—"interpreting it, understanding it, and so gaining the power to patronize it."[68] Daniel's acceptance of a racial destiny, for example, enacts

Cambridge UP, 1982), 10–11; Gregory Castle, *Reading the Modernist Bildungsroman* (Gainesville, FL: UP of Florida, 2006), 48.

[67] See Stefanie Markovits, *The Crisis of Action in Nineteenth-Century English Literature* (Columbus, OH: Ohio State UP, 2006), 111–12.

[68] Daniel Cottom, *Social Figures: George Eliot, Social History, and Literary Representation* (Minneapolis, MN: U of Minnesota P, 1987), 125. For a similar reading, see Carpenter, 58. For translation as a moral activity in Eliot's thinking, see Susan E. Hill, "Translating

the lesson that Gwendolen learns at the level of individual morality, namely that we must sometimes find purpose in that which constrains our desires. As Daniel took on the burden of a mystical heritage, so will Gwendolen accept the consequences that her own daily choices bring back upon her. He explains to her:

> Looking at your life as a debt may seem the dreariest view of things at a distance; but it cannot really be so. What makes life dreary is the want of motive: but once beginning to act with that penitential, loving purpose you have in your mind, there will be unexpected satisfactions—there will be newly-opening needs—continually coming to carry you on from day to day. You will find your life growing like a plant.   (658)

Aamir Mufti is only the latest critic to find this relationship subtly colonialist, since it posits Oriental ethnicity as a moral resource for the English subject.[69] Yet the novel tends to regard Gwendolen's situation as an inversion of imperial privilege, since it transfigures the metropolitan self's aloofness from racial commitment into the lesser virtue of making do with small duties as they come. Arnold's metropolitan Englishman is superior to the Celt or the Teuton insofar as he can reflect from a distance upon their provincial virtues; Eliot's metropolitans, by contrast, live within a diminished, realist version of the story acted out by her heroic Jews. This is why Gwendolen, instead of feeling superior to Daniel's plot, ultimately comes to regard herself as a marginal character within it:

> And Gwendolen?—She was thinking of Deronda much more than he was thinking of her—often wondering what were his ideas "about things," and how his life was occupied ... [W]hat would he tell her that she ought to do? "He said, I must get more interest in others, and more knowledge, and that I must care about the best things—but how am I to begin?" She wondered what books he would tell her to take up to her own room, and recalled the famous writers that she had either not looked into or had found the most unreadable, with a half-smiling wish that she could mischievously ask Deronda if they were not the books called "medicine for the mind." Then she repented of her sauciness, and when she was safe from observation, carried up a miscellaneous selection—Descartes, Bacon, Locke, Butler, Burke, Guizot—knowing, as a clever young lady of education, that these

Feuerbach, Constructing Morality: The Theological and Literary Significance of Translation for George Eliot," *Journal of the American Academy of Religion* 65.3 (1997): 635–53.

[69] Aamir Mufti, *Enlightenment in the Colony: The Jewish Question and the Crisis of Postcolonial Culture* (Princeton, NJ: Princeton UP, 2007), 107–8. See also Susan Meyer, "'Safely to their own borders': Proto-Zionism, Feminism, and Nationalism in *Daniel Deronda*," *ELH* 60.3 (1993): 733–58; Nancy Henry, "George Eliot and the Colonies," *Victorian Literature and Culture* 29.2 (2001): 413–33.

authors were ornaments of mankind, feeling sure that Deronda had read them, and hoping that by dipping into them all in succession, with her rapid understanding she might get a point of view nearer to his level. (467–8)

This passage, which begins Chapter 44, recalls the opening of *Middlemarch*'s Chapter 29, in which Eliot famously interrupts a sentence about Dorothea Brooke with the question, "Why always Dorothea?"[70] There, Eliot's goal was to question our prioritizing of particular centers of consciousness in both art and life. Here, however, the would-be shift of focalization from one character to another is hijacked by the fact that Gwendolen has already begun to see Daniel more than herself as the center of her own story. Many-sidedness becomes the capacity to see your own situation as just one possible plotline among many; where Daniel comes to envision a world in which multiple races are linked by "separateness with communication" (620), Gwendolen learns to place herself within the mind of another protagonist and see how his perspective might reconfigure her own plot. As Daniel exits London, with its overstuffed bookshops, and enters his own heroic narrative, it is Gwendolen who remains behind as Eliot's secular reader—a figure whose reading is not a private experience but rather a habit of outward attention that displaces her from the center of the story.

---

[70] Eliot, *Middlemarch: A Study of Provincial Life*, ed. David Carroll (1871–72; New York, NY: Oxford UP, 1996), 261.

4

A More Liberal Surrender

Aestheticism, Asceticism, and Walter Pater's Erotics of Conversion

The idea of conversion has become a key point of interest for scholars who argue for a historical continuity between liberal individualism and the construction of religion as belief. By emphasizing the "*self-conscious* selection and integration of new elements into [one's] identity," Talal Asad writes, Protestant (especially evangelical) discourses on conversion played a crucial role in modeling modern subjectivity at home and disseminating it through missionary activity abroad.[1] Conversion, as Peter van der Veer puts it, became a Foucauldian technology of the self that connected "the European development of modern notions of personhood ... to the missionary project" and underwrote what Raymond Williams describes as a key conceit of European modernity: that change is at some level intrinsically good.[2] For this reason it is perhaps not surprising that the writers canvassed in this study tended to regard abrupt religious change as anathema to the development of a many-sided personality. Matthew Arnold decried "violent revolution in the words and externals of religion" as a species of Hebraism, while in *Daniel Deronda*, as we have seen, George Eliot produced something of a conversion novel against conversion—the story of a character who finds a vocation by "converting" to an identity that he was already unconsciously inhabiting.[3]

This chapter explores the tensions between Victorian aesthetic liberalism and the idea of conversion by examining an even more radical variation on the anti-conversion plot: Walter Pater's *Marius the Epicurean*

---

[1] Talal Asad, "Comments on Conversion," in Peter van der Veer (ed.), *Conversion to Modernities: The Globalization of Christianity* (New York, NY: Routledge, 1996), 265.

[2] Van der Veer, introduction to *Conversion to Modernities*, 9, 18. For more on the relationship between missionary conversion and modernization, see Webb Keane, *Christian Moderns: Freedom and Fetish in the Mission Encounter* (Berkeley, CA: U of California P, 2007).

[3] *The Complete Prose Works of Matthew Arnold*, ed. R. H. Super (11 vols.; Ann Arbor, MI: U of Michigan P, 1960–77), 8: 142.

(1885). The novel narrates the life of a second-century Roman who acquires an intense attraction to the early Christian Church. It is structured like a philosophical *Bildungsroman*, with Marius growing up amid the folk religions of the Campagna before traveling to Rome, where, at the court of Marcus Aurelius, he passes first through an Epicurean phase and then through a Stoic phase before falling in with a small Christian congregation.[4] Yet the novel's suggestion is that Christianity entices Marius, not because it offers him some new philosophical lodestar, but rather because it recovers and preserves many of the pagan forms of his youth. Adapting E. B. Tylor's concept of cultural survivals, Pater describes Christianity as a receptive medium that salvages relics of past culture and then synthesizes them into new aesthetic formations. As such, Marius's turn to Christianity represents less a philosophical break than a turn to many-sidedness which internalizes the contradictory inheritances of history through a kind of aesthetic play.

By telling this story, *Marius* reworks the form of the *Bildungsroman* even more dramatically than *Deronda*. For where *Deronda* employs two distinct plots of *Bildung* to map out different possible relationships between individual many-sidedness and the social, *Marius*, I argue, eliminates the form's constitutive tension between self and society almost entirely. Instead of a protagonist who cultivates his identity in dialectical tension with social demands, Pater offers one whose growth is wholly fed by the historical evolution of his culture. In this way Pater's revised *Bildungsroman* also provincializes Europe by effectively de-privileging the metropolitan plot of self-development. All of the major figures in this study embraced deterministic accounts of religion usually ascribed to Europe's others as resources for the Western individual. In Arnold and Eliot, however, this move had the effect of reinstating European privilege; the Arnoldian alien is neither Jew nor Greek, Teuton nor Celt, but can draw upon each of these narrower types, much as Gwendolen Harleth learns the lessons of Daniel's ethnicity by translating them into the realist idiom of her own plot. Pater, by contrast, imagines that even the most refined scheme of aesthetic cultivation will require submitting to an intensely local set of determinants. Consequently, *Marius* comes much closer to the modernist conception of culture as an enclosed social whole,

[4] For maps of Marius's philosophical course, see Ulrich Knoepflmacher, *Religious Humanism and the Victorian Novel: George Eliot, Walter Pater, and Samuel Butler* (Princeton, NJ: Princeton UP, 1965), 195–223; R. V. Osborne, "*Marius the Epicurean*," *Essays in Criticism* 1 (1951): 387–403; Billie Andrew Inman, "The Organic Structure of *Marius the Epicurean*," *Philological Quarterly* 41.2 (1962): 475–91. For a survey of major criticism, see Franklin E. Court, "The Critical Reception of Pater's *Marius*," *English Literature in Transition, 1880–1920* 27.2 (1984): 124–39.

replacing the progressive teleology of the *Bildungsroman* with a flattened global imaginary in which equally holistic cultures keep returning to their own grounds for sustenance.

At a more granular level, *Marius* dramatizes how the ethos of many-sidedness curiously replicates the logic of *askesis*. On the face of it, by replacing an evangelical plot of conversion with a narrative of conversion as renaissance—the creative recuperation of older aesthetic forms—Pater is rejecting, in even stronger terms than Arnold, the ascetic impulse that links certain versions of Christianity to bourgeois modernity. As against the project of improving the self by casting away its flawed parts, Pater imagines a self that can harmonize all of its inherited attachments and impulses. At the same time, however, *Marius* portrays many-sidedness itself as a form of *askesis*, since it obliges the subject to give up the luxury of picking and choosing and instead to submit to the determining forces of the past. Jonathan Freedman and James Eli Adams have both described the bourgeois affinities of Victorian aestheticism, and indeed Pater's expansive aesthetic character turns out to be far more deeply inscribed within the tradition of inner-worldly asceticism than it might seem.[5] Just as Arnoldian culture fought to avoid becoming another ideal of "one thing needful," so does Pater's many-sidedness flirt with forms of self-sacrifice en route to aesthetic individuality.

In all of these ways, *Marius the Epicurean* obliges us to confront a broader question that looms over this study: What sort of critical stance does many-sidedness ultimately represent? For if the conversion plot was, as Gauri Viswanathan claims, the ultimate Victorian trope of cultural dissent, then by refusing it many-sidedness would seem to risk becoming a version of conservatism—a *mere* liberality that refuses to take strong positions.[6] At some level, of course, this paradox constitutes the core polemic of many-sidedness: its attempt to turn the tables on Dissenting liberalism by showing that the individuality it craves can better be developed by a practice of radical restraint. But does this fact prevent many-sidedness from gaining any real oppositional traction? Pater plays with this question in *Marius*, we might say, so as to deflect the charge that his brand of aestheticism amounts to a species of cultural apostasy. Around 1860, while still an undergraduate at Oxford, Pater reportedly underwent a Christian deconversion that saw him read extensively in philosophy—

[5] James Eli Adams, *Dandies and Desert Saints: Styles of Victorian Masculinity* (Ithaca, NY: Cornell UP, 1995); Jonathan Freedman, *Professions of Taste: Henry James, British Aestheticism and Commodity Culture* (Stanford, CA: Stanford UP, 1990).

[6] Gauri Viswanathan, *Outside the Fold: Conversion, Modernity, and Belief* (Princeton, NJ: Princeton UP, 1998).

"Heraclitus, Pythagoras, Plato, and the moderns Schelling and Hegel"—
and begin "indulging in 'Mephistophelian sneers' . . . at religion in whatever form, and in attacks on the Bible after the manner of Voltaire."[7]
All this lay the groundwork for the controversy surrounding *Studies in the
History of the Renaissance* (1873), which Pater's contemporaries famously
interpreted as a paean to materialism and solipsism. Margaret Oliphant,
writing in *Blackwood's*, censured Pater's "grand pursuit of self-culture" as a
"new version of that coarse old refrain of the Epicureans' gay despair, 'Let
us eat and drink, for to-morrow we die.'"[8] In many ways *Marius* represents Pater's attempt to respond to this narrative about himself. The third
edition of *The Renaissance* (1888) saw Pater add a footnote that directed
readers toward *Marius* as a corrective to some of the dangerous tendencies
ascribed to his study.[9] Around the same time, Pater's friends began to
notice a vaguely Anglo-Catholic turn in his outlook. Mary Arnold Ward,
the author of that quintessential Victorian crisis-of-faith novel, *Robert
Elsmere* (1888), described her Oxfordshire neighbor as making a "hesitat-
ing and wistful return towards Christianity, and Christianity of the
Catholic type."[10] Indeed, Pater himself would explain to Violet Paget
that *Marius* was meant to define a "religious phase possible for the modern
mind."[11] Yet the novel accomplishes something much stranger than this
by suggesting that aestheticism's so-called deviance—its passivity and
openness to manifold influences—is more truly conservative than the
orthodoxy of Pater's critics. The novel's aesthetic Christianity attains a
Dissenting potency, not because it pushes back against its culture, but
rather because its receptivity and inconsistency are able to entertain
elements of the past that more rigorous philosophical positions screen out.

---

[7] Thomas Wright, *The Life of Walter Pater* (2 vols.; London, UK: Everett, 1907),
1: 170, 1: 169. See Dennis Donoghue, *Walter Pater: Lover of Strange Souls* (New York, NY:
Knopf, 1995), 27–8.
  [8] Margaret Oliphant, "New Books," *Blackwood's Edinburgh Magazine* 114 (1873), 608;
quoted in Donoghue, 58. See also Matthew Potolsky, "Fear of Falling: Walter Pater's
Marius the Epicurean as a Dangerous Influence," *ELH* 65.3 (1998): 701–29.
  [9] See *The Works of Walter Pater* (8 vols.; London, UK: Macmillan, 1900–01), 1: 233.
All subsequent citations from these volumes will be noted in parentheses.
  [10] Mrs. Humphry Ward (Mary Arnold Ward), *A Writer's Recollections* (London, UK:
W. Collins, 1918), 120.
  [11] *The Letters of Walter Pater*, ed. Lawrence Evans (Oxford, UK: Clarendon P, 1970),
79. The latter is quoted in Maureen Moran, "Pater's 'Great Change': *Marius the Epicurean*
as Historical Conversion Romance," in Laurel Brake, Lesley Higgins, Carolyn Williams
(eds.), *Walter Pater: Transparencies of Desire* (Greensboro, NC: ELT P, 2002), 173. For
more on the religious arc of Pater's career, see Leslie Higgins, "A 'Thousand Solaces' for the
Modern Spirit: Walter Pater's Religious Discourse," in *Victorian Religious Discourse*, ed.
Jude V. Nixon (New York, NY: Palgrave, 2004), 189–204.

RENAISSANCE, SURVIVALS, AND
AESTHETIC CULTURE

Walter Pater's major critical writings of the 1860s and 1870s follow Arnold in positing many-sidedness as an alternative ethos for modernity. In his "Preface" to *The Renaissance*, for example, Pater explains that what attracts him to the period is the way in which it sought to bring together as many modes of knowledge and experience as possible—"to reconcile forms of sentiment which at first sight seem incompatible, to adjust the various products of the human mind to each other in one many-sided type of intellectual culture, to give humanity, for heart and imagination to feed upon, as much as it could possibly receive" (1:30). While in most eras "[a]rt and poetry, philosophy and religious life...are each of them confined to its own circle of ideas," he writes, early modern Europe experienced "an age productive in personalities, many-sided, centralised, complete," in which "artists and philosophers...[did] not live in isolation, but breathe[d] a common air" and affirmed a common faith "that nothing which has ever interested living men and women can wholly lose its vitality" (1:xiii–iv, 1:49). Consequently, the word "renaissance," as Pater uses it, comes to name less a historical period than an inclusive stance toward history that models his own critical project. In the "Preface," Pater tells us that his goal is to reject the classical-medieval binary that typically underwrites the idea of a capital-R *Renaissance* and give the term

> a much wider scope than was intended by those who originally used it to denote only that revival of classical antiquity in the fifteenth century which was but one of many results of a general excitement and enlightening of the human mind, and of which the great aim and achievements of what, as Christian art, is often falsely opposed to the Renaissance, were another result. This outbreak of the human spirit may be traced far into the middle age itself, with its qualities already clearly pronounced, the care for physical beauty, the worship of the body, the breaking down of those limits which the religious system of the middle age imposed on the heart and the imagination.   (1:xii)

If renaissance is an impulse that brings together different sides of human life in the faith that they are complementary, then studying it requires that we look for the continuities linking historical periods and movements— Christian and classical, medieval and pagan, twelfth-century France and eighteenth-century Germany—that might seem to be in conflict.

Importantly, Pater's humanistic perennialism has a distinctly scientistic bent. Much as Arnold had constructed a vision of many-sidedness by figuring diverse strains of human character as the fixed traits of different races, so does Pater treat the objects of aesthetic experience as involuntary sensory bombardments that we cannot choose but instead must work to harmonize. Although "[m]any attempts have been made by writers on art and poetry to define beauty in the abstract" (1:vii), he explains in the "Preface," "the first step towards seeing one's object as it really is, is to know one's own impression as it really is, to discriminate it, to realise it distinctly" (1:viii). Consequently, the aesthete's work is less like a metaphysician's than like a chemist's:

> The aesthetic critic, then, regards all the objects with which he has to do, all works of art, and the fairer forms of nature and human life, as powers or forces producing pleasurable sensations, each of a more or less peculiar or unique kind. This influence he feels, and wishes to explain, analysing it and reducing it to its elements. To him, the picture, the landscape, the engaging personality in life or in a book, *La Gioconda*, the hills of Carrara, Pico of Mirandola, are valuable for their virtues, as we say, in speaking of a herb, a wine, a gem; for the property each has of affecting one with a special, a unique, impression of pleasure. Our education becomes complete in proportion as our susceptibility to these impressions increases in depth and variety. And the function of the aesthetic critic is to distinguish, analyse, and separate from its adjuncts, the virtue by which a picture, a landscape, a fair personality in life or in a book, produces this special impression of beauty or pleasure, to indicate what the source of that impression is, and under what conditions it is experienced. His end is reached when he has disengaged that virtue, and noted it, as a chemist notes some natural element, for himself and others. (1:ix)

In this passage Pater dismisses the practice of critical abstraction only to reintroduce it via the notion of "disengagement," which figures critical thinking as something closer to chemical extraction. Rather than generalize about beauty as a principle, the Paterian critic "reduces" beauty "to its elements" by specifying "the source of that impression" and its "conditions." "Our education," he writes, "becomes complete in proportion as our susceptibility to these impressions increases in depth and variety" (1:ix).

This conception of many-sidedness as a quantitative enrichment of the self through careful, empirical attention goes back Alexander Baumgarten's original definition of the term *aesthetic* and generates the notorious problem of agency in the "Conclusion" to *The Renaissance*.[12] If human life, according to Pater, is an uncontrollable flood of sensations—"the passage and dissolution of impressions, images, sensations . . . that continual vanishing away, that strange, perpetual weaving and unweaving of ourselves" (1:236)—then the personality that can internalize as many as

[12] See Freedman, 10.

possible will recover a surprising autonomy. "A counted number of pulses," he writes, "is given to us of a variegated, dramatic life," and "our one chance lies in expanding that interval, in getting as many pulsations as possible into the given time" (1:236).[13] Carolyn Williams thus argues that Pater's primary goal is to recuperate some measure of transcendental subjectivity by positing a heroic "overseeing self" to police this stream of impressions.[14] Yet such a claim underestimates the degree to which Pater is positively attracted to this deterministic account of experience precisely because it forecloses an abstract intellectualism that would sacrifice possible impressions to the fetish of philosophical consistency:

> With this sense of the splendour of our experience and of its awful brevity, gathering all we are into one desperate effort to see and touch, we shall hardly have time to make theories about the things we see and touch ... The theory or idea or system which requires of us the sacrifice of any part of this experience, in consideration of some interest into which we cannot enter, or some abstract theory we have not identified with ourselves, or what is only conventional, has no real claim upon us. (1:237–8)

David DeLaura notes that Pater tends to be less ambivalent than Arnold in his attraction to the physical sciences, and indeed embraces the sometimes relativistic consequences of a scientific materialism.[15] For in fact his real fear is that abstract thinking might shut down possible avenues of experience altogether. In Pater's mind, atomistic materialism, much like Arnoldian polygenesis, commits the critic to an assessment of plurality and heterogeneity that cannot be abstracted too easily into facile universalism or a tyrannizing one-sidedness.

Pater's interest in using physical determinism to frame the project of many-sidedness would drive his work in the 1870s beyond the rhetoric of science and toward the anthropological concept of survival, which was becoming a keyword for a number of major theorists. During the 1860s, as we saw in Chapter 1, a wide array of Victorian social scientists began to take up models of evolutionary progress. One major fascination of this

[13] In taking this complex view of aesthetic agency, Benjamin Morgan shows, Pater was following Hegel's attempt to ground consciousness in sensory experience without reducing it to such; see "Aesthetic Freedom: Walter Pater and the Politics of Autonomy," *ELH* 77.3 (2010): 743–9. For other accounts of the reading that led Pater to his "Conclusion," see Billie Andrew Inman, *Walter Pater's Reading: A Bibliography of His Library Borrowings and Literary References, 1858–1873* (New York, NY: Garland, 1981); F. C. McGrath, *The Sensible Spirit: Walter Pater and the Modernist Paradigm* (Tampa, FL: U of South Florida P, 1986).

[14] Carolyn Williams, *Transfigured World: Walter Pater's Aesthetic Historicism* (Ithaca, NY: Cornell UP, 1989), 31.

[15] See David DeLaura, *Hebrew and Hellene in Victorian England* (Austin, TX: U of Texas P, 1969), 174–5, 193–4, 228–30.

work was the question of why certain biological or cultural forms endured while others died out. In his 1864 *Principles of Biology*, for instance, Herbert Spencer expounded upon the recent work of Charles Darwin by coining the phrase "survival of the fittest" to describe the process whereby those organisms most able to fulfill "the conditions to life" managed to "survive and propagate."[16] Meanwhile E. B. Tylor, first in an 1867 address to the Royal Institution entitled "On the Traces of the Early Mental Condition of Man," and then in his pathbreaking *Primitive Culture* (1871), would define "survivals" as "processes, customs, opinions, and so forth, which have been carried on by force of habit into a new state of society different from that in which they had their original home."[17] The tradition of saying "God bless you" when a friend sneezes, for instance, preserves (according to Tylor) a primitive belief in the identity of breath and soul.[18] If "culture," as Tylor famously defined it, was a "complex whole which includes knowledge, belief, art, morals, law, custom," and advanced in "uniform...stages of development" around the world, then survivals were culture's detritus, anachronistic remnants from particular historical periods that somehow lingered into later ones while their meanings became obscure.[19]

The key thing to notice about Spencer's and Tylor's understandings of "survival" is that they define diametrically opposed processes. Spencer's survivals are things that endure because they prove themselves more fit in the struggle for existence; Tylor's, meanwhile, are essentially *unfit* for their cultural moments and yet stick around anyway. In Chapter 1, we saw how Tylor's anthropology, though ostensibly picturing the steady progress of reason over custom and superstition, contained an unmistakable element of determinism. In this case, the fact that survivals are things that persist in spite of anyone's choice made the concept especially appealing to writers interested in decadence—in the persistence of form beyond function or the autonomy of parts over the whole.[20] William Morris's 1888 essay on "The Revival of Architecture," for example, acknowledges that new buildings constructed after Gothic models occasionally sink to the status of

[16] Herbert Spencer, *The Principles of Biology* (2 vols.; London, UK: Williams and Norgate, 1864), 1: 453, 1: 445. See Marvin Harris, *The Rise of Anthropological Theory* (New York, NY: Crowell, 1968), 128.

[17] E. B. Tylor, *Primitive Culture: Researches into the Development of Mythology, Philosophy, Religion, Language, Art, and Custom* (2 vols.; London, UK: John Murray, 1871), 1: 15.

[18] Tylor, *Primitive Culture*, 1: 92–3; see also "On the Traces of the Early Mental Condition of Man," *Proceedings of the Royal Institution* 5 (1867): 91.

[19] Tylor, *Primitive Culture*, 1: 1.

[20] For this classic definition of decadence, see Havelock Ellis, "Introduction" to J. K. Huysmans, *Against the Grain* (1884), trans. John Howard (1922; New York, NY: Boni, 1924), xii.

"semi-Gothic survivals," aesthetic forms no longer bearing any live relationship to the social conditions that bred them.[21] In *The Picture of
Dorian Gray* (1891), meanwhile, Oscar Wilde's Lord Henry remarks
that "[t]he mutilation of the savage has its tragic survival in the self-
denial that mars our lives."[22] For Wilde, identifying certain behaviors as
survivals allows him to suggest how they are charged with contradictory
layers of motive, both conscious and unconscious, thus reminding us of
the historical links between Tylor's doctrine of survivals and emerging
forms of depth-psychology.[23]

Pater himself would become acquainted with Tylor's work thanks to his
conversations at Oxford with Tylor's main disciple, Andrew Lang, who
held an Open Fellowship at Merton College and (as we will see in
Chapter 5) was using Tylor to rethink the work of medieval French
balladiers such as Villon and Ronsard.[24] For his own part, Pater latched
onto the idea of survivals because it resonated with the "Conclusion" in
describing a process halfway between passive reception and active recuperation. It also allowed him to extend his narrative of cultural revival back
beyond classical Greece and into the twilight of prehistory. If *The Renaissance* had traced the recurrence of a "universal pagan sentiment" (1:201)
through Western art since the Greeks, then Pater's *Greek Studies* (1895), a
collection of lectures delivered at Oxford in the 1870s, would reimagine
this paganism as a primitive survival from the very dawn of civilization.[25]
In "The Bacchanals of Euripides" (1878), for example, Pater refers to the
Dionysian *Thiasus* ritual as "a religious custom, in which the habit of an
earlier world might seem to survive" (7:57). In this way Pater's use
of Tylor previews how Victorian anthropology would help transform
Classics during the 1890s, as James Frazer and a group sometimes called
the Cambridge Ritualists—Jane Harrison, Gilbert Murray, A. B. Cook,
Lewis Farnell—replaced the Apollonian vision of classical Greece valorized

[21] William Morris, "The Revival of Architecture," *Fortnightly Review* 43 (1888): 670.

[22] Oscar Wilde, *The Major Works* (New York, NY: Harper Collins, 1966), 29.

[23] See Christopher Herbert, *Culture and Anomie: Ethnographic Imagination in the
Nineteenth Century* (Chicago, IL: U of Chicago P, 1991), 253–60.

[24] Robert Crawford, "Pater's Renaissance, Andrew Lang, and Anthropological Romanticism," *ELH* 53.4 (1986): 856–60. For more on Pater's anthropological influences, see
James Kissane, "Victorian Mythology," *Victorian Studies* 6.1 (1962): 5–28; Linda Dowling,
Language and Decadence in the Victorian Fin de Siècle (Princeton, NJ: Princeton UP, 1986),
117–20; William F. Shuter, *Rereading Walter Pater* (New York, NY: Cambridge UP,
1997), 100–6; and Stefano Evangelista, "'Outward Nature and the Moods of Men':
Romantic Mythology in Pater's Essays on Dionysus and Demeter," in *Walter Pater:
Transparencies of Desire*, 107–18.

[25] Ernest Renan had noted back in the 1840s that an interest in the primitive was
frequently the flipside of an interest in lateness, decadence, and overrefinement. See Matei
Calinescu, *Five Faces of Modernity* (1977; Durham, NC: Duke UP, 1987), 163–4.

by Matthew Arnold with a Dionysian Greece still vitally connected to ancient tribal society.[26]

Yet by reimagining the many-sided character as one that was fed by survivals of primitive culture, Pater was not just deepening the temporal scope of "renaissance" but also asking some vexing questions about what happens to cultural forms as they endure through history. Do survivals survive by dint of a virtue that they possess or for more capricious reasons? Moreover, does the process of survival diminish cultural forms or add something to them as well? Pater is ambiguous on both points. On the one hand, he sometimes portrays myths as surviving because they carry a profound resonance with human nature, a sort of Spencerian fitness after all:

> The myth of Demeter and Persephone... illustrates the power of the Greek religion as a religion of pure ideas—of conceptions, which having no link on historical fact, yet, because they arose naturally out of the spirit of man, and embodied, in adequate symbols, his deepest thoughts concerning the conditions of his physical and spiritual life, maintained their hold through many changes, and are still not without a solemnizing power even for the modern mind, which has once admitted them as recognized and habitual inhabitants and, abiding thus for the elevation and purifying of our sentiments, long after the earlier and simpler races of their worshippers have passed away, they may be a pledge to us of the place in our culture, at once legitimate and possible, of the associations, the conceptions, the imagery, of Greek religious poetry in general, of the poetry of all religions. (7:151)

By this account, subsequent literary adaptations of a myth act as a cloak that hides the splendor of the earlier tradition (7:20–1). This sounds a bit like Max Müller's thesis that the ancient nature-mysticism at the origins of religion inevitably diminished as sacred texts were transmitted over time. Yet while Pater was indeed familiar with Müller's work, his more characteristic move in the *Greek Studies* is to describe survival as something that *adds* significance to cultural objects.[27] For instance, Pater calls the myth of Demeter and Persephone "a relic of the *earlier* inhabitants of Greece" that over centuries "asserted its interest, little by little, and took a complex hold on the minds of the Greeks, becoming finally the central and most popular subject of their national worship" (7:81). Later, in an essay on the cult of Dionysus, he describes how "the religious imagination of the Greeks" took

---

[26] E. E. Evans-Pritchard, *Theories of Primitive Religion* (New York, NY: Oxford UP, 1965), 72–3; Frank Turner, *The Greek Heritage in Victorian Britain* (New Haven, CT: Yale UP, 1981), 115–34; Robert Ackerman, *The Myth and Ritual School: J. G. Frazer and the Cambridge Ritualists* (New York, NY: Garland, 1991).

[27] For Pater and Müller, see Pater, 7: 30–1, and Evangelista.

fragments of primitive culture and gradually, by "a unifying or identifying power," "wel[ded them] into something like the identity of a human personality" (7:29).[28]

In such passages Pater effectively ventures a third possible relationship between survival and fitness. Where Spencer's survivals survive because they possess an intrinsic fitness, and Tylor's survive despite being essentially unfit, Pater's survivals often seem to acquire their fitness simply by sticking around long enough. In fairness, Tylor himself imagined something like this process insofar as his examples of survivals tend to be objects whose original functions have been "transmuted" into aesthetic value.[29] He points to the early modern "practical coat" that has become the Victorian gentleman's evening wear and to the ostensibly ornamental details of the Victorian drawing room, which seem aesthetic to us only because we have forgotten their origins:

> It needs but a glance into the trivial details of our own daily life to set us thinking how far we are really its originators, and how far but the transmitters and modifiers of the results of long past ages. Looking round the rooms we live in, we may try here how far he who only knows his own time can be capable of rightly comprehending even that. Here is the "honeysuckle" of Assyria, there the fleur-de-lis of Anjou, a cornice with a Greek border runs round the ceiling, the style of Louis XIV and its parent the Renaissance share the looking glass between them. Transformed, shifted, or mutilated, such elements of art still carry their history plainly stamped upon them.[30]

Yet Tylor, unlike Pater, always regards use-value as primary and aesthetic value as secondary. As it happens, this description of "the rooms we live in" strongly and perhaps deliberately echoes a passage in *The Stones of Venice* (1851–53) in which John Ruskin describes the various products of alienated labor—objects whose decorative qualities have come at the expense of their history—that fill English homes.[31] Pater, by contrast,

---

[28] For an extended reading of Pater's account of myth-generation, see C. Williams, 235–58.

[29] Harris, 165.

[30] E. B. Tylor, *Anthropology: An Introduction to the Study of Man and Civilization* (1881; New York, NY: D. Appleton, 1898), 16; *Primitive Culture* 1: 16. See Harris, 166–7. During the 1910s and '20s, Tylor's last major disciple, R. R. Marett, would devote several essays to this idea that "inasmuch as survivals survive . . . they are not quite dead after all," but rather "help to constitute and condition the living present." *Psychology and Folk-Lore* (London, UK: Methuen, 1920), 102.

[31] "And now, reader, look round this English room of yours, about which you have been proud so often, because the work of it was so good and strong, and the ornaments of it so finished. Examine again all those accurate mouldings, and perfect polishings, and unerring adjustments of the seasoned wood and tempered steel. Many a time you have exulted over them, and thought how great England was, because her slightest work was done so

radically flattens the cultural field to the single level of acquired signifi-cance and envisions historical development as amplifying or refining existing forms rather than producing new ones.

What is perhaps most inventive about Pater's rethinking of Tylorian survivals is the way that it anticipates the modernist view of culture as a holistic circulatory system perpetually recycling its own forms. As we have already seen, the Victorian period saw the word "culture" acquire three broad senses: culture as individual cultivation, culture as Tylor's "Culture, or Civilization," and culture as a particular way of life.[32] The first and second senses are both liberal and teleological, projecting stories of pro-gress onto the life of the individual and the history of humankind, as against the third sense, which is conservative and holistic. Christopher Herbert, however, argues that Tylor's account of survivals historically linked the second and third senses of the word. As the detritus within Tylor's story of smooth civilizational progress, survivals reveal the extent to which culture does *not* merely replace primitive forms with more advanced ones but instead is constituted by forms whose functions have become primarily symbolic.[33] Pater's use of the concept nicely illustrates this shift; more curiously still, it has a way of merging the first and third senses of culture as well. For if Paterian self-culture is a process fed by the recuperation of historical survivals that have thickened into holistic culture, this means that, for Pater, the most "cultured" self in the liberal sense is also the subject of "culture" in its holistic, modernist sense. If George Eliot had imagined recuperated racial heritage as a supplement for cosmopolitan individuality, then Pater derives a kind of modernity from the individual's self-conscious inscription within the totality of a single historical culture. Hence what James Eli Adams has identified as a recur-ring figure in Pater's work: the modern subject who achieves high aesthetic sensitivity by summing up the whole prior history of his or her society in the flesh. Such figures include the Giaconda of Pater's essay on Leonardo da Vinci, or the "new Giaconda" whom he describes in an unpublished draft essay called "The Aesthetic Life" as "modernity made visible."[34]

In consequence, Pater's work ultimately imagines a global relativism that Arnold's, for instance, does not. If Arnold's cosmopolite learns to

thoroughly. Alas! if read rightly, these perfectnesses are signs of a slavery in our England a thousand times more bitter and more degrading than that of the scourged African, or helot Greek." *The Genius of John Ruskin*, ed. John D. Rosenberg (Charlottesville, VA: U of Virginia P, 1964), 178.

[32] Adam Kuper, *Culture: The Anthropologists' Account* (Cambridge, MA: Harvard, 1999), 5–9; Raymond Williams, *Keywords: A Vocabulary of Culture and Society* (1976; New York, NY: Routledge, 2011), 76–82.

[33] Herbert, 260–5.   [34] Adams, 224; see also C. Williams, 43–6.

internalize the talents and limitations of different global cultures, the Paterian ego possesses a cultivated shape that bespeaks its origins in a particular place under specific influences. For example, take "The Child in the House" (1878), which along with Pater's *Imaginary Portraits* (1887) uses a concrete biographical sketch to flesh out the phenomenology of the "Conclusion." The text describes how our growing personalities are fed by all of the tiny details of the worlds we grow up in, which become meaningful to us because of the arbitrary significance they assume over time. "So powerful," Pater writes, is our attraction to certain aesthetic forms,

> and yet accidents like those I have been speaking of so mechanically deter-
> mine it; its essence being indeed the early familiar, as constituting our ideal,
> or typical conception, of rest and security. Out of so many possible condi-
> tions, just this for you and that for me, brings ever the unmistakable
> realization of the delightful *chez soi*; this of the Englishman, for me and
> you, with the closely-drawn white curtain and the shaded lamp; that, quite
> other, for the wandering Arab, who folds his tent every morning, and makes
> his sleeping-place among haunted ruins, or in old tombs.   (8:179)

For Pater, the Englishman cherishes his white curtains and the Arab his tent because each has become familiar to a particular group of people through long usage. Reflecting on this particularity of origin, in turn, promises gives the self an awareness of its own limitation within a world of differences.

MARIUS THE EPICUREAN AND CONVERSION AS SURVIVAL

In *Marius the Epicurean* (1888), a sort of expanded imaginary portrait, Pater turns his account of a many-sidedness fed by historical culture into a theory of the sacred. Anticipating to some degree the work of Émile Durkheim, who would derive religion from the psychic gravity that the social whole exercises upon the self, *Marius* identifies religion with the individual's deep attachment to the long-surviving cultural forms that have shaped his or her consciousness. Specifically, the novel proposes that early Christianity gained its power over a decadent Roman Empire not by offering new doctrines but rather by channeling a deep history of Western cultural forms. As a product of Roman folk religion, Marius feels drawn to the myth of Jesus because in it he sees gathered up "images of hope... from that jaded pagan world"—"Hercules wrestling with Death for possession of Alcestis, Orpheus taming the wild beasts, the

Shepherd ... carrying the sick lamb upon his shoulders"—all united in a new narrative that transfigures their old meanings (3:104). Pater also describes the nascent Church's liturgy as recalling a Greek chorus: "the voices burst out once more presently, in richer and more varied melody, though still of an antiphonal character ... somewhat after the manner of a Greek chorus," but with a more marked "novelty of poetic accent" and "genuine expansion of heart" (3:132). In this way early Christianity fulfills Pater's idiosyncratic concept of renaissance as an openness to the totality of human experience. Just as "Pico Della Mirandola" (1871) had cele- brated the early modern attempt "to reconcile Christianity with the religion of ancient Greece" and "to adjust the various products of the human mind to one another in one many-sided type of intellectual culture" (1:30), so does *Marius*'s eponymous protagonist find in Chris- tianity the same impulse that attracts him to Epicureanism—the instinct to take in more of life rather than less:

> Not pleasure, but a general completeness of life, was the practical ideal to which this anti-metaphysical metaphysic really pointed. And towards such a full or complete life, a life of various yet select sensation, the most direct and effective auxiliary must be, in a word, Insight. Liberty of soul, freedom from all partial and misrepresentative doctrine which does but relieve one element in our experience at the cost of another ... insight through culture, into all that the present moment holds in trust for us, as we stand so briefly in its presence. From that maxim of *Life as the end of Life*, followed, as a practical consequence, the desirableness of refining all the instruments of inward and outward intuition, of developing all their capacities, of testing and exercising one's self in them, till one's whole nature become one complex medium of reception, toward the vision—the "beatific vision," if we really cared to make it such—of our actual experience in the world. (2:146–7)

Christianity, in Pater's rereading, is an Epicureanism whose goals extend beyond sensation and toward "a general completeness of life." It is an "anti-metaphysical metaphysic" that offers freedom from those ideas about the world that would cause us to miss "all that the present moment holds in trust for us." Thus Pater, like Arnold before him, embraces the notion that religious establishments might function as a medium that encourages self-cultivation. For Marius, the rites of Christianity represent "a venerable system of sentiment and idea, widely extended in time and place," which is "rich in the world's experience; so that, in attaching oneself to it, one lets in a great tide of that experience, and makes, as it were with a single step, a great experience of one's own" (3:28).

Pater's revisionist portrait of the early Church generates a series of narrative paradoxes as *Marius* creatively upends key elements of the *Bildungsroman*, the historical novel, and the conversion plot. Most strikingly,

Marius becomes a narrative of religious change that frames all significant transformations as moments of recuperation. If the modernist understanding of culture that Pater's work anticipates was in many ways a critique of missionary conversion, with its insistence that a universally true creed should override local value systems, *Marius* projects this critique back onto the foundational conversion narrative of Western culture.[35] It does so both by reimagining Christianity as contiguous with classical paganism and, more locally, by recasting what might appear to be moments of personal transformation as sites of many-sided expansion. In particular, its notion of survival as cultural appreciation rewrites what William James called a "twice-born" narrative of qualitative transformation as a "once-born" narrative of quantitative accumulation.[36] Over the novel's final chapters, Marius befriends members of the Church, becomes enamored of their ceremonies, then dies of a plague and is named a martyr to the faith, "according to their generous view in this matter" (3:224). Nowhere does Marius explicitly convert to Christianity; instead, he is incorporated posthumously into Church hagiography, where he lives on in the memory of others. Like the myths of Greece and Rome, and like Virgilian pastoral, Marius himself becomes a survival of an "older art, here arranged and harmonised . . . by no sudden and abrupt creation, but rather by the action of a new principle upon elements, all of which had in truth already lived and died many times" (3:96–7). Indeed, Pater interprets Christianity's focus on memorializing the physical body, and its hope for the body's eventual resurrection, as a rebuke to immaterial salvation. Instead of looking toward the soul's transcendence of the body in a heavenly realm, he suggests the early Church cherished the bodies of the deceased as material survivals to be transvalued through sacred rites:

> Clearly, these people, concurring in this with the special sympathies of Marius himself, had adopted the practice of burial from some peculiar feeling of hope they entertained concerning the body . . . The complete and irreparable disappearance of the dead in the funeral fire, so crushing to the spirits, as he for one had found it, had long since induced in him a preference for that other mode of settlement to the last sleep, as having something about it more homelike and hopeful, at least in outward seeming.   (3:101)

Much as Eliot valorized books as physical heirlooms of their own histories, so does this portrait of an early Christian necropolis see Pater transfer a value that might otherwise be located in an otherworldly realm—the

---

[35] See Ruth Benedict, *Patterns of Culture* (1934; New York, NY: Houghton-Mifflin, 2005), 251–78; Keane, 128.

[36] William James, *The Varieties of Religious Experience: A Study in Human Nature* (1902; London, UK: Longmans, Green, 1920), 80.

immaterial transcendence of the soul, like the inner content of books—onto the physicality of the object. In Pater's historical Christianity, the dead live on only when their memory is yoked to tangible sites: the tomb of Marius's father, we are told, provides him with "that secondary sort of life which we can give to the dead, in our intensely realized memory of them—the 'subjective immortality'" (2:24).

Along similar lines, the story of Marius's non-conversion is organized around a series of seeming epiphanies that turn out to change very little. John McGowan has shown how modernist writers such as Yeats reinvented the epiphany as an experience that told more about the self than about some external truth.[37] Likewise, Pater takes moments that might initially resemble cruxes of a conversion plot and diffuses their force so that they become isolated moments of erotic surrender that progressively enrich a cultured life. If Eliot characters such as Daniel Deronda and Gwendolen Harleth, according to David Kurnick, experience "a panoramic or alienated perspective" on social life with "a rush of erotic energy" (600–1), this seems even more markedly true in *Marius*. In the second half of the novel, as Marius begins to grow impatient with Marcus Aurelius's rigid Stoicism, he experiences a series of revelations while traveling (like Paul of Tarsus) that prepare him for some kind of Christian faith. During a trip on the Emperor's business across the Campagna, Marius pauses to rest in an olive garden and witnesses an estranged vision of himself crossing a landscape, "passing from point to point" (3:68) like an externalized version of the subject in the "Conclusion." This initial vision provokes Marius to reflect upon the importance of companionship in his life, which leads him to envision a second figure on the plain beside him, "a self not himself, beside him in his coming and going" (3:69), and to "formulat[e] at last, as the necessary exponent of our own and the world's life, that reasonable Ideal to which the Old Testament gives the name of Creator, which for the philosophers of Greece is the Eternal Reason, and in the New Testament the Father of Men" (3:70). Although this vision comes to Marius "like the break of day over some vast prospect" (3:72), he does not stop there but instead abstracts the notion of a divine companion further into a Platonic vision of the world as a single medium of ideas. "Might not this entire material world," the narrator asks, "the very scene around him, the immemorial rocks, the firm marble, the olive-gardens, the falling water, be themselves but reflections in, or a creation of, that one indefectible mind, wherein he too became conscious, for an hour, a day, for so many years?" (3:71). The climax of this sequence, however,

[37] John McGowan, "From Pater to Wilde to Joyce: Modernist Epiphany and the Soulful Self," *Texas Studies in Literature and Language* 32.3 (1990): 417–45.

sees Pater's narrator pull back and reframe it as nothing more than a series of accumulated impressions:

> Himself—his sensations and ideas—never fell again precisely into focus as on that day, yet he was the richer by its experience. But for once only to have come under the power of that peculiar mood, to have felt the train of reflections which belong to it really forcible and conclusive, to have been led by them to a conclusion, to have apprehended the *Great Ideal*, so palpably that it defined personal gratitude and the sense of a friendly hand laid upon him amid the shadows of the world, left this one particular hour a marked point in life never to be forgotten. It gave him a definitely ascertained measure of his moral or intellectual need, of the demand his soul must make upon the powers, whatsoever they might be, which had brought him, as he was, into the world at all. And again, would he be faithful to himself, to his own habits of mind, his leading suppositions, if he did but remain just there? Must not all that remained of life be but a search for the equivalent of that Ideal, among so-called actual things—a gathering together of every trace or token of it, which his actual experience might present?   (3:73)

Marius seems definitively altered by this apprehension of "the Great Ideal," but in fact the experience's lucidity is unusual rather than "conclusive": his "sensations and ideas," after which the volume is named, will never again attain the same clarity. Far from granting him philosophical closure, the vision sends him back into the world upon "a search for the equivalent of that Ideal, among so-called actual things..."

At the wider level of its historical narrative, *Marius* employs a rhetoric of prolepsis to present seemingly new cultural modes as being comprised of very old elements. In an essay on the Victorian genre of the historical conversion novel, Maureen Moran shows how texts such as Charles Kingsley's *Hypatia* (1853) and John Henry Newman's *Callista* (1855) sought to depict Christian orthodoxy at a moment when it was profoundly heterodox.[38] Pater, in effect, reverses the formula by showing the young Church's radicalism to consist precisely in its clearer continuity with the pagan past. In particular, his narrator has a habit of harping upon the word "already" so as to back-date the emergence of whatever cultural institution he is discussing—calling to mind the old poststructuralist use of "always already" to dramatize how ideology presents contingent truths as perennial or natural:

> The Mass, indeed, would appear to have been said continuously from the Apostolic age. Its details, as one by one they become visible in later history,

[38] Moran, 172–3. For more on *Marius*'s place within the conventions of the Victorian historical conversion novel, see Curtis Dahl, "Pater's *Marius* and Historical Novels on Early Christian Times," *Nineteenth-Century Fiction* 28.1 (1973): 1–24.

have already the character of what is ancient and venerable. "We are very old, and ye are young!" they seem to protest, to those who fail to understand them. Ritual, in fact, like all other elements of religion, must grow and cannot be made—grow by the same law of development which prevails everywhere else, in the moral as in the physical world. As regards this special phase of the religious life, however, such development seems to have been unusually rapid in the subterranean age which preceded Constantine; and in the very first days of the final triumph of the church the Mass emerges to general view already substantially complete. (3:127)

Already, in the reign of Antoninus Pius, the time was gone by when men became Christians under some sudden and overpowering impression, and with all the disturbing results of such a crisis. At this period, the larger number, perhaps, had been born Christians, had been ever with peaceful hearts in their "Father's house." (3:119)

The aesthetic charm of the catholic church [sic], her evocative power over all that is eloquent and expressive in the better mind of man...all this, as abundantly realised centuries later by Dante and Giotto, by the great medieval church-builders, by the great ritualists like Saint Gregory, and the masters of sacred music in the middle age—we may see already...towards the end of the second century. (3:124)

T. S. Eliot saw anachronism in Pater's suggestion that a Roman, encountering Christianity for the first time, would feel a distinctly Victorian nostalgia for it.[39] Yet Pater's claim is that what we call nostalgia is not the mark of a late or decadent age but represents the primary religious affect of all periods.

It might be said, of course, that in much of this *Marius* simply draws out certain ambiguities already endemic to the classical *Bildungsroman*. The novel's odd combination of flux and stasis, for instance—the fact that Marius keeps growing without really arriving anywhere—reflects the way that *Bildung* itself is, according to Thomas Pfau, a "tautological" notion, at once process and product.[40] However, by removing all friction between Marius and his society, *Marius* also illustrates Douglas Mao's claim that the *Bildungsroman* underwent a real transformation when it began to replace the humanistic model of self-cultivation with new physiological conceptions of the individual's determination by his or her

---

[39] T. S. Eliot, "Arnold and Pater" (1930), *Selected Essays, 1917–1932* (New York, NY: Harcourt, Brace, 1932), 346–57.

[40] Thomas Pfau, "From Mediation to Medium: Aesthetic and Anthropological Dimensions of the Image (*Bild*) and the Crisis of *Bildung* in German Modernism," *Modernist Cultures* 1.2 (2005), 141. *Marius* also speaks to Pfau's claim that the plot of *Bildung* constantly tempts the possibility of atavism: if *Bildung* is the unfolding of an image, or *Bild*, then it necessarily carries a danger of collapsing back into that image because it cannot contain anything that goes beyond it (see 159–60).

environment.[41] In particular, the novel does away with the tension between self and society that most critics have seen as the *Bildungsroman*'s key structural feature.[42] In *Marius*, we encounter not a self whose growth is shaped by the external pressure of social necessity but rather one that seems identical with the entire previous history of its culture, always taking on influences without ever achieving a moment of self-conscious differentiation. One symptom of this is the way that the novel avoids staging interactions between Marius and other characters in favor of a mostly internally focalized third-person narrative. Although Marius is supposed to accrue influences from the people he meets, these moments of influence, as Wolfgang Iser has shown, are narrated less as a series of dramatic encounters than as a progression of static "tableaux" that tend to gain their significance from the narrator's reflections rather than from any resolution at the level of the plot.[43]

In all of these ways, Marius comes to bear a striking resemblance to the hero of the colonial *Bildungsroman* as described by Jed Esty. The traditional *Bildungsroman*, Esty argues, shaped the energies of liberal individualism within the containing form of the nation, but in the colonial setting, with its ongoing deferral of national sovereignty and objectifying racial and cultural hierarchies, that dialectic of individual maturation was replaced by plots of perpetually inconclusive development.[44] *Marius*, as we have seen, provincializes the Western subject by removing it from a standard story of progress from pagan to medieval to modern and rooting it in the same organic, non-universal culture that Victorian liberalism typically projected onto colonized peoples. As such, its protagonist's profound stasis comes to reflect the condition of a reprovincialized Europe that does not occupy any exceptional historical trajectory.[45]

---

[41] Douglas Mao, *Fateful Beauty: Aesthetic Environments, Juvenile Development, and Literature 1860–1960* (Princeton, NJ: Princeton UP, 2010).

[42] Franco Moretti, *The Way of the World: The Bildungsroman in European Culture* (1987; London, UK: Verso, 2000), 3–13. See also G. B. Tennyson, "The *Bildungsroman* and Nineteenth-Century English Literature," in Rosario P. Armato and John M. Spalek (eds.), *Medieval Epic to the "Epic Theater" of Brecht: Essays in Comparative Literature* (Los Angeles, CA: U of Southern California P, 1968), 143–5.

[43] Wolfgang Iser, *Walter Pater: The Aesthetic Moment* (1960; New York, NY: Cambridge UP, 1987), 129–31. Iser is citing David Cecil, *Walter Pater. The Scholar-Artist* (New York, NY: Cambridge UP, 1955), 24.

[44] Jed Esty, *Unseasonable Youth: Modernism, Colonialism, and the Fiction of Development* (New York, NY: Oxford UP, 2011), 1–38.

[45] In this sense Esty corroborates Georg Lukàcs's claim that the post-1848 historical novel abandoned faith in active human political progress for a depiction of history as a series of meaningless costume-changes or irresistible evolutionary processes. See *The Historical Novel* (1937), trans. Hannah and Stanley Mitchell (1962; Lincoln, NE: U of Nebraska P, 1983), 171–250. Along similar lines, two of *Marius*'s best critics—Avrom Fleishman and Ulrich C. Knoepflmacher—have questioned its status as a historical novel on the grounds

Yet in fact Pater does preserve a certain agency for Marius by position-
ing him as what James Buzard calls an autoethnographic protagonist.
Buzard argues that, under the awareness of global differences precipitated
by colonialism, certain nineteenth-century novels sought to reimagine
England as just one global culture among many. Toward this end, they
gave their subjects a position of semi-detachment that allowed them to
participate in metropolitan culture while being aware of it *as* a culture: a
specific, local way of life that they did not choose. Novels such as *Bleak
House* (1853), Buzard shows, replaced the classical *Bildungsroman's* productive friction between self and society with an early version of anthropology's participant-observer dynamic.[46] In much the same fashion, Pater
gives his protagonist a reflexive self-consciousness that lets him regard his
own culture qua culture, immersing himself in it while describing that
immersion from without:

> Marius informed himself with much pains concerning the church at Cecilia's
> house.... And what he found... was the vision of a natural, a scrupulously
> natural love, transforming, by some new gift of insight into the truth of
> human relationships, and under the urgency of some new motive by him so
> far unfathomable, all the conditions of life. He saw, in all its primitive
> freshness and amid the lively facts of its actual coming into the world, as a
> reality of experience, that the regenerate type of humanity, which, centuries
> later, Giotto and his successors, down to the best and purest days of the
> young Raphael, working under conditions very friendly to the imagination,
> were to conceive as an artistic ideal.   (3:110–11)

In this passage, Marius's deepening attraction to Christian ritual is figured
as a sympathy for the *idea* of historical community that allows him to
become a center of consciousness for the narrator's anthropological
ruminations. The narration is structured largely around the repetitions
of "he found... He saw... He felt...," which frame the scene in terms of
Marius's immersed point of view. Yet the observations themselves, and the
stakes that they imagine, betray a theoretical distance that seems better
suited to the nineteenth-century narrator than to the second-century
participant. This back-and-forth movement between immersed and
detached perspectives recurs throughout the later episodes of the novel,
such as this scene, which finds Marius observing an early Mass:

---

that it contains no sense of active historical change. See Freedman, 25; Fleishman, *The
English Historical Novel* (Baltimore, MD: Johns Hopkins UP, 1971), 169–76; Knoepflmacher, 189–223.

[46] James Buzard, *Disorienting Fiction: The Autoethnographic Work of Nineteenth-Century
British Novels* (Princeton, NJ: Princeton UP, 2005), 8–12.

Coming thus unexpectedly upon this large assembly, so entirely united, in a silence so profound, for purposes unknown to him, Marius felt for a moment as if he had stumbled by chance upon some great conspiracy. Yet that could scarcely be, for the people here collected might have figured as the earliest handsel, or pattern, of a new world, from the very face of which discontent had passed away. Corresponding to the variety of human type there present, was the various expression of every form of human sorrow assuaged. What desire, what fulfillment of desire, had wrought so pathetically on the features of these ranks of aged men and women of humble condition? . . . Was some credible message from beyond "the flaming rampart of the world"—a message of hope, regarding the place of men's souls and their interest in the sum of things—already moulding anew their very bodies, and looks, and voices, now and here?   (3:131–2)

Marius enters the frame as an outsider, stumbling upon this novel yet ancient ceremony as a "conspiracy" or "pattern," a formation vibrant within yet cryptic from without. The passage then segues into a sequence of questions that are implicitly attributed to Marius's perspective, yet which also seem to come from a more distanced, even theoretical vantage point: What is the shared "desire" that centers this community? What is it that has "mould[ed] anew their very bodies, and looks, and voice," into a collective? As soon as the ritual ends, however, we are told that "the natural soul of worship" in Marius has "been satisfied as never before" (3:132, 3:141). Marius would seem to have received the benefits of total immersion (to adapt a phrase) while being able to come and go as a reflective individual.

PATER'S AESTHETIC *ASKESIS*

So far I have described *Marius the Epicurean* as an unconventional *Bildungsroman* that eliminates the genre's constitutive tension between individuality and socialization by reimagining personal development as a smooth, continuous process fed by the determining influences of historical culture. What becomes clearer as the novel progresses is that this move is part of an out-and-out polemic against what Pater calls "sacrifice" (3:17). Animal sacrifice recurs throughout *Marius* as a symptom of humankind's limited sympathies for otherness (see 2:234–47), while asceticism is denounced as the great, perennial alternative to many-sidedness:

In the history of the church, as throughout the moral history of mankind, there are two distinct ideals, either of which it is possible to maintain—two conceptions, under one or the other of which we may represent to ourselves men's efforts towards a better life. . . . The ideal of asceticism represents moral effort as essentially a sacrifice, the sacrifice of one part of human nature to another, that it may live that more completely in what survives of it; while the ideal of culture represents it as a harmonious development of all the parts of human nature, in just proportion to each other.   (3:121–2)

In many ways, of course, this passage reprises Arnold's contrast between Hebraism and Hellenism by pitting the centrifugal desire to balance "all the parts of human nature" against a centripetal ethos that disciplines the personality by denying certain drives or desires. But Pater's critique of sacrifice also extends the criticism of propositional attitudes in religion and philosophy that we saw in *The Renaissance*. The protagonist of "Emerald Uthwart" (1892), for instance, finds himself caught "in a system of fixed rules, amid which, it might be, some of his own tendencies and inclinations would die out of him through disuse" (8:211), while in "Two French Stories" (1872) Pater ventures that

> the student of the Renaissance has this advantage over the student of the emancipation of the human mind in the Reformation, or the French Revolution, that in tracing the footsteps of humanity to higher levels, he is not beset at every turn by the inflexibilities and antagonisms of some well-recognized controversy, with rigidly defined opposites, exhausting the intelligence and limiting one's sympathies.   (1:26)

Even Marcus Aurelius's Stoicism is disparaged as "a theory . . . of loss and gain" (3:17) that demands "the sacrifice of a thousand possible sympathies" (3:24). In contrast, a "system of symbolic usages" that emphasizes "the sacredness of time, of life and its events, and . . . of such gifts to men as fire, water, the earth" (2:9–10), can, as the paratactic structure of Pater's prose here suggests, open up an "enchanted region" where "there are no fixed parties, no exclusions," only a "unity of culture in which 'whatsoever things are comely' are reconciled, for the elevation and adorning of our spirits" (1:26–7).

Pater's critique of sacrifice aligns him even more closely than Arnold or Eliot with what Charles Taylor calls the "immanent counter-Enlightenment," a specific strain of secularist thought that affirms "the wrong we do, in pursuing our highest ideals, when we sacrifice the body, or ordinary desire, or the fulfillments of everyday life," and imagines a kind of alternative transcendence that comes when "[o]ur highest aspirations and our life energies are somehow lined up."[47] Hence the multiple resonances between Pater's work and that of Friedrich Nietzsche. In the *Greek Studies*, for example, Pater anticipates Nietzsche's claim that "ecstatic identification

---

[47] Charles Taylor, *A Secular Age* (Cambridge, MA: Harvard UP, 2007), 369, 640, 6.

with the totality of things takes one 'beyond good and evil' "[48] by pushing the idea of many-sidedness beyond Arnoldian balance and toward a vision of *ex-statis*:

> Coleridge, in one of his fantastic speculations, refining on the German word for enthusiasm—*Schwärmerei*, swarming, as he says, "like the swarming of bees together"—has explained how the sympathies of mere numbers, as such, the random catching on fire of one here and another there, when people are collected together, generates as if by mere contact, some new and rapturous spirit, not traceable in the individual units of a multitude.
>
> (7:56–7)

Meanwhile *Marius*'s critique of sacrifice echoes Nietzsche's distinction, in *On the Genealogy of Morals* (1887), between positive religions that project ego strength and negative religions that ask us to reject whole parts of ourselves for transcendent ideals.[49]

Yet the curious thing about *Marius the Epicurean* is the fact that its affirmation of many-sidedness becomes an ascetic ethos in its own right by demanding that its protagonist surrender a certain agency.[50] What the child Marius learns from his native folk religion is a "devout circumspection" that requires an Eliot-like attentiveness to "the claims of others" but also sounds suspiciously like a monastic vocation: it "made him anticipate all his life long as a thing towards which he must carefully train himself, some great occasion of self-devotion . . . that should consecrate his life . . . as the early Christian looked forward to martyrdom at the end of his course, as a seal of worth upon it" (2:21–2). Similarly, Marius's adolescent Epicureanism renders him a "passive spectator" (1:125) of the Heraclitan flux around him:

> To Marius the whole of life seemed full of sacred presences, demanding of him a similar collectedness . . . a sort of devout circumspection lest he should fall short at any point of the demand upon him of anything in which deity was concerned. . . . And from habit, this feeling of a responsibility towards the world of men and things . . . kept him serious and dignified amid the Epicurean speculations which in after-years much engrossed him, when he had learned to think of all religions as indifferent. (2:21–2)

"Demanding"; "devout circumspection"; "serious and dignified": these are phrases more redolent of asceticism than aestheticism. Yet they are both, for as Pater puts it, in one of the novel's most striking phrases, the key value that sustains Marius throughout his aesthetic education is above all

---

[48] Julian Young, *Nietzsche's Philosophy of Religion* (New York, NY: Cambridge UP, 2006), 142.
[49] See Young, 149–56.   [50] Adams also notes this irony; see 174–7.

"the impulse to surrender himself, in perfectly liberal inquiry about it, to anything that, as a matter of fact, attracted or impressed him strongly" (3:110). More abstractly, Marius's refusal to foreclose any possible avenue of self-development translates into a sacrifice of plot, as the very reluctance to commit to a vocation that frees him from bourgeois discipline also leaves him without any agential contours at all. In Iser's words, "plot is turned into a minus-function" as Marius "does not embrace any single concept of life but remains suspended among all the possibilities that experience affords him. As none of these can fulfill him, he can only go on from one experience to another, a process of extension that in turn is only possible *because* he rejects every concept and so retains his freedom."[51] The result is that Marius emerges as a character neither flat enough to be identified with a doctrinaire ideological position nor round enough to "master his own fate through action."[52]

This return of *askesis* within Pater's work finds its boldest expression in the "Lacedaemon" chapter of *Plato and Platonism* (1893), which proposes that, among all of the ancient Greeks, it was in fact the militaristic Spartans who most nearly achieved a "true and genuine Hellenism" (6:224).[53] Relocating Arnold's famous dualism within the Hellenic character itself, the lectures distinguish between the Ionian (aesthetic, many-sided, free) and the Dorian (disciplined, austere) impulses in Greek life, only to name the latter the best means to the former. This is because Sparta's totalizing regime of military education, Pater writes, drew "no sharp distinction between mental and bodily exercise" (6:224) but rather "conceived the whole of life as [a] matter of attention, patience, a[nd] fidelity to detail" (6:215). Their religion, although "strenuous" and "monastic," was also "cheerful" because it supported "that harmony of functions, which is the Aristotelian definition of health" (6:227). Indeed, Spartan military life becomes unabashedly aesthetic for Pater insofar as it pictures no end beyond itself: if one were to ask, "Why this strenuous task-work, day after day; why this loyalty to a system, so costly to you individually . . . ?", Pater conjectures that an "intelligent young Spartan might have replied: 'To the end that I myself may be a perfect work of art'" (6:232). In comparison with Hebrew or Christian righteousness, which have very specific payoffs in mind, Spartan military discipline looks curiously disinterested:

> *To what purpose?* Why, with no prospect of Israel's reward, are you as scrupulous, minute, self-taxing, as he? A tincture of asceticism in the Lacedaemonian rule may remind us again of the monasticism of the Middle Ages.

[51] Iser, 134.   [52] Ibid., 131.   [53] See Adams, 176–8, 215–16.

But then, monastic severity was for the purging of a troubled conscience, or for the hope of an immense prize, neither of which conditions is to be supposed here. In fact the surprise of Saint Paul, as a practical man, at the slightness of the reward for which a Greek spent himself, natural as it is about all pagan perfection, is especially applicable about these Lacedaemonians, who indeed had actually invented that so "corruptible" and essentially worthless parsley crown in place of the more tangible prizes of an earlier age. Strange people! Where, precisely, may be the spring of action in you, who are so severe to yourselves; you who, in the words of Plato's supposed objector that the rulers of the ideal state are not to be envied, have nothing you can really call your own, but are like hired servants in your own houses...? (6:233)

Earlier I argued that Pater's derivation of many-sidedness from an open-ness to the survivals of the past sees ethnographic culture merge with liberal self-culture. *Plato and Platonism* approaches the paradox from the other end by claiming that Sparta's totalizing regime of discipline ultim-ately produced the kind of holistic way of life that only a modernist ethnographer could describe. If Marius, in order to explain the rituals of Christianity to the modern reader, must assume the fieldworker's participant-observer voice, then Spartan self-discipline becomes a totalizing system that cannot wholly be depicted from the outside. As Pater puts it, "you couldn't really know it unless you were of it" (6:215).

Pater's return to *askesis* parallels a paradox that we have previously seen in Arnold and Eliot. Just as Arnoldian culture becomes a positive and exclusionary ideal through its very disavowal of Hebraism, and much as Eliot had worried (via *Daniel Deronda*) that a truly universal sympathy might become a detached egotism of its own, so does Marius's desire to take in more sides of experience require that he sacrifice the possibility of individual choice. Not only this, but at times Marius's many-sidedness also takes on the distinct flavor of bourgeois economic calculation.[54] McGowan reads the attentiveness defined in Pater's *Renaissance* as an affirmation of the present moment over any theory of delayed gratifica-tion, but in fact *Marius* shows that such attention can become a kind of hoarding—an attempt to draw moments out for as long as possible, or to accumulate the maximum number of subjective experiences within the time allotted.[55] Thus Jonathan Freedman portrays the "Conclusion" as an immanent critique of consumerism, one that is so intent upon maximizing its desires that it rejects the limited nature of material goods and seeks only

[54] Adams argues that Marius's self-control among the decadent patricians of Antonine Rome clearly positions him as a middle-class parvenu (189–90).
[55] McGowan, 420–3.

to accumulate experiences in the abstract.[56] Within *Marius* we see this irony in the fact that Marius's initial interest in Christianity is driven by a weird cost-benefit analysis. In considering what this new Church offers him, Marius reflects that his Epicureanism

> had been a theory, avowedly, of loss and gain (so to call it) of an economy. If, therefore, it missed something in the commerce of life, which some other theory of practice was able to include, if it made a needless sacrifice, then it must be, in a manner, inconsistent with itself, and lack theoretic completeness. (3:17)

This possibility, which inspires Marius to open himself to Christianity's eclectic aesthetic, returns at the very end of the novel, when Marius, lying on his deathbed, considers whether his "jealous estimate of gain and loss, to use life, not as the means to some problematic end, but, as far as might be, from dying hour to dying hour, an end in itself" has produced the best possible outcome (3:219).

From the standpoint of the present, *Marius* illuminates the ascetic thread running through contemporary forms of liberalism that have taken Mill's "variety of experiences" as their goal. The bucket list of experiences that one must check off before one dies, or the fascination with Buddhist mindfulness—all affirm the value of the present moment over delayed gratification, yet all, like Marius, display a highly purposeful rigor. Viewed within a wider historical perspective, Pater's return to *askesis* illustrates Pierre Hadot's claim that classical philosophy across the spectrum was conceptualized as a way of life centered upon forms of ascetic practice. Even Epicureanism, Hadot writes, sought to maximize the subject's immanent experience by way of an "*askesis* of desire" that involved limiting oneself to natural and necessary pleasures:

> Like the Stoic, the Epicurean finds perfection in the present moment. For him, the pleasure of the present moment does not need to last in order to be perfect. A single instant of pleasure is as perfect as an eternity thereof. Here, Epicurus is heir to the Aristotelian theory of pleasure. For Aristotle, just as the act of vision is complete and finished, in its specificity, at each moment of its duration, so pleasure is specifically complete at each moment. Pleasure is not a movement which unfolds within time, nor does it depend on duration. It is a reality in itself which is not situated within the category of time.[57]

For this reason, Hadot collapses not just the gap between Epicureanism and Stoicism but also that between classical philosophy and the early

---

[56] Freedman, 63–71.
[57] Pierre Hadot, *What is Ancient Philosophy?*, trans. Michael Chase (Cambridge, MA: Harvard UP, 2002), 197.

Christian ascetics, who regarded themselves as Christianizing philosophy
and indeed drew heavily upon Stoic and Epicurean exercises of self-
examination. Michel Foucault, however, argues that the crucial break
came in the work of Descartes, who taught modernity to decouple self-
knowledge from technologies of the self altogether. Aestheticism, for
Foucault, represented the first significant post-Christian attempt to reinte-
grate embodied practices into self-knowledge.[58] When Baudelaire wrote
that the *flâneur*'s personal regime "borders upon the spiritual and stoical,"
and mimics in many ways "the strictest monastic rule," he was reacquaint-
ing liberalism with the idea that individualism is a matter not just of self-
knowledge but also of self-making.[59]

Marius's most distinctive contribution to the aestheticist rediscovery
of bodily discipline is to suggest that suffering itself might play a role in
individual cultivation as a secular virtue. Both Talal Asad and Charles
Taylor note that physical suffering has long been something of a scandal
for those versions of secular modernity built around the affirmation of
immanent goods.[60] *Marius*, however, reconsiders the Christian passion
(with its etymological connection to "passive") as a resource for aesthetic
individuality by entertaining the possibility that susceptibility to the pain
of others might be one necessary consequence of the aesthete's openness to
experience. Midway through the novel, Marius reflects to himself that the
"power of sympathy" is linked to "the capacity for suffering," since it offers
a "power of insight" into "the pain one actually sees" (3:182–3). This link
is confirmed when Marius first glimpses an icon of Jesus and feels a shock
of recognition at the sight of another young man sacrificing bits of himself
to others "voluntarily, one by one":

> It was the image of a young man giving up voluntarily, one by one, for the
> greatest of ends, the greatest gifts; actually parting with himself, above all,
> with the serenity, the divine serenity, of his own soul; yet from the midst of
> his desolation crying out upon the greatness of his success, as if foreseeing
> this very worship. As centre of the supposed facts which for these people were
> become so constraining a motive of hopefulness, of activity, that image
> seemed to display itself with an overwhelming claim on human gratitude.

---

[58] See Michel Foucault, "On the Genealogy of Ethics: An Overview of a Work in
Progress," *The Foucault Reader*, ed. Paul Rabinow (New York, NY: Pantheon, 1984),
371–2; and Alice Ramos, "Technologies of the Self: Truth, Asceticism, and Autonomy,"
Journal of French and Francophone Philosophy 6.1–2 (2010): 20–9.

[59] Charles Baudelaire, "The Painter of Modern Life," in *The Painter of Modern Life and
Other Essays*, ed. and trans. Jonathan Mayne (New York, NY: Phaidon, 1995), 28. See
Adams, 210.

[60] Taylor, 650; Asad, *Formations of the Secular: Christianity, Islam, Modernity* (Stanford,
CA: Stanford UP, 2003), 67–99.

What Saint Lewis of France discerned, and found so irresistibly touching, across the dimness of many centuries, as a painful thing done for love of him by one he had never seen, was to them almost as a thing of yesterday.

(3:138–9)

Imagery soon becomes prophecy as Marius, upon hearing of the arrest of several of his new Christian friends, exploits a rumor that there is one pagan among them by insisting that it is not himself but in fact Cornelius, who is then released (3:212). Marius too is eventually freed, but only after contracting a plague, and soon succumbs to disease and fatigue. In what is meant to be his culminating act of self-expansion, Marius conspicuously re-enacts the ultimate act of sacrifice and the inspiration for a million monastic vocations. This death-drive within many-sidedness ultimately gives Marius's *Bildung* the shaping *sjuzhet* that it has previously lacked. Marius's growth is not curbed by reconciliation with society by way of vocation; rather, it finds an immanent terminus in his willingness to sacrifice himself to a world that has permeated his experience so thoroughly.

MANY-SIDEDNESS AND THE POSSIBILITIES OF DISSENT

Tracing Marius's metamorphosis from expansive aesthete to suffering Christ-figure ultimately brings us to the question of politics: what sort of oppositional stance can Pater's brand of aesthetic liberalism actually offer? For just as Jesus the literary figure has stood both for passive suffering and for heroic resistance to authority, so can Pater's many-sided self be taken either as a lightning-rod of Victorian cultural apostasy or as a deeply conservative figure who affirms in his person the collective inheritance of the past. Many readers, of course, found Pater's aestheticism subversive precisely because it seemed to privilege the passive over the active virtues.[61] But such a gloss does scant justice to the sort of Dissenting posture that the novel figures. For *Marius*, radical aestheticism is the great custodian of Western culture, while the supposed orthodoxies of medieval Catholicism and modern Dissent are both fringe formations that break with substantial portions of Europe's past. By extension, the novel figures Christianity itself both as an organic reconciliation of the West's contradictory cultural inheritances and as a voice of continual dissatisfaction with the given—"a permanent protest established in the world, a plea, a perpetual after-thought, which humanity henceforth would ever possess in

---

[61] See Adams, 174–6.

reserve, against any wholly mechanical and disheartening theory of itself and its conditions" (3:221).

This problem emerges with special clarity if we read *Marius* alongside Oscar Wilde's major essays, which use the figure of Jesus to question the oppositional possibilities of aestheticism. In "The Critic as Artist" (1891), Wilde argues, much like Pater, that aesthetic criticism can facilitate an eclectic mastery over the past by allowing us to channel inherited instincts toward self-conscious ends. The "culture" borne by "racial experience," Wilde writes,

> can be made perfect by the critical spirit alone... For who is the true critic but he who bears within himself the dreams, and ideas, and feelings of myriad generations, and to whom no form of thought is alien, no emotional impulse obscure? And who the true man of culture, if not he who by fine scholarship and fastidious rejection has made instinct self-conscious and intelligent...?[62]

"The Soul of Man Under Socialism" (1891), in turn, explores the reverse side of this assertion by insisting that many of the activities with which classical liberalism associates agency, most notably wage labor and the acquisition of property, actually diminish the ego by alienating it into external objects. Under socialism, however, individuals will be released from the "sordid necessity" of earning a livelihood and allowed to invest all of their energies in self-development.[63] Jesus, for Wilde, is the historical figure who best embodied this paradoxical possibility. By enjoining his followers to give away their possessions to the poor, Wilde writes, Jesus was not preaching selfless altruism so much as telling them to unburden their personalities so that they might grow unencumbered:

> What Jesus meant, was this. He said to man, "You have a wonderful personality. Develop it. Be yourself. Don't imagine that your perfection lies in accumulating or possessing external things... It involves sordid pre-occupation, endless industry, continual wrong. Personal property hinders Individualism at every step."[64]

Yet this dimension of Jesus's character also unsettles Wilde. By telling his followers to disavow worldly striving, Jesus was not just enjoining them to be like the lilies that Wilde would later wear in his lapel, but also choosing the path of martyrdom over revolution. Instead of constructing a new society in which the individual was released from the tyranny of labor, he

---

[62] Oscar Wilde, *The Major Works* (New York, NY: Harper Collins, 1966), 1041.
[63] Ibid., 1079.   [64] Ibid., 1085.

rejected society outright and thus resigned himself to suffer at its hands. "Christ made no attempt to reconstruct society," Wilde writes, "and consequently the Individualism that he preached to man could be realised only through pain or in solitude"; he became "a God realising his perfection through pain," whereas the Wildean aesthete affirms that "[p]ain is not the ultimate mode of perfection [because] it has reference to wrong, unhealthy, unjust surroundings.[65]

If "The Soul of Man Under Socialism" faults Jesus for working out an imperfect compromise between a disinterested aestheticism and the practice of cultural dissent, Wilde's own public persona sought to reconcile these two impulses through its peculiar brand of social performance. As a public figure, the Wildean aesthete refuses practical labor while still doing much by performing an outsized personality. The time that he refuses to waste in practical work is time that he spends performing *himself*, a labor that does not accrue in alienated objects but instead vanishes into the air of the Paterian present moment. Only in *De Profundis* (1905)—written after "Sorrow had made my days her own and bound me to her wheel"—would Wilde follow Pater in imagining self-sacrifice itself as an avenue of aesthetic expansion.[66] Jesus, he writes to his estranged Bosie, "realised in the entire sphere of human relations that imaginative sympathy which in the sphere of Art is the sole secret of creation. He understood the leprosy of the leper, the darkness of the blind, the fierce misery of those who live for pleasure, the strange poverty of the rich . . . [and that] '*Whatever happens to another happens to oneself*.'"[67] In this way his example offers the believer a path to "an extended, a Titan personality."[68]

Pater, I would like to propose in closing, finds a different rapprochement between anti-bourgeois aestheticism and iconoclastic politics in the figure of the Dissenting collectivity. Heather Love has argued that Pater was no less of a performer than Wilde, but that his performances emphasized deferral in a way that Wilde's flamboyant confrontations did not. Specifically, Love invokes Eve Sedgwick's concept of queer performativity to argue that Pater resisted the orthodoxies of his day through a "combination of reticence and virtuosic stylistic performance" that offered critical pushback by dramatizing its own marginality and powerlessness.[69] Love's reading resonates tellingly with that of Rachel Teukolsky, who has argued that *Marius*'s Church dramatizes the work of countercultural

[65] Ibid., 1102, 1103.   [66] Ibid., 923.   [67] Ibid., 923.   [68] Ibid., 926.
[69] Heather K. Love, "Forced Exile: Walter Pater's Queer Modernism," in Douglas Mao and Rebecca L. Walkowitz (eds.), *Bad Modernisms* (Durham, NC: Duke UP, 2006), 27.

artistic coteries.[70] Reading Love and Teukolsky together, we might say that Pater is attracted to the work of creative collectivities because they serve as vehicles through which quiet or self-marginalizing individuals can become instigators of long-term historical change. In the moment, such collectivities force their members to sacrifice personal will and desire. Viewed in retrospect, however, they exhibit the very transformational possibilities that their individual members have renounced. *Plato and Platonism*, for instance, argues that the rigidly hierarchical societies of both Sparta and Plato's Republic suppressed individual freedoms in a way that ultimately figured a revolutionary aesthetic. Much as Arnold's *Celtic Literature* premises English many-sidedness upon the supposed fixity of Celtic, Saxon, and Norman traits, so does Plato's Republic, according to Pater, tell its citizens that they are "actually made of different stuff" and "appointed to this rather than to that order of service" (6:249) in order to model a complex whole that subsequent readers can take as an image of self-culture. Within the Republic, "[d]eveloping [the citizen] to the utmost on all his various sides" is discouraged insofar as it risks damaging the "unity of the whole" (6:240). Yet on the whole the Republic itself becomes an image of the complex totality of a cultivated individual, much like the medieval Church, with its "unity or harmony enforced on disparate elements, unity as of an army, or an order of monks, organic, mechanic, liturgical" (6:242–3).

Along similar lines, the early Christian community that Marius witnesses at Cecilia's house generates new cultural possibilities through an essentially conservative process of curation, or what Teukolsky calls "tasteful recombination"—that is, by rearranging elements of the pagan past in ways that draw out countervailing tendencies already present within the culture:

> All around, in those well-ordered precincts, were the quiet signs of wealth, and of a noble taste—a taste, indeed, chiefly evidenced in the selection and juxtaposition of the material it had to deal with, consisting almost exclusively of the remains of an older art, here arranged and harmonized, with effects, both as regards colour and form, so delicate as to seem really derivative from some finer intelligence in these matters than lay within the resources of the ancient world. (3:96)[71]

Although this process, as we have seen, subsumes Marius's individuality into Church iconography, in so doing it also grafts him onto a different kind of paternity. For the fact that Cecilia's chapel is set in a *house* casts it

---

[70] Rachel Teukolsky, *The Literate Eye: Victorian Art Writing and Modernist Aesthetics* (New York, NY: Oxford UP, 2009), 140–5.
[71] Ibid., 143.

as a reinvented family organized around unconventional forms of filiation. Cecilia herself is a "wealthy Roman matron" (3:99) whose "antique severity" (3:106) presides over a "strange family" (3:108), one that, true to its general practice, teases out unexpected possibilities within the old Roman veneration of the patriarchal family:

> And what [Marius] found, thus looking, literally, for the dead among the living, was the vision of a natural, scrupulously natural, love, transforming, by some new gift of insight into the truth of human relationships, and under the urgency of some new motive . . . Chastity—as he seemed to understand, the chastity of men and women, amid all the conditions, and with the results proper to such chastity, is the most beautiful thing in the world and the truest conservation of that creative energy by which men and women were first brought into it. The nature of the family, for which the better genius of old Rome had sincerely cared, of the family and its appropriate affections— all that love of one's kindred by which obviously one does triumph in some degree over death had never been so felt before. (3:110–11)

The filiation that this family offers is linked less by procreation than by memorialization. Although Cecilia's "chaste" society is not necessarily celibate, it primarily channels "that creative energy by which men and women" are brought into the world toward the work of recuperation and survival. Children are crucial to its life, but mostly in the form of meticulously curated child-graves: "beds of infants, but a span long indeed . . . decked in some instances with the favorite toys of their tiny occupants—toy-soldiers, little chariot-wheels, the entire paraphernalia of a baby-house . . ." (3:102). Crucially, it is only through membership in this community that Marius, unmarried and stricken down in his youth, will be able to "link himself to the generations to come in the world he was leaving":

> Yes! through the survival of their children, happy parents are able to think calmly, and with a very practical affection, of a world in which they are to have no direct share; planting with a cheerful good-humour, the acorns they carry about with them, that their grand-children may be shaded from the sun by the broad oak-trees of the future. That is nature's way of easing death to us. It was thus too, surprised, delighted, that Marius, under the power of that new hope among men, could think of the generations to come after him.
> (3:221–2)

Here Pater returns to the language of survivals to perform a strange inversion: where most people are only survived by their children, Marius's progeny will be the cultural survivals that he helps transmit through Christianity, including of course himself.

Christianity, in short, comes to epitomize the paradoxical stance of Paterian Dissent by expressing the entire past of its culture while working as a destabilizing element with it—suppressing the individuality of its members while giving them agency as members of an unorthodox cultural formation. In historical terms, Pater sees in the second-century Church a third way between Dissent and Establishment, one that offers insurgent values yet also avoids the reactionary fanaticism that will later consume it under the stress of persecution. Marius, he tells us,

> had lighted, by one of the peculiar intellectual good-fortunes of his life, upon a period when, even more than in the days of austere *ascêsis* which had preceded and were to follow it, the church was true for a moment, truer perhaps than she would ever be again, to that element of profound serenity in the soul of her Founder, which reflected the eternal goodwill of God to man ... the minor "Peace of the church," as we might call it, in distinction from the final "Peace of the church," commonly so-called, under Constantine ... [which,] in many ways, does but establish the exclusiveness, the puritanism, the ascetic gloom which, in the period between Aurelius and the first Christian emperor, characterised a church under misunderstanding or oppression, driven back, in a world of tasteless controversy, inwards upon herself. (3:118–19)

This Christianity is minor but not oppositional, neither digging in its heels against a persecuting society nor enjoying the rights of legitimate violence. Its Dissenting edge, rather, comes from the fact that its many-sidedness always exceeds whatever philosophical system happens to carry the day. As such, it is a site at which strange new possibilities will take shape—not in Marius's lifetime, nor perhaps even in Pater's, but eventually.

5

National Supernaturalism
Andrew Lang, World Literature, and the Limits of Eclecticism

Folk tales "point, beyond all doubt, to rude efforts on the part of primitive man to realize to himself the phenomena of nature by personifying them and attaching to them explanatory fables"; they represent "the flotsam and jetsam of the ages, still beating feebly against the shore of the nineteenth century," and once they have "died out" they "will never again be heard on the hillsides, where they probably existed for a couple of thousand years . . ."[1] These words, published in 1890, would seem to epitomize the outlook of Victorian evolutionary anthropology. Folk tales, the writer tells us, are not the property of particular races or nations but instead draw upon the stock of archaic beliefs, particularly animism, that all human beings held at one time. This is why "man, all the world over, when he is tired of the actualities of life, seeks to unbend his mind with the creations of fantasy."[2] Yet this passage was not written by the sort of liberal imperialist who usually took up E. B. Tylor's evolutionism, but rather by Douglas Hyde, Irish folklorist, champion of spoken Gaelic, and, from 1938 to 1945, the first President of the Republic of Ireland. In effect, Hyde was inverting the standard polemic of literary nationalism that Herder had established in the eighteenth century. Instead of portraying the Irish literary voice as ethnically distinct, he was presenting it as the best modern articulation of humankind's primitive religious unconscious. Nor was he alone. As Gregory Castle and others have shown, although evolutionary anthropology had originally been developed to discredit concepts of national or racial identity, by the end of the nineteenth century it had become a tool by which the likes of Hyde, J. M. Synge, and William Butler Yeats asserted the unique significance of Ireland to world

---

[1] Douglas Hyde, *Beside the Fire: A Collection of Irish Gaelic Folk Stories* (London, UK: David Nutt, 1890), xxxvi, x, xli–xlii.
[2] Ibid., ix.

literature.[3] For these writers, calling the Irish voice a survival of "the ancient religion of the world" allowed them to present it both as singular in character and as universal in its appeal.[4] Like Arnold and Eliot, they were using the mediating term of religion to imagine how ethnic inheritance might feed into a cosmopolitan modernity.

This chapter takes up the case of the writer who, perhaps more than any other, lay the groundwork for this move: Andrew Lang. Born in the border country of Scotland and trained in Classics at Oxford, where he attended Matthew Arnold's lectures and ran in aestheticist circles, Lang went down to London in 1874 to enter the burgeoning periodical market and would soon become one of the most prolific and contradictory figures in Victorian letters.[5] In a literary career that spanned four decades, Lang published critical essays, translations of French ballads and Greek poetry, adventure novels, essays in anthropology, and, most famously of all, a series of fairy-tale collections known as the Colored Fairy Books: *The Blue Fairy Book* (1889), *The Red Fairy Book* (1890), *The Green Fairy Book* (1892), and many more. Nathan Hensley has called him a cultural "mediator," "an agent of connection" who linked different strands in a literary network, and indeed his work has a way of pulling together the various strains in this study: the mid-Victorian anthropological debates of Prichard and Müller, the Oxbridge aestheticism of Arnold and Pater, and Eliot's world of literary periodicals.[6] Most notably for our purposes, Lang did much to popularize Tylor's new evolutionary anthropology and in fact used Tylor's doctrine of "survivals" to wage a literary polemic on behalf of the imperial gothic fiction of H. Rider Haggard and Robert Louis Stevenson.[7] The appeal of such

[3] See Mary Helen Thuente, *W. B. Yeats and Irish Folklore* (Totowa, NJ: Gill and Macmillan, 1980); John Hutchinson, *The Dynamics of Cultural Nationalism: The Gaelic Revival and the Creation of the Irish Nation State* (London, UK: Allen and Unwin, 1987); Stephen Regan, "W. B. Yeats and Irish Cultural Politics in the 1890s," in Sally Ledger and Scott McCracken (eds.), *Cultural Politics at the Fin de Siècle* (London, UK: Routledge, 1995), 66–84; Gregory Castle, *Modernism and the Celtic Revival* (New York, NY: Cambridge UP, 2001), 1–97; Sinéad Garrigan Mattar, *Primitivism, Science, and the Irish Revival* (New York, NY: Oxford UP, 2004).

[4] W. B. Yeats, "The Celtic Element in Literature," *Cosmopolis* 10 (1898): 677.

[5] The best overviews of Lang's life can be found in Roger Lancelyn Green, *Andrew Lang* (Leicester, UK: Ward, 1946) and Eleanor De Selms Langstaff, *Andrew Lang* (Boston, MA: Twayne, 1978). For Lang and Arnold, see Eric Sharpe, "Andrew Lang and the Making of Myth," *Ethnography is a Heavy Rite: Studies of Religion in Honor of Juha Pentikäinen*, ed. Juha Pentikäinen, Nils G. Holm, and Hannu Kilpeläinen (Helsinki, Finland: Åbo Akademi, 2000), 59–60.

[6] Nathan Hensley, "What is a Network? (And Who Is Andrew Lang?)," *RaVON* 64 (October 2013), paragraph 5—citing Bruno Latour, *We Have Never Been Modern*, trans. Catherine Porter (1991; Cambridge, MA: Harvard UP, 1993), 81.

[7] See Robert Michalski, "Towards a Popular Culture: Andrew Lang's Anthropological and Literary Criticism," *Journal of American Culture* 18.3 (1995): 13–17. For broader

new-fashioned romance, according to Lang, was that it resonated with those relics of primal religiosity—animism, belief in magic, belief in spirits—that persisted deep within the modern psyche. We enjoy "the books of the railway stall" in addition to "the old books, the good books, the classics," he wrote in the *Contemporary Review*, "because the barbaric element has not died out of our blood, and because we have a childish love of marvels, miracles, man-eating giants, women who never die, 'murders grim and gray,' and Homer's other materials."[8]

In promoting writers who spoke to the savage survivals buried within the modern self, Lang was ostensibly distancing himself from both Romantic racialism and aesthetic liberalism, the two strains of thought that the previous authors in this study had wound together. He dismissed the thesis that particular stories belonged to certain races or nations by insisting that folk tales from Kenya to Finland all expressed a savage consciousness that was universal in its aesthetic appeal. But he also rejected the high aestheticism of Arnold and Pater, with its Oxonian hauteur, for an omnivorous kind of many-sidedness that could relish primordial folk-lore and modern pulp fiction alongside the poems of Virgil or Milton. Nevertheless, the fact is that Lang's work very much follows that of Arnold, Pater, and Eliot in conflating religion with race so as to make it a resource for a many-sided individuality. As Lang saw it, in order for primitive literary survivals to give the modern self a true heterogeneity, they had to represent pure products of an alien worldview, an occult state of mind that was fundamentally out of place in the nineteenth century. In this way, I will argue, the otherness of primitive religiosity comes to take over the role that race has played in Arnold: that of guaranteeing for modernity an internal heterogeneity that cannot be rationalized away. Just as Arnold had used racial polygenesis to dramatize a project of cultural hybridity, so would Lang leverage the essential alienness of folk tales to enhance a modern eclecticism. Race and religion once again blur into each other as religion becomes something whose intransigence captures the frisson of ethnicity without attendant notions of cultural property.

Lang's peculiar return to a rhetoric of Romantic authenticity would give him a highly mixed legacy as the nineteenth century gave way to the twentieth. On the one hand, as I have suggested, it would prove founda-tional for the work of Yeats and his fellow travelers in the Irish Literary

---

accounts of the imperial gothic, see Patrick Brantlinger, *Rule of Darkness: British Literature and Imperialism, 1830–1914* (Ithaca, NY: Cornell UP, 1988); John McClure, *Late Imperial Romance* (New York, NY: Verso, 1994); Gail Chang-Liang Low, *White Skins/Black Masks: Representation and Colonialism* (London, UK: Routledge, 1996).

[8] Andrew Lang, "Realism and Romance," *Contemporary Review* 52 (1887): 684, 689.

Renaissance, who learned from Lang that presenting the Irish voice as the echo of a universal occult sensibility allowed one to frame Irish folk literature as simultaneously articulating a culturally distinct point of view *and* informing a global literary modernism. On the other hand, Lang's tendency to inflect Tylorian evolutionism with the language of Romantic authenticity alienated him from British anthropology at the precise moment when it was becoming a respectable academic discipline. Not only did it discourage Lang from embracing newer accounts of folklore as the product of textual diffusion and appropriation, but it also pushed him to advocate the still more dubious position that folklore offered modern readers insight into actual supernatural phenomena: ghosts, extrasensory perception, telepathic powers. To Lang's mind, the best way to grant folklore an essential otherness was to consider that it might bear witness to dimensions of reality for which science could not yet account. Although Lang still features prominently in many histories of anthropology, his work—not unlike that of his old rival, Max Müller—was too Romantic, too eclectic, and too dilettantish for a discipline just beginning to garner mainstream respectability. (As it happens, Lang was the last major figure in British anthropology not to hold a university post. The anthropologist R. R. Marret once recalled an aging Lang grumbling that he could have become a "really big 'swell' in anthropology" had it been an actual profession.[9])

I end this study with Lang because his work, taken as a whole, suggests some of the wider resonances that many-sidedness, as a secularist ethos, would have in the twentieth century and beyond. Arnold and Pater, as we have seen, were constantly trying to distinguish their ethics of many-sidedness from the bourgeois liberalism of the marketplace; Lang, by contrast, explicitly transformed many-sidedness into a middlebrow eclecticism of picking and choosing. In his hands, many-sidedness defines simultaneously a personal aestheticism and a sweet tooth for mass culture, an unabashed commercialism and a Romantic amateurism, an interest in the social sciences and a credulous supernaturalism. What is more, I argue, Lang's way of detaching the frisson of Romantic authenticity from ideas of national or racial property produces a now-familiar kind of pop spirituality in which specific cultural objects become liquidated into universal spiritual currency. Viewed from a century hence, Lang shows how many-sidedness could inspire not just Pater's religion of art, or Eliot's dialectical historicism, but also the idea that religion and ethnicity were spiritual commodities available to an eclectic, literary self through

[9] George Stocking, *Victorian Anthropology* (New York, NY: Free P, 1987), 263. See also R. L. Green, 74.

popular fiction and occult media. In all this Lang corroborates Jonathan Freedman's suggestion that aestheticism's lasting power lay in its failure to fully distinguish itself from middle-class culture, and it is in this light that Lang's own shortcomings as both a critic and an anthropologist should be judged.[10]

FOLKLORE THEORY FROM RACE TO EVOLUTION

The enterprise that the Victorians first dubbed "folklore" took shape in England during the seventeenth century as aristocratic gentlemen and Anglican clergy began to collect old stories and songs from among the rural poor.[11] Some early compilations of "popular antiquities" nostalgic-ally celebrated the manners and sentiments of a bygone England; Thomas Percy's *Reliques of Ancient English Poetry* (1765), for instance, would have an important impact upon the later ballad revivalism of Samuel Taylor Coleridge and Walter Scott.[12] Most early antiquarian collections, how-ever, had a strongly iconoclastic bent. Henry Bourne's *Antiquities Vulgares* (1736), for example, presented popular tradition as a tissue of "heathen errors renewed and enlarged by the medieval church" and hoped, by bringing them to light, to hasten their demise.[13] Bourne's text would provide the basis for John Brand's *Observations on Popular Antiquities* (1777), which was later reworked by Sir Henry Ellis into the most influential antiquarian compendium of the late eighteenth and early nine-teenth centuries, *Observations on Popular Antiquities: Chiefly Illustrating the Origin of Our Vulgar Customs, Ceremonies and Superstitions* (1813).[14]

Although the Brand-Ellis mode of antiquarianism had few direct links to eighteenth-century conjectural history, the two traditions did have overlapping agendas. Both balanced the impulse to condemn lingering forms of irrational thought against a more sympathetic curiosity about their persistence. As Brand remarked, it was fascinating to observe how the beliefs and customs of the "Common People" had somehow managed to "furvive the Reformation" and other "Shocks, by which even Empires have been overthrown," "out-liv[ing] the general Knowledge of the very

---

[10] Jonathan Freedman, *Professions of Taste: Henry James, British Aestheticism and Com-modity Culture* (Stanford, CA: Stanford UP, 1990), 3.
[11] William John Thoms coined the term "folk-lore" in a letter to the *Athenaeum* in 1846. See Richard Dorson, *The British Folklorists: A History* (Chicago, IL: U of Chicago P, 1968), 1, 80–1; and, more broadly, Philippa Levine, *The Amateur and the Professional: Antiquarians, Historians and Archaeologists in Victorian England, 1838–1886* (New York, NY: Cambridge UP, 1986).
[12] Dorson, 2.   [13] Ibid., 12.   [14] Ibid., 13–25.

Caufes that gave rife to them."[15] In this last phrase particularly Brand seems to anticipate Tylor's theory of survivals, as did John Aubrey when he argued that the natives of North America offered an image of the savagery once inhabited by prehistoric Britons.[16]

If antiquaries like Brand and Aubrey are seldom remembered today, it is because their early version of folklore studies would be dramatically eclipsed toward the end of the eighteenth century by a Romantic-nationalist model of folklore that took identity rather than history as its object of study. James Macpherson's Ossian poems, whatever their subsequent notoriety in the history of literary fraud, played a key role in this change. In 1760, Macpherson published a collection of *Fragments of Ancient Poetry, Collected in the Highlands of Scotland*, followed soon after by *Fingal* (1761) and *Temora* (1763), all purportedly the work of the ancient bard Ossian.[17] As Joep Leerssen notes, Macpherson's shift in titles—from taxonomic labels to proper names—reveals a metamorphosis in the antiquary's work from the hunting of historical relics to the wholesale recovery of a representative national voice.[18] Indeed, it was chiefly the experience of reading Michael Denis's German translation of Macpherson that moved Johann Gottfried von Herder, that seminal theorist of Romantic nationalism, to argue in his "Extract from a Correspondence about Ossian and the Songs of Ancient Peoples" (1773) that the works of bards like Ossian, Homer, and Shakespeare were the media through which the *Geist* of a people attained articulation.[19]

Herder was responding to a Germany whose population was divided both territorially and religiously and whose aristocracy tended to disdain regional dialects in favor of French. In his mind, recovering and publishing authentic German folk tales represented the first step toward generating a national consciousness that would enable state-formation.[20] Herder's claims, and his own volume of *Volkslieder* (1778–79), would resonate widely, inspiring such volumes as Ludwig Tiecke's *Minnelieder aus dem*

---

[15] John Brand, *Observations on Popular Antiquities* (Newcastle-upon-Tyne, UK: T. Saint, 1777), v, iv, iii. See Dorson, 13–25.

[16] Stuart Piggott, *Ruins in a Landscape: Essays in Antiquarianism* (Edinburgh, UK: Edinburgh UP, 1976), 112.

[17] For an overview, see Joep Leerssen, "Ossian and the Rise of Literary Historicism," *The Reception of Ossian in Europe*, ed. Howard Gaskill (New York, NY: Continuum, 2004), 109–25.

[18] Ibid., 125.

[19] William A. Wilson, "Herder, Folklore, and Romantic Nationalism," *The Journal of Popular Culture* 6.4 (1973): 821; Bruce Lincoln, *Theorizing Myth: Narrative, Ideology, and Scholarship* (Chicago, IL: U of Chicago P, 2000), 232.

[20] For the political background to folklore studies in Germany, see Uli Linke, "Folklore, Anthropology, and the Governance of Social Life," *Comparative Studies in Society and History* 32.1 (1990): 117–48.

Schwäbischen Zeitalter (1803), Clemens Brentano's and Achim von Arnim's *Des Knaben Wunderhorn* (1805–08), and above all Jacob and Wilhelm Grimm's seminal collection of *Kinder-und-Hausmärchen* (1812–15). Over the next two decades, similar collections would emerge from across the disorganized territories of Eastern Europe thanks to the Slovaks Jan Kollár and Pavel Josef Šafárik, the Czech nationalist František Ladislav Čelakovský, the Serb Vuk Karadžić, and the Pole Kazimierz Boratyński. In Finland, Elias Lönnrot went so far as to collate a broad collection of folk songs into a new national epic, the *Kalevala*, in 1835.[21]

Within Great Britain, despite the ignominious shadow cast by the Ossian controversy, Scottish and Irish folklorists would spend the early decades of the nineteenth century zealously striving to follow the Grimms' model. Walter Scott's *Minstrelsy of the Scottish Border* (1802–03), published in the wake of the Act of Union, was only the most celebrated of dozens of texts that sought to become touchstones of what Katie Trumpener has called "survival in destruction."[22] In Scotland, Allan Cunningham published several collections of rural traditions, including *Remains of Nithsdale and Galloway Song* (1810) and *Traditional Tales of the English and Scottish Peasantry* (1822); Robert Chambers brought out collections like *Popular Rhymes of Scotland* (1826) and *Scottish Jests and Anecdotes* (1832); and Hugh Miller's *Scenes and Legends of the North of Scotland* (1838) offered "a pioneer collection of local narratives . . . seen in their full context of village society and history."[23] Among Irish folklorists, Thomas Crofton Croker's *Fairy Legends and Traditions of the South of Ireland* (1825) set a new benchmark for field collections, while Thomas Keightley, who had aided Croker in his tale-gathering, would follow suit with his own *Fairy Mythology* (1828) and *Tales and Popular Fictions* (1834).[24] But perhaps the most accomplished Celtic folklorist in mid-Victorian Britain was John Francis Campbell of Islay, whose four-volume *Popular Tales of the West Highlands, Orally Collected* (1860–62) derived from years of fieldwork and came, in Richard Dorson's estimation, remarkably close to matching the achievement of the Grimms.[25]

By the mid-Victorian years it was, a bit curiously, Max Müller who in England had become most strongly associated with this ethnocentric way of reading folklore. Although Müller, as we have seen in Chapter 1, rejected the thesis that different mythologies expressed the spirits of distinct races, his work did much to popularize the notion that England

---

[22] Katie Trumpener, *Bardic Nationalism: The Romantic Novel and the British Empire* (Princeton, NJ: Princeton UP, 1997), 8.
[23] Dorson, 140; see 118–52.   [24] Ibid., 44–57.   [25] Ibid., 393–401.

owed its rich store of folk tales to its ancient Indo-European birthright and thus became loosely associated with a certain kind of Romantic nationalism.[26] In volumes such as *The Mythology of the Aryan Nations* (1870), disciples of Müller like George William Cox and Robert Brown documented the existence of single folklore tradition extending from the modern English nursery back into Indian antiquity.[27]

This race-based approach to folklore would be challenged in the 1870s by the rise of E. B. Tylor's evolutionary anthropology. For Tylor, folk tales represented neither unique racial utterances, nor fragments of deformed language, but in fact survivals of archaic human belief. Tylor himself was hesitant to attack Müller directly, preferring instead to present to his approach as being complementary to the German's: "Progress, degradation, survival, revival, modification, are all modes of the connexion that binds together the complex network of civilization."[28] The real assault on Müller's thesis would come from Andrew Lang, who became Tylor's bulldog in much the same way that Thomas Huxley had been Darwin's. During his years at Oxford, first as a Snell Exhibition fellow at Baliol College and later on an Open Fellowship at Merton College from 1868 to 1874, Lang ran in aestheticist circles and began to dabble in traditional French ballad forms, as evinced in 1872's *Ballads and Lyrics of Old France* and 1884's *Rhymes à la Mode*. This interest in ballad literature, however, also steered Lang toward the study of cultural survivals and hence the work of Tylor, whose acquaintance he made in 1872.[29] As his career moved beyond Oxford and into the world of London literary journalism, Lang would become a fierce advocate of the survival theory of mythology and a vocal opponent of Müller's old decay-of-language thesis.[30]

---

[26] Tomoko Masuzawa notes how odd it is that Müller has frequently been the poster-boy for versions of Romantic race theory he never really supported. A chief source of the confusion is the scholarly legend that he was responsible for coining "Aryan" as a politically charged substitute for the hyphenated "Indo-European." See *The Invention of World Religions* (Chicago, IL: U of Chicago P, 2005), 208, 242–3.

[27] See Dorson, 174–81.

[28] E. B. Tylor, *Primitive Culture: Researches Into the Development of Mythology, Philosophy, Religion, Language, Art, and Custom* (2 vols.; London, UK: John Murray, 1871), 1: 16. Despite this conciliatory tone, Tylor fundamentally disputed whether language had played a meaningful role in the creation of myths, writing that "I am disposed ... differing here in some measure from Professor Max Müller's view of the subject ... [to] take material myth to be the primary, and verbal myth to be the secondary formation" (1:271).

[29] See Robert Crawford, "Pater's Renaissance, Andrew Lang, and Anthropological Romanticism," *ELH* 53.4 (1986): 849–79; Andrew Lang, "Edward Burnett Tylor," *Anthropological Essays Presented to Edward Burnett Tylor in Honour of His 75th Birthday, Oct. 2, 1907* (Oxford, UK: Clarendon, 1907), 1–2.

[30] For overviews of Lang's debates with Müller, see Dorson, 206–12; Eric L. Montenyohl, "Andrew Lang's Contribution to English Folk Narrative Scholarship,"

Lang initiated the hostilities with an essay entitled "Mythology and Fairy Tales," published in the *Fortnightly Review* in 1873. The German, Lang insisted, had arranged the sequence of literary history upside-down. Where Müller held that centuries of oral transmission had caused the high nature-myths of the ancient Aryans to degenerate first into classical mythology and thence into the *Märchen* of European peasants, Lang took the global ubiquity of certain tales to suggest that they actually represented the raw materials out of which more polished myths and epics had developed. "[F]ar from being the detritus of a higher mythology," he wrote, those "low" or "savage" stories preserved an ancient condition of the human mind that gave credence "to magic, or Shamanism, to kinship with the beasts, and to bestial transformations."[31] While "civilised peoples," he continued, "have elaborated these child-like legends into the chief Romantic myths, as of the Ship Argo, and the sagas of Heracles and Odysseus," still "[u]ncivilised races, Ojibbeways, Eskimo [sic], Samoans, retain the old wives' fables in a form far less cultivated—probably nearer the originals."[32]

Inverting Müller's model of literary history, Lang argued, allowed one to solve two problems that had bedeviled traditional philology. First, it explained why European folk tales so strongly resembled stories from Africa or Polynesia, whose languages had experienced no ancient contact with the Indo-European tongues. The likeness, Lang argued, resulted from the fact that "[s]imilar conditions of mind" inevitably "produce similar practices, apart from identity of race, or borrowing of ideas and manners."[33] Versions of the Grimms' "Goose Girl," for instance, could be found upon multiple continents either because "the West Highlanders, and Zulus, and Germans got their story from the old French" or because "there are necessary forms of the imagination, which in widely separated peoples must produce identical results"; he let the reader decide which seemed more likely.[34] Second, Lang argued, Tylor's evolutionary model helped account for the fact that classical myths, the supposed cornerstone of the Western literary imagination, featured conspicuously barbaric elements. Homer's epics contained episodes that scandalized modern readers because they had been built out of older narratives that expressed primitive ideas about the kinship between humans and animals or the

Western Folklore 47.4 (1988), 270–8; Sharpe; Marjorie Wheeler-Barclay, *The Science of Religion in Britain, 1860–1915* (Charlottesville, VA: U of Virginia P, 2010), 115–18.

[31] Lang, "Mythology and Fairy Tales," *Fortnightly Review* 13 (1873): 620.

[32] Lang, "Literary Fairy Stories," introduction to Frederik Van Eeden, *Little Johannes* (1887), trans. Clara Bell (London, UK: William Heinemann, 1895), v, vi.

[33] Lang, *Custom and Myth*, (London, UK: Longmans, Green, 1884), 21–2.

[34] Lang, "Mythology and Fairy Tales," 622.

inner life of objects.[35] In his introduction to Margaret Hunt's edition of *Grimm's Household Tales* (1884), for instance, Lang produced a chart of such ideas and their parallel manifestations in both savage and European narratives:

1. SAVAGE IDEA.
Belief in kinship with Animals.

Savage Tale.	*European Tale.*
Woman marries an elephant.	Man weds girl whose brothers
Woman marries a whale.	are ravens.
Woman gives birth to crows.	Queen accused of bearing puppies
Man marries a beaver.	or cats.
Girl wooed by frog.	Girl marries a frog.
Girl marries serpent.	Girl marries a tick.
	[...]

7. SAVAGE IDEA.
Husband and wife are forbidden to see each other, or to name each other's names.

Savage Tale.	*European Tale.*
Wife disappears (but not apparently	Husband or wife disappear
because of infringement	when seen, or when the
of taboo).	name is named. (These
Wife disappears after infringement	acts being prohibited by
of taboo.	savage custom.)
	[...]

9. SAVAGE IDEA.
Human strength, or soul, resides in this or that part of the body, and the strength of one man may be acquired by another who secures this part.

Savage Tale.	*European Tale.*
Certain giants take out their hearts	The giant who has no heart in
when they sleep, and are	his body.
overcome by men who secure	The man whose life or force depends
the hearts.	on a lock of hair, and is lost
	when the hair is lost.[36]

---

[35] Lang, *Myth, Ritual and Religion* (2 vols.; London, UK: Longmans, Green, 1887), 1: 255–326.

[36] Lang, "Introduction. Household Tales; Their Origins, Diffusion, and Relation to the Higher Myths," *Grimm's Household Tales*, trans. Margaret Hunt (vol. 1 of 2; London, UK: George Bell and Sons, 1884), lvii–lvix.

Elsewhere in the same essay, Lang enumerated the many plot parallels between the Jason cycle, the Finnish *Kalevala*, and Henry Callaway's collection of *Nursery Tales, Traditions, and Histories of the Zulus* (1868).[37]

Folklore, in short, was not a patchwork of linguistic confusions but rather the articulation of a unique worldview that had once underpinned the "religious imagination" of peoples everywhere.[38] Such a claim would make Lang's and Tylor's work attractive to Sigmund Freud, whose *Totem and Taboo* (1913) cited both in arguing that the culture of the civilized bore a deep connection to that of so-called savages.[39] In its more immediate Victorian context, Lang's work took up the project, anticipated by Pater's *Greek Studies*, of primitivizing the classical—that is, reimagining Greek mythology as the missing link between high Western civilization and the savagery that it so often defined itself against. This notion becomes a satirical device in much of Lang's short fiction. In a story entitled "The End of Phaecia," a missionary named Thomas Gowles finds himself shipwrecked upon an island that harbors the last remnants of classical Greek culture. After making an ethnographic survey of the islanders' customs, barely escaping a sacrificial fire, and then wiping out the natives with a disease, Gowles describes his ordeal to the head of the Classical Department at the British Museum:

> When I described the sacrifice I saw on landing in the island, he exclaimed, "Great Heavens! The Attic Thargelia." He grew more and more excited as I went on, and producing a Greek book, "Pausanias," he showed me that the sacrifice of wild beasts was practiced sixteen hundred years ago in honour of Artemis Elaphria....When I had finished my tale, he burst out into violent and libelous language. "You have destroyed," he said, "with your miserable modern measles and Gardiner guns, the last remaining city of the ancient Greeks. The winds cast you on the shore of Phaecia, the island sung by Homer; and, in your brutal ignorance, you never knew it. You have ruined a happy, harmless, and peaceful people, and deprived archaeology of an opportunity that can never return!"[40]

The joke here is not simply that Gowles's evangelical Philistinism is oblivious to the difference between ancient Greece and modern Polynesia—he considers subsequent archaeological expeditions to the island "a shameful waste of public money," given "so many darkened

---

[37] Ibid., xlvii–xlviii.   [38] Lang, "Mythology and Fairy Tales," 620.

[39] For the connections between Lang, Tylor, and Freud, see Kathy Alexis Psomiades, "Hidden Meaning: Andrew Lang, H. Rider Haggard, Sigmund Freud, and Interpretation," *RaVON* 64 (October 2013); Peter Melville Logan, *Victorian Fetishism: Intellectuals and Primitives* (Albany, NY: SUNY P, 2010), 115–36.

[40] Lang, "The End of Phaecia," *In the Wrong Paradise, and Other Stories* (London, UK: Kegan Paul, Trench, 1886), 105–6.

people still ignorant of our enlightened civilization"—but also that the modern insistence upon that difference is perhaps even less credible.[41] In dismissing these classical Greeks as mere savages, Gowles attains an insight that the museum head, who valorizes them as uniquely precious relics, cannot: that their sort of culture is ubiquitous and ordinary, rather than a special phenomenon of Western civilization.

By 1878, Lang had gathered around himself a group of like-minded researchers who formed the core of a new organization called the London Folk-Lore Society.[42] The Society initiated a journal, the *Folk-Lore Record*, and soon eclipsed the Anthropological Institute as a center of anthropological theorizing.[43] Like the old Ethnological Society of the 1840s, it consisted largely of middle-class professionals who pursued antiquarian and scientific research in their free hours. Alfred Nutt worked primarily as a publisher in London and printed a series of *Popular Studies in Mythology, Romance and Folk-Lore* designed to promote the findings of folklore for a wider audience.[44] No less than Lang, Nutt strongly opposed racial readings of folk tales, writing that there was a "grave difference of opinion . . . between those who consider the chief object of folk-lore to be the reconstruction of particular chapters in the past history of the race, and those who regard it as the study of certain psychical phenomena of man in a particular stage of culture."[45] Edwin Sidney Hartland, a solicitor in Swansea, took a similarly hard Tylorian line, arguing that the incidents in folk tales were "not arbitrary or capricious, but the logical result of principles accepted by a people in the state of savagery."[46] George Laurence Gomme, who worked for London's Metropolitan Board of Works, was an ardent "exhorter, encourager, organizer, and promoter of folklore researches," while Edward Clodd, a banker and friend of Herbert Spencer, authored anthropological primers for children such as *The Childhood of the World* (1872) and *The Childhood of Religions* (1896).[47]

Although Müller would see his brand of comparative mythology lose ground to evolutionism, he also proved an astute critic of the new paradigm's shortcomings. For one thing, he criticized the evolutionists' habit of cherry-picking second-hand observations about non-European peoples that fit their preconceptions of how savages should think and

---

[41] Ibid., 106.

[42] Dorson, in his bid to construct a canon of British folklore scholarship, calls Lang's circle the "Great Team"; see 202–5.

[43] Stocking, *Victorian Anthropology*, 262.   [44] Dorson, 229–39.

[45] Alfred Nutt, "Recent Archaeological Research II," *Archaeological Review* 3 (1889): 74.

[46] E. S. Hartland, *Folklore: What Is It, and What Is the Good of It?* (London, UK: David Nutt, 1904), 27. See Dorson, 239–48.

[47] Dorson, 224, 248–57.

behave. "When we read some of the more recent works on anthropology," he observed in the *Nineteenth Century*, "the primordial savage seems to be not unlike one of those hideous India-rubber dolls that can be squeezed into every possible shape, and made to utter every possible noise."[48] In the days of Rousseau, he noted, European travelers had returned home with reports of noble savages; today, "partly owing . . . to a desire of finding the missing link between man and monkeys, descriptions of savages . . . abound which ma[ke] us doubt whether the Negro was not a lower creature than the gorilla."[49] Müller also accused Lang and the Folk-Lore Society of being dilettantes who made ambitious pronouncements about "the customs and myths of people whose language they do not understand" and who would have done well to "confine their critical remarks to the languages of which they know at least the alphabet and grammar."[50] It was certainly interesting to argue "that the Fijians . . . look upon shooting stars as the departing souls of men," but before comparing this belief to what seemed like parallel traditions in other societies, one needed first to understand what exactly it meant within the local dialect.[51] Yet in spite of Müller's criticisms—many of which would be repeated by anthropologists in the twentieth century—the evolutionary view of folklore began to gather clout, thanks in no small part to the wider literary and cultural narrative that Lang would build around it.

LANG, PRIMITIVISM, AND MANY-SIDED POPULISM

Lang's advocacy in the *Fortnightly* and other journals would help evolutionary anthropology gain widespread intellectual currency during the 1870s and '80s.[52] Yet at no point were Lang or Tylor arguing anything that had not been maintained, in a broad sense, by conjectural historians during the eighteenth century. For Lang, at least, the urgency behind this anthropological polemic came from its connection to a contemporary controversy about the function of modern literature: the so-called "romance and realism" debates between adventure novelists like H. Rider Haggard

---

[48] F. Max Müller, "The Savage," *Nineteenth Century* 17 (1885): 111.

[49] Müller, *Lectures on the Origin and Growth of Religion* (London, UK: Longmans, Green, 1878), 91.

[50] Müller, *Contributions to the Science of Mythology* (2 vols.; London, UK: Longmans, Green, 1897), 1: 24, 1: xxvi.

[51] Müller, *Lectures on the Origin and Growth of Religion*, 87.

[52] See Stocking, *After Tylor: British Social Anthropology, 1888–1951* (Madison, WI: U of Wisconsin P, 1995), 50–63.

and proponents of realist fiction such as Henry James and William Dean Howells.[53] These debates were a response to the unprecedented expansion of the reading public instigated by the Elementary Education Act of 1870 and the fragmentation of the literary market that it helped produce.[54] With more and more readers consuming ever-cheaper materials, the question arose of exactly what sort of literature would best cultivate the new reading masses, and would frequently be answered in the language of evolutionary social science.[55] James and Howells, for their part, argued that a more factual, even scientific style of novel could help train the public in the ways of modern rationality and discourage the childish mental tendencies endemic to sensation fiction or historical romances. In "The Art of Fiction" (1884), James lamented that modern novels had been "vulgarised" by the "overcrowding" of the market and by a focus on "happy endings," while Howells insisted that the modern reader needed to relinquish the juvenile preference for linear storytelling and learn to make sense of psychological narratives instead.[56]

Lang, meanwhile, belonged to a group of writers who defended the new genre fiction by maintaining that it preserved primitive elements worth retaining in the modern world. Haggard, for example, argued in the *Contemporary Review* that "the love of romance is probably coeval with the existence of humanity," resonating equally among "savage races" and in "the cultured breast," while Lang insisted that "the whole of the poetic way of regarding Nature" was a "savage survival."[57] Though "the Coming Man may be bald, toothless, highly 'cultured,' and addicted to tales of introspective analysis,"

[53] For an overview, see Anna Vaninskaya, "The Late-Victorian Romance Revival: A Generic Excursus," *English Literature in Transition, 1880–1920* 51.1 (2008): 57–79; for Lang's place in the debates, see Joseph Weintraub, "Andrew Lang: Critic of Romance," *English Literature in Transition* 18.1 (1975): 5–15.

[54] On the connection between the Victorian romance revival and the expansion of the literary market, see N. N. Feltes, *Literary Capital and the Late Victorian Novel* (Madison, WI: U of Wisconsin P, 1993) and Nicholas Daly, *Modernism, Romance, and the Fin de Siècle* (New York, NY: Cambridge UP, 1999).

[55] See Stephen Arata, *Fictions of Loss in the Victorian Fin de Siècle* (New York, NY: Cambridge UP, 1996), 89–95; Julia Reid, *Robert Louis Stevenson, Science, and the Fin de Siècle* (London, UK: Palgrave, 2006); Christine Ferguson, *Language, Science, and Popular Fiction in the Victorian Fin-de-Siècle: The Brutal Tongue* (Burlington, VT: Ashgate, 2006), 47–70.

[56] Henry James, "The Art of Fiction" (1884), in *Partial Portraits* (London, UK: Macmillan, 1899), 383; see W. D. Howells, "Henry James, Jr.", in Ulrich Halfmann, Donald Pizer, and Ronald Gottesman (eds.), *Selected Literary Criticism* (3 vols.; Bloomington, IN: Indiana UP, 1993), 1: 317–23.

[57] H. Rider Haggard, "About Fiction," *Contemporary Review*, 51 (1887): 172; Lang, "Realism and Romance," 690.

I don't envy him when he has got rid of that relic of the ape, his hair; those relics of the age of combat, his teeth and nails; that survival of barbarism, his delight in the last battles of Odysseus, Laertes' son... [T]he natural man within me, the survival of some blue-painted Briton or of some gypsy, was equally pleased with a *true* Zulu love story, sketched in two pages, a story so terrible, so moving, in the long, gallant fight against odds, and the awful unheard-of death-agony of two Zulu lovers, that I presume no civilized fancy could have invented the incidents that actually occurred.[58]

Similar pleasures, Lang continued, could be found in Stevenson, whose gift "is not only to have been a fantastic child, and to retain, in maturity, that fantasy ripened into imagination," but also to have "kept up the habit of dramatising everything, of playing, half consciously, many parts, of making the world 'an unsubstantial fairy place.'"[59] Reading Charles Kingsley requires that "we must be boys again," while Dickens's practice of describing humans as object-like (and vice-versa) recalls Tylor's thesis that "early man, and simple natural men, and children, regard all nature as animated... transfer[ing] to all things in the universe the vitality of which they are conscious themselves."[60]

Lang, in short, took up Tylor for the very un-Tylorian (and distinctly Paterian) reason that he liked survivals and wished to see more of them in modern literature. In so doing, he established a precedent for modernists like T. S. Eliot and D. H. Lawrence, who would parlay Tylor's account of the occult continuities between modern and savage mentalities into literary projects that broke with Victorian realist decorum.[61] Unlike some twentieth-century primitivists, however, Lang's goal was not an atavistic return to a more primal state of being but instead an ethos of many-sidedness. As against the Hebraism of the realist novel, with its "minute portraiture of modern life and analysis of modern character," so "limited in scope, and frequently cramped in style," Langian romance, like Arnoldian culture, seeks to use the differential pressure of otherness to create space for heterogeneity within the modern character.[62] J. W. Burrow notes how, in

[58] Lang, "Realism and Romance," 689.
[59] Lang, "Mr. Stevenson's Works," *Essays in Little* (New York, NY: Scribner, 1891), 25.
[60] Lang, "Charles Kingsley," *Essays in Little*, 159; "Charles Dickens," *Fortnightly Review* 6 (December 1898): 947–8.
[61] For overviews, see Michael Bell, *Primitivism* (London, UK: Methuen, 1972); John B. Vickery, *The Literary Impact of the Golden Bough* (Princeton, NJ: Princeton UP, 1973); Marc Manganaro, *Culture, 1922: The Emergence of a Concept* (Princeton, NJ: Princeton UP, 2002).
[62] "Realism and Romance," 688. In an essay entitled "The Evolution of Literary Decency" Lang would argue that the triumph of didacticism and realism in Victorian fiction reflected both "the rise of a larger reading middle class" (368) and the evangelical movement. "The Evolution of Literary Decency," *Blackwood's Edinburgh Magazine* 167 (1900): 363–70.

the classical model of *Bildung*, the "most cultivated individual[s]...are the ones which can most successfully assimilate and most fully contain the various cultural and moral commitments...entered into by mankind in the course of history," including "the primitive and poetic virtues of earlier civilizations,"[63] and this was more or less Lang's take on the matter. "Fiction," Lang wrote, "is a shield with two sides, the silver and the golden: the study of manners and of character, on one hand," and "on the other, the description of adventure, the delight of Romantic narrative."[64] What was necessary was not to elect one over the other but rather to affirm that "we might have many delights, among others 'the joy of adventurous living,' and of reading about adventurous living."[65] "The advantage of our mixed condition, civilized at top with the old barbarian under our clothes," Lang concluded, is "that we can enjoy all sorts of things."[66] The Lang writing here is the one who had been swept up in the Swinburne craze of the 1860s, whose early *Ballads in Blue China* had followed the revival "of old French ballad forms into English verse that had begun with the Villon translations of Swinburne and Rossetti," and of whom George Saintsbury ventured that "[no]body, undergraduate or don, Oxonian or Cantab., about the year 1869 possessed" more "knowledge of ancient and modern literature, coupled with power to make use of it in a literary way."[67]

Lang also, however, turned the Arnoldian version of many-sidedness on its head by making it a rationale for omnivorous pop-culture consumption. If many-sidedness was an ethos ambiguously poised between pluralism and elitism—celebrating the variety of human experience, but also privileging a certain detachment from it—Lang inclined toward the former extreme.[68] Writing that "the world will not take Mr. Matthew Arnold's advice about neglecting the works of our fleeting age," Lang argued that, "[h]owever much we may intellectually prefer the old books, the good books, the classics, we find ourselves reading the books of the railway stall."[69] In an essay on Mark Twain, meanwhile, he confessed that "I have lived with the earliest Apostles of Culture, in the days when Chippendale was first a name to conjure with, and Japanese art came in like a raging lion, and Ronsard was the favourite poet, and Mr. William Morris was a poet too, and blue and green were the only wear...And

[63] J. W. Burrow, introduction to Wilhelm von Humboldt, *The Limits of State Action*, trans. Burrow (New York, NY: Cambridge UP, 1969), xxi.

[64] Lang, "Realism and Romance," 684.   [65] Ibid., 689.

[66] Ibid., 690.   [67] R. L. Green, 33, 61, 53.

[68] For more on this ambiguity, see Christine Bolus-Reichert, *The Age of Eclecticism: Literature and Culture in Britain, 1815–1885* (Columbus, OH: The Ohio State UP, 2009), 6–7.

[69] Lang, "Realism and Romance," 683, 684.

yet ... I find myself delighting in a great many things which are under the ban of Culture."[70] In this sense Lang's work renders explicit what Daly takes to be a suppressed theme of the Victorian romance revival: that such fiction was a product of mass culture instead of a holdout against it.[71] The romance that Lang defended was, in Anna Vaninskaya's words, "a commodity in an increasingly fragmented mass market," a result of "the economics of publishing, the material methods of book production and distribution," and in particular "[t]he triumph of the cheap one-volume first edition, aided by methods of modern advertising."[72] Lang found it extremely apt that William Morris should have made the Icelandic Sagas available "for a shilling," since they reflected above all the tastes of "the people."[73]

The populist bent with which Lang inflected the idea of many-sidedness also made him especially keen to avoid Arnold's language of racial character. In an 1897 essay on the Celtic literary renaissance, Lang criticized Arnold's *Study of Celtic Literature* on the grounds that deriving the melancholy poetic strain in the English character from the Celtic blood in the population not only flew in the face of ethnological evidence but also unnecessarily limited the reach of his claims. If Arnold had happily detached "Hebraism" and "Hellenism" from actual racial inheritances, then why not do this with the Celts? "If [the Englishman] could get the Greek way, untaught of and undescended from Greeks, why in the world should he not be born with the Celtic way, with no aid from a drop of Celtic blood? Shakespeare had 'the Greek note' as well as 'the Celtic note' ... "[74] The value of such qualities, Lang continued, lay in their universality as remnants of a primal savagery that knew no ethnic provenance. The nature-mysticism often attributed to the Celts, for example, was just as evident in the mythology of the Iroquois or Zulus, because in reality "every savage—the Maori, the Red Indian, the Zulu—is as full of second sight as any man of Moidart."[75] "What is called 'Celtic' in poetry or in superstition is really early human," and what had kept the Irish or the Welsh from turning their oral traditions into a great modern literature was not the inefficacy of Celtic sentiment but in fact colonialism: "Their development ... was diverted by Christianity, and stunted by foreign conquest. Their educated classes were Anglicised, or Frenchified. They never enjoyed the chances of Greece, Rome, France, Italy, Germany, Spain, and England ... "[76]

[70] Lang, "The Art of Mark Twain," *The Illustrated London News* 98 (1891): 222.
[71] Daly, 9.   [72] Vaninskaya, 58–9.
[73] Lang, "The Sagas," *Essays in Little*, 147, 151.
[74] Lang, "The Celtic Renascence," *Blackwood's Edinburgh Magazine* 161 (1897): 183.
[75] Ibid., 188.   [76] Ibid., 188, 191.

Lang's populist inflection of many-sidedness would give his work another quality that differentiated it from modernist primitivism: a profoundly anti-formalist prejudice. Where T. S. Eliot's primitivism viewed myth as a deep structure that could restore order to a fragmented modern world, Lang pictured modernity as a cramped space that needed disruption from without.[77] For this reason Lang was reluctant to equate "romance" with any particular formal structures and instead associated it with a quality of mind that chafed at the restrictions of bourgeois rationality. Although his chart of folklore motifs, cited above, bears some resemblance to Vladimir Propp's well-known lists of folk tale functions, it actually purports to bear witness to the universality of certain ideas rather than to the ubiquity of discrete formal units.[78] For this reason J. R. R. Tolkien, delivering the annual Andrew Lang Lecture at the University of St. Andrews in 1938, would fault Lang for privileging the cultural contents over the aesthetic forms of folk tales.[79] Yet Lang's preoccupation with folklore's content *was* an aesthetic choice, since in his mind the pleasure of an old story came from the sense that it offered a window onto a radically other way of being. Realism was a kind of structural formula, but romance was an experience of release from literary and social structures. As Lang put it in an 1888 essay in the *St. James Gazette*, savage romance "admits us into the region where men are more brave and women more beautiful, and passions more intense than in ordinary experience."[80]

Hence the strange fact that, although Lang typically defined romance as a plot-driven genre—"the simple 'yarn'," "stories told for the story's sake"—his emphasis was less on plot as a formal element than upon a certain mindset provoked by absorption in linear narrative.[81] In the words of Stevenson's "Gossip on Romance" (1882), romance should be so "absorbing and voluptuous" that it leaves us "rapt clean out of ourselves":

> Crusoe recoiling from the footprint, Achilles shouting over against the Trojans, Ulysses bending the great bow, Christian running with his fingers in his ears, these are each culminating moments in the legend, and each has been printed on the mind's eye forever. Other things we may forget; we may

---

[77] See T. S. Eliot, "Ulysses, Order, and Myth," *The Dial* 75.5 (1932): 480–3.

[78] See Vladimir Propp, *Morphology of the Folktale*, ed. Louis A. Wagner and trans. Lawrence Scott (1958; Austin, TX: U of Texas P, 1968).

[79] J. R. R. Tolkien, "On Fairy Stories" (1939), *The Tolkien Reader* (New York, NY: Ballantine Books, 1966), 18, 31.

[80] Cited in Weintraub, 9.

[81] Lang, "A Dip in Criticism," *Contemporary Review* 54 (1888): 500; "Realism and Romance," 689.

forget the words, although they are beautiful; we may forget the author's comment, although perhaps it was ingenious and true.[82]

Romance, in Christine Ferguson's paraphrase, produces a kind of "linguistic amnesia" that directs our attentions away from the particulars of a text and toward iconic images that hypostasize in the mind's eye.[83] For Lang, the function of such literature was to direct the reader beyond bookish immersion and toward an imagined world of direct action. Modern romancers, he argued,

> have, at least, seen new worlds for themselves; have gone out of the streets of the over-populated lands into the open air; have sailed and ridden, walked and hunted; have escaped from the fog and smoke of the towns. New strength has come from fresher air into their brains and blood... [T]hey have found so much to see and to record, that they are not tempted to use the microscope, and to pore for ever on the minute in character.[84]

Thus defined, romance ironically comes to look a lot like realism insofar as it aims for an immediacy to life beyond the "unhealthy" mediations of form and convention. This is why Lang would define the Saga simply as a literary mode marked by "true pictures... of strange customs and lost beliefs," and claim that Haggard's novels possessed an undeniable "*vraisemblance*" thanks to their author's "practical knowledge and experience of savage life and wild lands."[85]

THE ROMANTICISM OF SURVIVALS AND THE NEW DIFFUSIONISM

In short, Lang's work points toward the manifold connections between aestheticism, an expanding print market, and *fin de siècle* commodity culture. At once an Oxford aesthete, an unabashed populist, and a canny commercializer—someone who frequently decried *Yellow Book* decadence but whose 1887 *Aucassin and Nicolete* was released in "550 small and 60 large paper copies, printed in red and black on Japanese vellum, with etched title-page and other decorations by Jacomb Hood"[86]—Lang reminds us that, in Jonathan Freedman's phrase, aestheticism was part of an emerging "culture of consumerism" as well as "the growth in organization, sophistication, and extensiveness of the

---

[82] Robert Louis Stevenson, "A Gossip on Romance," *Longman's Magazine* 1 (1882): 69, 72.
[83] Ferguson, 57.   [84] Lang, "Mr. Kipling's Stories," *Essays in Little*, 200.
[85] Lang, "The Sagas," *Essays in Little*, 142; "She," *The Academy* 83 (1912): 274–5.
[86] R. L. Green, 118.

mass-circulation press."[87] Aestheticism, for Freedman, represents an attempt to take stock of the clutter of modernity, not through some radically new Positivist regime, but instead through an essentially middle-class ethos of personal taste-making.

Lang's populist posture, however, was undercut by a certain tendency, which he shared with Arnold, to overfetishize those illiberal energies that his criticism purported to contextualize and situate. Both Lang and Arnold were constructing imperialist aesthetics that imagined how a many-sided modernity might be enhanced by absorbing narrower traits like the sentimentality of the Celt, the moralism of the Semite, or the imaginativeness of the Tylorian savage. But in both cases what is ostensibly an eclectic willingness to experience "many delights" becomes a highly mimetic form of desire. Arnoldian culture, as we have seen, not only incorporates Hebraism's "fire and strength" but also comes to mirror its intolerance. Lang's eclecticism, meanwhile, is possessed by a longing not just to recuperate but also to return to a kind of savagery. In his defining account of "imperial gothic" fiction, Patrick Brantlinger argued that romance-revivalists like Lang were riven by "anxieties about the ease with which civilization can revert to barbarism," but in fact Lang and his fellow travelers embraced that possibility quite openly.[88] Where Lang had relished "the old barbarian under our clothes" and fretted that the "Coming Man" would be "bald, toothless, highly 'cultured,' and addicted to tales of introspective analysis," Haggard would dedicate *Nada the Lily* (1892) to Sompsen, who had once earned the respect of three thousand Zulu warriors by telling them "that for every drop of blood they shed of his, a hundred avengers should rise from the sea," thus demonstrating "that white heroes have as savage a splendor as they."[89] In such moments, Gail Chang-Liang Low shows, England's imperial success is imagined to hinge upon an ability to mirror back the virtues of those it has conquered.[90] Or, in Lang's phrase, "Not for nothing did Nature leave us all savages under our white skins."[91]

This narrowing tendency within Lang's vision of many-sidedness—its inclination to revel in a stereotypical primitivism that it ostensibly regards as but one side of fiction—has attracted much comment from postcolonial critics of children's literature.[92] For our purposes, the key thing to

---

[87] Freedman, 52, 51.   [88] Brantlinger, 229.

[89] Martin Green, *Dreams of Adventure, Deeds of Empire* (London, UK: Routledge, 1980), 231.

[90] See Low, 1–9.   [91] Lang, "Romance and Realism," 689.

[92] See Anna Smol, "The 'Savage' and the 'Civilized': Andrew Lang's Representation of the Child and the Translation of Folklore," *Children's Literature Association Quarterly* 21.4 (1996): 177–83; Sarah Hines, "Collecting the Empire: Andrew Lang's Fairy Books (1889–1910)," *Marvels and Tales* 24.1 (2010): 39–56. For similar readings of Victorian

recognize is that it implicitly subverts Lang's populist polemic by celebrating the savage's *un*popularity. Supposedly Lang's primitive represents a facet of popular taste that will inevitably prevail against elite opinion, but in actuality Lang more often seems to value him insofar as, like Arnold's Celt, he stands on the losing side of history, and is therefore able to give modernity something that it cannot generate within itself. As Harold Orel puts it, Lang's work expressed a "basically...Jacobite" sympathy for the lost cause, "the little against the big, the one against the multitude."[93] Hence his strange habit of portraying many of his favorite authors as *outré* curiosities instead of wildly successful commercial artists. "I do not anticipate for Mr. Kipling a very popular popularity," Lang wrote in one early review; for "his favorite subjects are too remote and unfamiliar for a world that likes to be amused with matters near home and passions that do not stray far from the drawing-room or the parlor...He is not in tune with our modern civilization, whereof many a heart is sick; he is more at home in an Afghan pass than in the Strand."[94] Along similar lines, Lang described Haggard's *She* as reading like "the perished literature of some lost and wandering star, some world unlike ours," and dubbed Stevenson, whose consummate professionalism Lang knew well, "an amateur of boyish pleasures" who had tossed off *Treasure Island* "by way of mere diversion and child's play."[95]

Indeed, Lang's valorization of an unpopular otherness in the DNA of romance carried a distinct whiff of the Romantic ethnocentrism he had ostensibly disavowed. Brad Evans has argued that Victorian evolutionary anthropology shared with the racial anthropology it supplanted a tendency to essentialize folk tales as the receptacles of a rare consciousness belonging only to certain peoples, and Lang's work certainly provides evidence for this claim.[96] In Lang's work, the concept of savage psychology effectively recapitulates the function of racial spirit in explaining particular culture formations as the repositories of a "lost authenticity" (to borrow James

---

children's literature generally, see Jacqueline Rose, *The Case of Peter Pan, or The Impossibility of Children's Fiction* (London, UK: Macmillan, 1984); Jo-Ann Wallace, "De-Scribing *The Water-Babies*: 'The Child' in Post-Colonial Theory," in Chris Tiffin and Alan Lawson (eds.), *De-Scribing Empire: Post-colonialism and Textuality* (London, UK: Routledge, 1994), 171–93; and Bill Ashcroft, "Primitive and Wingless: The Colonial Subject as Child," in Wendy S. Jacobson (ed.), *Dickens and the Children of Empire* (London, UK: Palgrave, 2000), 184–202.

[93] Harold Orel, *Victorian Literary Critics* (London, UK: Macmillan, 1984), 133; see also R. L. Green, 111.

[94] "Andrew Lang on Rudyard Kipling," *The Review of Reviews* 2 (1890): 217.

[95] Lang, "A Dip in Criticism," 499; "Mr. Stevenson's Works," 29.

[96] Brad Evans, *Before Cultures: The Ethnographic Imagination in American Literature, 1865–1920* (Chicago, IL: U of Chicago P, 2005), 69.

Clifford's phrase).[97] In particular, Lang's universal primitive often reads like a proxy for the Highland chieftain of Walter-Scott Romanticism. Scott remained his favorite touchstone for those qualities that he felt were becoming scarce in modern literature—"for my part," he wrote, "I think and hope that Scott can never die, till men grow up into manhood without ever having been boys"—and he persistently attributed Stevenson's "power of touching us with a sense of the supernatural," "his gay courage," and above all the "eternal child" in him to his border-country roots.[98] The savage impulse in romance, which Lang typically celebrates in the language of populism, here feels attached to a specifically identitarian form of nostalgia.

In more pragmatic terms, Lang's implicit association of the savage with lost authenticity transformed his customary anti-formalism into a deep pessimism regarding the very literary projects he advocated. Throughout Lang's criticism, for instance, his demand that modern novelists produce more romance is shadowed by a persistent skepticism toward their capacity to do so, since romance, as Lang understands it, resides in an endangered quality of mind instead of in some replicable formal structure. Literary savagery is not a trope to be learned or adapted but rather a quality of being that, once gone, can never be regained. Where T. S. Eliot's "mythic method" and Haggard's imperial romance were both prescriptive programs for redeeming society through literature, Lang cautioned that "there can be...no Romantic school."[99] For while "[a]ny clever man or woman may elaborate a realistic novel according to the rule," romance "bloweth where she listeth," and "education will never restore the power of uttering verses such as those which Shakespeare and Goethe, and even Euripides, it is said, have deigned to borrow from the popular store."[100]

In particular, Lang would frequently cast doubt upon the genre of the *Kunstmärchen*, or literary fairy tale. "We can never quite recover the old simplicity, energy, and romance" of the original *Hausmärchen*, he wrote in his introduction to Clara Bell's translation of Frederick Van Eeden's *Little Johannes* (1895), a modern Dutch fairy tale.[101] This theme even runs through what remain the most commercially enduring productions of Lang's career, the so-called Colored Fairy Books that he released each

[97] James Clifford, *The Predicament of Culture: Twentieth-Century Ethnography, Literature, and Art* (Cambridge, MA: Harvard UP, 1988), 4.

[98] Lang, "The Poems of Walter Scott," *Essays in Little*, 180; "Mr. Stevenson's Works," 25. For more on Lang, Stevenson, and their self-consciously Scottish milieu, see Robert Crawford, *Devolving English Literature* (1992; Edinburgh, UK: Edinburgh UP, 2000), 151–75; Penny Fielding, *Writing and Orality: Nationality, Culture, and Nineteenth-Century Scottish Fiction* (Oxford, UK: Clarendon, 1996), 132–52.

[99] Lang, "Realism and Romance," 691.

[100] Ibid.; "French Peasant Songs," *Cornhill* 33 (1876): 608.

[101] Lang, "Introduction" to *Little Johannes*, xv–xvi.

Christmas for the lucrative holiday book market.[102] Roger Lancelyn Green credits Lang's series with reviving the popularity of the fairy tale genre in the Anglo-American world, and it is certainly true that, with their Henry J. Ford illustrations, they were beautifully designed objects that remain highly collectible over a century later.[103] But in fact the series is shot through with a kind of fatalistic self-deprecation. Each volume opens with an introduction in which Lang simulates a comic dialogue between child readers and himself; the children greedily demand more stories each year, causing Lang to confess that he cannot create new tales to tell, only trek farther afield in the global archive to find them. In the introduction to *The Violet Fairy Book* (1901), Lang notes that he "is accustomed to being asked, by ladies, 'Have you written anything else except the Fairy Books?'" and must always explain that "he is not the author of the stories in the Fairy Books... [H]e did not invent them 'out of his own head,'" even though, "save these, [he] has written almost everything else, except hymns, sermons, and dramatic works."[104] Lang's introduction to *The Lilac Fairy Book* (1910) declares that "nobody can write a new fairy tale... only mix up and dress up the old,"[105] while his introduction to *Little Johannes* explains that there is a significant difference between the unconscious processes that produced the original fairy tales and the artifice that in modern times has sought to construct new ones:

> The slow evolution of romance is all unlike what occurs when a poet chooses some wild-flower of popular lore, and cultivates it in his garden, when La Fontaine, for example, selects the Fable; when the anecdote is developed into the *fabliau* or the *conte*, when Apuleius makes prize of *Cupid and Psyche*... when Fenelon moralises the fairy tale, or Madame d'Aulnoy touches it with courtly wit and happy humor, or when Thackeray burlesques it, with a kindly mockery, or when Dr. Frederik van Eeden, or Dr. MacDonald, allegorises the nursery narratives.[106]

Moralizing, allegorizing, mockery, burlesque: all represent forms of commentary after the fact. Such is also the approach of Lang's own excursions into the *Kunstmärchen* genre, including *The Princess Nobody* (1884), *The Gold of Fairnilee* (1888), and *Prince Prigio* (1889), whose characters are often self-consciously aware of the rules that govern their literary world.

[102] See Glenn S. Burne, "Andrew Lang's *The Blue Fairy Book*: Changing the Course of History," *Touchstones: Reflections on the Best in Children's Literature* (3 vols.; West Lafayette, IN: Children's Literature Association, 1987), 2: 140–50.

[103] See Seth Lerer, *Children's Literature: A Reader's History, from Aesop to Harry Potter* (Chicago, IL: U of Chicago P, 2008), 220.

[104] Lang, *The Violet Fairy Book* (London, UK: Longmans, Green, 1901), vii.

[105] Lang, *The Lilac Fairy Book* (London, UK: Longmans, Green, 1910), viii.

[106] Lang, "Introduction," *Little Johannes*, vii–viii.

In *Prince Prigio*, a king is seeking a way to dispose of his eldest son, Prigio, and so sends his three sons off to fight a dragon in full knowledge that, as these stories go, the youngest is bound to succeed. But Prigio understands the narrative conventions of his world too, and thus manipulates his Quixotic younger brothers by declaring that he does not believe in fire drakes, allowing the two siblings to charge off to their doom.[107] Later in the story, after being given a set of magical clothes against his knowledge, Prigio proves too rationalistic to take their magic seriously: "the Prince was so extremely wise, and learned, and scientific, that he did not believe in fairies, nor in fairy gifts. 'It is indigestion,' he said to himself: 'those sausages were not of the best; and that Burgundy was extremely strong. Things are not as they appear.'"[108]

What emerges in such texts is the figure of the editor as the paragon of Langian many-sidedness. By assuring his readers that he was "the Editor and not the author of the Fairy Tales, just as a distinguished man of science is only the Editor, not the Author of Nature," Lang was imagining a self that did not create new ideas but rather took inheritances from the past and creatively arranged them.[109] Statements like these have led critics in recent years to reappraise Lang as a figure who allows us to think about literary production in ways that dispense with the vaunted figure of the solitary creator-genius. As Jonah Siegel notes, Lang's understanding of creativity as the recuperation of survivals seems to anticipate postmodern critiques of the originary author, as well as accounts of literature as the product of networks.[110] Thus Letitia Hemans shows how Lang's evolutionary view of literary history liberated the modern writer from proprietary notions of plagiarism, while Molly Clark Hillard compares Lang to the collector of Walter Benjamin's *Arcades Project* (1927–40).[111] But the key thing to notice here is that Lang tended to view his brand of eclecticism as a form of diminished or second-hand creativity. Lang did not appreciate his own practice as a freewheeling celebration of printed commodities but instead viewed it as a parodic version of the ancient bard's comprehensiveness. His late volume on Tennyson, for example, argues that "the life and work of Tennyson present something like the

---

[107] Lang, *Prince Prigio* (Bristol, UK: J. W. Arrowsmith, 1889), 19–25.
[108] Ibid., 44.
[109] Lang, *The Crimson Fairy Book* (London, UK: Longmans, Green 1903), v.
[110] Jonah Siegel, "Lang's Survivals," *RaVON* 64 (October 2013).
[111] Hensley; Letitia Henville, "Andrew Lang's 'Literary Plagiarism': Reading Material and the Material of Literature," *RaVON* 64 (October 2013); Molly Clark Hillard, "Trysting Genres: Andrew Lang's Fairy Tale Methodologies," *RaVON* 64 (October 2013), paragraphs 8, 10. All three essays appear in a special issue of *Romanticism and Victorianism on the Web*, "The Andrew Lang Effect," edited by Hensley, which considers how Lang's account of survivals, disciplinarity, and literary networking reflects upon questions of authorial agency.

normal type of what . . . the life and work of a modern poet ought to be": "because even poetry now is affected by the division of labor," he explained, "[w]e do not look to the poet for a large share in the practical activities of existence: we do not expect him, like Aeschylus and Sophocles, Theognis and Alcaeus, to take a conspicuous part in politics and war; or even, as in the Age of Anne, to shine among wits and in society. Life has become, perhaps, too specialised for such multifarious activities."[112] The great irony of his career is that his vision of many-sidedness opened up an enthusiastic participation in 1880s–90s print culture while also rendering him skeptical toward its ultimate possibilities.

Lang's sense of belatedness ultimately led him to take the losing side of certain key discussions that began to percolate within the Folk-Lore Society during the 1890s. Chief among these was a renewed debate over diffusion as a major folklore paradigm. From its beginnings, the Society had been defined by its opposition to Müller and his thesis that mythology represented the product of linguistic migration. With Müller's views now largely *passé*, however, there emerged room within the Society for younger members to revisit the idea that diffusion, and in particular textual diffusion, was responsible for the worldwide ubiquity of certain stories.[113] Lang's fellow Scot William Clouston, for instance, produced a substantial body of work that documented the transmission of written folk tales from Asia to Europe during the late medieval period. In essays on the Arabian Nights and in translations of shorter texts like *The Book of Sindibad* (1884) and *The Tale of Beryn* (1887), Clouston built a convincing case that many European folk tales were really "secondary forms of Oriental originals" that had been imported as texts instead of orally.[114] Moses Gaster, a Romanian rabbi living in London, argued that most European folk tales had originated not in the oral lore of ancient peoples but rather in printed collections such as the *Pantchatantra*, which had been translated from Arabic and Syrian into Greek and thence dispersed throughout Europe some time after the tenth century.[115] But arguably the most

---

[112] Lang, *Alfred Tennyson* (Edinburgh, UK: Blackwood, 1901), 1. Like Homer, whose status as a historical figure Lang would address in a full volume, Lang himself was subject to rumors that he was a fabrication whose works had in fact been produced by multiple, anonymous hands. See George Gordon, "Andrew Lang" (1927), *Concerning Andrew Lang: Being the Andrew Lang Lectures Delivered Before the University of St. Andrews, 1927–1937* (Oxford, UK: Clarendon P, 1949), 4.

[113] For an overview of this second wave of Society folklorists, see Dorson, 266–315.

[114] W. A. Clouston, *Popular Tales and Fictions: Their Migrations and Transformations* (2 vols.; London, UK: Blackwood, 1887), 1:2. See Dorson, 257–65.

[115] Dorson, 273–5. See Moses Gaster, *Ilchester Lectures on Greeko-Slavonic Literature and Its Relation to the Folk-Lore of Europe during the Middle Ages* (London, UK: Trübner, 1887), and "The Modern Origin of Fairy-Tales," *Folk-Lore* 5 (1887): 339–51.

vocal advocate of the new diffusionism was Joseph Jacobs, a Sydney-born Jewish historian who joined the Folk-Lore Society during the 1880s. Like Lang, Jacobs was an accomplished man of letters whose output included journalism, literary reviews, and a series of fairy-tale books that, according to Dorson, "rivaled that of Lang in appeal and exceeded his in scholarship": *English Fairy Tales* (1890), *Celtic Fairy Tales* (1892), *Indian Fairy Tales* (1892), and others.[116] Jacobs also edited scholarly editions of such globetrotting narratives as *The Fables of Aesop* (1889, 1894) and *The Most Delectable History of Reynard the Fox* (1895).[117]

What we see emerging in Clouston and Jacobs is diffusion as a third way for folklore, a paradigm that avoided the essentialism of both race and evolution and enabled a more literary approach to folk tales. Like Müller before them, Clouston and Jacobs challenged Lang's view that such tales offered unmediated access to an endangered condition of the human mind by showing how they had arisen through modern processes of borrowing, adaptation, and exchange. Unlike Müller's largely speculative etymology, however, Clouston's and Jacobs's method drew substantially upon modern archival evidence. Given the prominence of Lang within the Folk-Lore Society, many of the new diffusionists chose to downplay this emerging clash of perspectives, but Jacobs threw down the gauntlet in a paper on "The Science of Folk-Tales and the Problem of Diffusion" which he delivered at the first International Folk-Lore Congress in London in 1891. Lang's practice of mining folk tales for survivals, Jacobs argued, showed inadequate regard for the tales as literary productions, for "to study *them* is not to study the tale."[118] Moreover, he continued, deriving folklore from savage psychology did less to explain its contemporary appeal than Lang thought. After all, "English children of the last century adopted from Perrault the story of *Puss in Boots*, but they did not therefore believe in talking animals."[119] The reality, according to Jacobs, was that such tales had spread so widely because their "fantastic elements" appealed to the imagination and the willing suspension of disbelief.[120]

Jacobs's work, with its focus on diffusion over comparative national categories or universal genealogies, bears a certain resemblance to world-literature scholarship in our own day.[121] In the immediate context of the

---

[116] Dorson, 269.   [117] Ibid., 266–70.

[118] Joseph Jacobs, "The Science of Folk-Tales and the Problem of Diffusion," *The International Folk-Lore Congress, 1891: Papers and Transactions*, ed. Joseph Jacobs and Alfred Nutt (London, UK: David Nutt, 1892), 76.

[119] Ibid., 79.   [120] Ibid.

[121] See, for example, the essays collected in Antoinette Burton and Isabel Hofmeyr (eds.), *Ten Books That Shaped the British Empire: Creating an Imperial Commons* (Durham, NC: Duke UP, 2015).

1890s it set off a series of debates over the theoretical orientation of the Folk-Lore Society.[122] Many of Lang's colleagues were attracted to the new diffusionism insofar as it opened up a more exciting archive than Tylor's practice of collating second-hand missionaries' and travelers' reports. Indeed, one might think that textual diffusion, as a paradigm, would have appealed to Lang, since it made folklore look like an object of popular circulation in line with the proverbial "books of the railway stall." Lang himself, however, mustered considerable resistance to Jacobs's model because it denied that folk tales were relics of a savage mentality at all.[123] Lang had opposed Müller because he wanted folklore to be rooted in a certain condition of mind, not the freaks and sports of circulating language, and he now opposed Jacobs for the same reason. As in the case of his anti-formalism, and his skepticism about *Kunstmärchen*, Lang's actual populist practice was undercut by a Romantic cult of lost authenticity. Despite all his interest in survivals and in the circulation of cultural artifacts, he could not abide a view of folk tales as *mere* circulating objects that lacked any essential connection to a deep and differential past.

As Jacobs's star continued to rise, however, it behooved Lang to gradually allow textual diffusion a greater role in the global spread of folk tales.[124] Seemingly in compensation, however, he also began to alter his account of folklore's origins so as to reconstitute its alterity on grounds that diffusion could not affect. Folk tales, for the late Lang, increasingly represented not expressions of savage superstition but rather witnesses to genuine supernatural phenomena: actual ghosts, actual second sight, actual extrasensory perception. These were not new interests for Lang, who had co-founded London's Society for Psychical Research in 1882.[125] In the context of his debate with Jacobs, however, they slowly became the driving force behind his interest in folklore. In an 1893 essay in the *Contemporary Review* entitled "Superstition and Fact," Lang suggested that the worldwide popularity of certain folk tales might be taken as evidence of hitherto unrecognized human mental powers. The ubiquity of fairy tales worldwide, he argued, stemmed not just from "similar phenomena of culture" but also from "similar abnormal experiences."[126] Lang offered an example of this new method the next year in *Cock Lane and Common-Sense* (1894), a collection

---

[122] Dorson, 298–311.
[123] See, for instance, Lang's debate with Jacobs over the origins of "Cinderella": Lang, "Introduction," Marian Roalfe Cox, *Cinderella: Three Hundred and Forty-five Variants* (London, UK: The Folk-Lore Society, 1893), vii–xxiv; Jacobs, "Cinderella in Britain," *Folk-Lore* 6 (1893): 269–84.
[124] See *The Orange Fairy Book* (London, UK: Longmans, Green, 1906), vi–vii.
[125] See Dorson, 212–16.
[126] Lang, "Superstition and Fact," *Contemporary Review* 64 (1893): 887.

of essays that compared modern European reports of "'ghosts,' 'wraiths,' 'second-sight,' and clairvoyance" to motifs in folklore, concluding that "[m]an may have faculties which savages recognise, and which physical science... often cast[s] aside as a survival of superstition."[127] Lang admitted that, while the evidence was still on the side of Tylor's animism-hypothesis, he was now inclined to leave the door open to alternatives. "[T]he most plausible theory" as to the origins of supernatural belief remained that "our savage ancestors were subject to great mental confusion"; yet who could say with certainty "that Lord Crawford, Sir David Brewster, Mr. Crookes, Mr. Hamilton Aide, and many others, were deceived by conjuring (on all occasions), or saw tables and people float about in the air, because of the traditional influence exercised by savage hallucinations"?[128]

Cock Lane provoked an angry rebuttal from Folk-Lore Society President Edward Clodd, whose 1895 Presidential Address denounced Lang for tarnishing the field he had once labored to make respectable.[129] The fact is, however, that Lang's attempt to root folklore in supernatural phenomena was simply his most creative attempt to construe it as something that enhanced modernity from within. If it was now much harder to claim that folk tales preserved unblemished traces of primitive psychology, then reimagining them as witnesses to occult marvels still allowed them to expand the purview of a many-sided self.[130] As Lang wrote in his "Notes on Ghosts" (1890), moderns find themselves attracted to ghost stories because "[w]e still long for a margin undiscovered, where hope and romance may dwell."[131]

YEATS'S OCCULT UNIVERSALISM

This chapter has placed Andrew Lang in a line of Victorian prose writers who rethought the relationship between religion, race, and individuality through the idea of many-sidedness. Like Arnold, Eliot, and Pater before

---

[127] Lang, *Cock Lane and Common-Sense*, (London, UK: Longmans, Green, 1894), 29, 338.
[128] Ibid., xiv, xv.
[129] Edward Clodd, "Presidential Address," *Folk-Lore* 6 (1895): 54–82; see Dorson, 215–16. On Lang's willingness to jeopardize the respectability of early anthropology by cross-fertilizing it with even less established bodies of knowledge, see Roger Luckhurst, "Knowledge, Belief and the Supernatural at the Imperial Margin," in Nicola Bown, Carolyn Burdett, and Pamela Thurschwell (eds.), *The Victorian Supernatural* (New York, NY: Cambridge UP, 2004), 197–216.
[130] For occultism as supplementary to modernity, see Alex Owen, *The Place of Enchantment: British Occultism and the Culture of the Modern* (Chicago, IL: U of Chicago P, 2007); Michael Saler, "Modernity and Enchantment: A Historiographic Review," *The American Historical Review* 111.3 (2006): 692–716.
[131] Lang, "Notes on Ghosts," *Forum* 10 (1890): 452.

him, Lang imagined that the survivals of ancient religion could feed an eclectic modern individuality. But, as we have also seen, Lang's variation on the theme began to work against him as the turn of the century approached. As an anthropologist, Lang's resistance to the new diffusionism and his attempt to use psychical research to explain the origins of folklore (he once styled himself a "psycho-folklorist") found him ever more isolated in anthropological and folklore circles after 1900.[132] As a literary critic, meanwhile, his insistence that modern readers should recover and enjoy "primitive" literature increasingly became a kind of middlebrow reductivism that won him ridicule among literary tastemakers. Although elements of his thinking anticipate some of the more adventuresome directions of modernism, particularly primitivism, he ultimately found himself resistant to all such newfangled literary projects and was, in turn, shunned by their exponents. Henry James, in an 1888 letter to Robert Louis Stevenson, complained that "Lang, in the *Daily News*, every morning, and I believe in a hundred other places, uses his beautiful thin facility to write everything down to the lowest level of Philistine twaddle," while to Edmund Gosse he dismissed Lang's "'cultivation'... of the puerile imagination and fourth-rate opinion."[133]

Viewed from a century's distance, however, Lang's polemic for many-sidedness turns out to have had a peculiar endurance as a way of thinking about religion and ethnicity as resources for modernity. Freedman maintains that aestheticism, as an enterprise, succeeded through a certain failure, insofar as it ultimately became part of the cultures of professionalism and commodification that it seemed to reject.[134] Lang in many ways exemplifies this pattern, for in fact his failure to become either a respectable anthropologist or a proto-modernist allowed his work to inform a now-familiar way of commodifying ethnic particularity under the sign of universal occult spirituality. As it happens, the closing decades of the nineteenth century would see a wave of new folk tale collections that stressed both the distinctly Celtic character of the tales and the notion that they bore witness to a supernatural world. Such collections were the product of a revived literary nationalism along the Celtic fringe and included Jeremiah Curtin's *Tales and Fairies of the Ghost World* (1895), D. E. Jenkins's *Beddgelert, Its Facts, Fairies, and Folk-Lore* (1899), Lady Jane Wilde's *Ancient Legends, Mystic Charms, and Superstitions of Ireland* (1887), and, most famously, the early work of W. B. Yeats, Isabella Augusta, Lady Gregory, and

---

[132] See Lang, "Protest of a Psycho-Folklorist," *Folklore* 6 (1895): 236–48.
[133] R. L. Green, 157.   [134] Freedman, 3.

J. M. Synge.[135] During the 1880s Yeats came under the influence of the nationalist activist John O'Leary, who directed him toward folklore studies, and in particular Arnold's lectures on Celtic literature.[136] He soon began publishing collections like *Fairy and Folk Tales of the Irish Peasantry* (1888) and *Irish Fairy Tales* (1892), which drew upon "the writings of... socio-cultural evolutionists such as James Frazer, Andrew Lang, Alfred Nutt, and Edward Clodd."[137] Gregory developed an interest in Irish folklore after she, like Yeats, took up Republican politics, and would spend the closing years of the century gathering folklore in County Galway and publishing them in *A Book of Saints and Wonders* (1906) and *The Kiltartan Wonder Book* (1910).[138] The playwright and poet Synge conducted ethnographic research on the Aran Islands during the 1890s and used it to argue in his *Aran Islands Journal* (1907) that beneath the islanders' nominal Catholicism lay a much deeper substratum of paganism.[139]

Exactly what chord had Lang struck? In effect, his late work showed that identifying folklore with primitive occult consciousness could solve what Trumpener identifies as a basic challenge of literary nationalism: presenting literary materials as distinctive while also defining their relevance to a larger world.[140] Or, in *Daniel Deronda*'s phrase, balancing separateness with communication. By framing folk tales as windows onto an occult religiosity at the origins of all human culture, Lang was able to continue insisting that they represented talismans of some premodern mindset without also limiting their interest. This move, as John and Jean Comaroff have shown, has become foundational to so-called New Age spirituality in our own day. In effect, New Age attempts to translate ethnic alterity into universal occult currency through a process of simultaneous spiritualization and commodification. It first abstracts a culture into some ostensibly universal spiritual essence and then attaches that essence to specific commodities like Native American dream-catchers or Japanese Zen tea sets, which can be marketed as resources for the metropolitan consumer's self-development.[141]

In the hands of the Irish Literary Renaissance, however, this same move offered a way to blend the rhetorics of authenticity and universalism by identifying Irishness with a universal occult instinct. As John Hutchinson has shown, Yeats and his circle sought not to reanimate some primordial Gaelic civilization but rather "to create a synthetic Anglo-Irish nation,

---

[135] See Dorson, 392–439.   [136] Hutchinson, 130–1.   [137] Mattar, 17–18.
[138] Ibid., 185–239.   [139] Ibid., 130–84.   [140] Trumpener, 166.
[141] See John L. and Jean Comaroff, *Ethnicity, Inc.* (Chicago, IL: U of Chicago P, 2009), 12; and, for a more general account, Paul Heelas, *The New Age Movement: The Celebration of the Self and the Sacralization of Modernity* (Oxford, UK: Blackwell, 1996).

which would provide Ireland with a cultural mission within the world English-language civilization now emerging" as well as reconcile literary nationalism with a liberal politics rooted in their ties to the Irish Protestant Ascendancy.[142] Their strategy, in effect, was to use Langian folklore theory to shift the locus of national identity from Irish land, Gaelic dialect, and Roman Catholicism onto a generic supernaturalism that spoke to all human beings everywhere.[143] In an 1898 essay entitled "The Celtic Element in Literature," for instance, Yeats wrote that "[w]hen Matthew Arnold thought he was criticising the Celts, he was really criticising the ancient religion of the world," since once upon a time "every people in the world believed that trees were divine, and could take a human or grotesque shape and dance among the shadows of the woods."[144] "All old literatures are full of this way of looking at things," Yeats continues, but the Celtic nations—thanks, tragically, to centuries of political brutalization—have preserved an especially rich store of it, one that promises to enrich the world in years to come.[145] Where Arnold's account of Celtic literature had been defensive and recuperative, Yeats would venture that the Celts offered modernity something it could not possibly do without—for "literature dwindles to a mere chronicle of circumstances...unless it is constantly flooded with the passions and beliefs of ancient times, and...of all the fountains of the passions and beliefs of ancient times in Europe, the Slavonic, the Finnish, the Scandinavian, and the Celtic, the Celtic alone has been for centuries close to the main river of European literature."[146]

Yeats also followed Lang in applying Tylorian anthropology to active occult inquiry. "Lang," writes Sinéad Garrigan Mattar, "appealed to Yeats in a manner that none of his fellows did, because he believed that psychical research and occult religion were relevant to the study of the primitive paranormal."[147] Beginning in the late 1880s, Yeats would join Lang's Society for Psychical Research as well as the Theosophical Society and the Hermetic Order of the Golden Dawn, and like Lang would insist that folklore studies and occultism could provide complementary explanations of psychic phenomena.[148] Writing in the Theosophist magazine *Lucifer* in 1889, Yeats reflected that "it would be interesting if some spiritualist or occultist would try to explain the various curious and intricate spiritual-istic beliefs of peasants. When reading Irish folk-lore, or listening to Irish

---

[142] Hutchinson, 215.
[143] Regan, 71–3. See also R. F. Foster, "Protestant Magic: W. B. Yeats and the Spell of Irish History," in *Paddy and Mr. Punch: Connections in Irish History and English History* (London, UK: Penguin, 1993), 83–105.
[144] Yeats, "The Celtic Element in Literature," *Cosmopolis* 10 (1898): 677, 676.
[145] Ibid., 677.   [146] Ibid., 684.   [147] Mattar, 77; see 71–3.
[148] Thuente, 33. For Yeats's broader occult milieu, see Owen, 51–84.

peasants telling their tales of magic and fairyism and witchcraft, more and more one is convinced that... there must be" some insight into new faculties of the human mind; "Even if it is all dreaming, why have they dreamed this particular dream?"[149] As Hutchinson puts it, "Yeats was little interested in the Irish past as such but rather in a vast cosmic history" that would see Ireland serve as the vanguard of "a new regenerative era... a new and higher cycle of human history," since it "alone... had retained the full imaginative vision of the folk over the generations."[150] Alongside Lang, Jane Wilde was Yeats's favorite tale collector because she was open to the notion that "the mythology of a people reveals their relation to a spiritual and invisible world."[151]

Like Lang before him, Yeats found that attempting to integrate folklore with occultism left one with few allies. On the one hand, it separated him from the more traditional ethno-nationalism of the Gaelic League and moved both O'Leary and, in later years, Seamus Heaney to accuse him of forging a nationalism devoid of political salience.[152] It also found scant favor among orthodox Tylorians, who shared with the nationalists a historicist scruple about recording the exact terminology and language of folk tales. For his own part, Yeats did recognize a certain gulf between a literary use of folklore that stressed its perennial spiritual relevance and a more exacting historicism. "The imaginative impulse," he wrote, "is our great need from folklore," and it was the privilege of a "single mind" to create a "unity and design" that oral tradition alone could not achieve.[153] Appropriately, as Castle shows, Yeats's own tale collections eschewed ethnographic fidelity and instead tried to enhance their materials intuitively from within. *Fairy and Folk Tales of the Irish Peasantry* (1888) mixes new poems by William Allingham, Samuel Ferguson, and Yeats with tales adapted by Crofton Croker, Douglas Hyde, Letitia McClintock, Samuel Lover, Standish O'Grady, Jane Wilde, and others.[154] *Celtic Twilight* (1893) relies more heavily on Yeats's own ethnographic collecting but still takes literary liberties, while 1904's *Stories of Red Hanrahan* articulates

---

[149] W. B. Yeats, "Irish Fairies, Ghosts, Witches, etc.", *Lucifer* 3 (1889): 399. Quoted in Thuente, 34.

[150] Hutchinson, 132, 133.

[151] Jane Francesca Wilde, *Ancient Legends, Mystic Charms, and Superstitions of Ireland* (London, UK: Ward and Downey, 1888), xi. Quoted in Thuente.

[152] Regan, 77. See Seamus Heaney, "A Tale of Two Islands: Reflections on the Irish Literary Revival," *Irish Studies* 1 (1980): 1–20.

[153] Cited in Thuente, 88; Yeats, *The Celtic Twilight* (1893; London, UK: A. H. Bullen, 1902), 233. See James Pethica, "Yeats, Folklore, and Irish Legend," in Marjorie Howes and John Kelly (eds.), *The Cambridge Companion to W. B. Yeats* (New York, NY: Cambridge UP, 2006), 137.

[154] Castle, 54.

a "conception of the folk poet as an outcast who alone can articulate the deeper concerns of his culture."[155]

By and large, of course, this meant that Yeats "found his constituency more and more among sections of the Protestant sub-Ascendancy . . . around whom a vigorous 'Celtic' arts and crafts movement was also emerging."[156] What is perhaps most intriguing here is that even the Gaelic-Leaguer Hyde would move toward the Langian model of folklore during the halcyon years of the Celtic Renaissance. Hyde, of course, had long stressed the importance of grasping folk tales in their native languages. "[F]olklore," he wrote, "is presented in an uncertain and unsuitable medium, whenever the contents of the stories are divorced from their original expression in language."[157] In the introduction to *Beside the Fire* (1890) he faulted most of the seminal Irish folklorists for sacrificing linguistic fidelity to literary style. "Crofton Croker," he wrote, "is, alas! too often his own original," for "[t]he fact is that he learned the groundwork of his tales from conversations with the Southern peasantry, whom he knew well, and then elaborated this over the midnight oil . . ."[158] Yet Hyde too would feel the necessity of framing Irish folklore as being potentially of interest to anyone by stressing its antiquity over its Irishness. Irish fairy tales, he wrote in that same introduction, appeal to all "whose minds are so primitive that they retain with pleasure those tales which the more sophisticated invariably forget."[159] Hyde's turn to primitivism, in other words, was less about preserving Irish alterity than about making a pitch to Anglophone readers; he was willing to identify with the gaze of stadial history because it defined the relevance of these stories in the broadest terms possible. Rather than speaking among themselves, Irish voices would be able to address an emerging European literary modernity, "participat[ing] as equals in world civilization as they had in their golden age."[160]

---

[155] Pethica, 137. [156] Hutchinson, 218. [157] Hyde, xvii.
[158] Ibid., x–xi. [159] Ibid., xvii. [160] Hutchinson, 223.

Coda
Aesthetic Secularism

By recovering writers like Arnold and Pater as theorists of the secular, *Cultivating Belief* is in some sense trying to recuperate the aesthetic itself as a useful term for thinking about secularity. For in fact one reason why these non-fiction prose writers fell out of favor as touchstones of Victorian studies was because of their ties to a dated account of the relationship between secularism and aesthetics. Beginning with T. S. Eliot, critics portrayed works such as *Marius the Epicurean* and *Literature and Dogma* as attempts to sacralize the external trappings of religious doctrines that could no longer be believed.[1] Arnold and his sort moved to associate religion with ritual or with race, the argument went, because such things preserved, metonymically, the residue of a spiritual outlook that Darwin and the Higher Criticism had denied them.

More recent critics have rejected this familiar storyline as being some-what narrow in its cultural and political scope. After all, the fear that religion was under threat from modern scholarship was something that kept only a relatively small group of intellectuals and middle-class readers up at night. Moreover, it could be said, this story of substitution turns on a thin account of aesthetics as an external form for holding meaningful contents. To call aesthetics a hollow shell from which the spirit can flee is to posit an awfully weak vision of the aesthetic itself. *Cultivating Belief*, however, ventures that Arnold, Eliot, and Pater show us a different possible relationship between secularism and aesthetics. Instead of represent-ing a husk that preserves the warmth of its vanished contents, the aesthetic, for these writers, provides a structure of experience called many-sidedness that recuperates religion as one possible site of values among many. Many-sidedness, as both an ethos and an intellectual framework, does not try to

---

[1] T. S. Eliot, "Arnold and Pater" (1930), in *Selected Essays, 1917–1932* (New York, NY: Harcourt, Brace, 1932), 346–57. For a more recent example, consult Hilary Fraser, *Beauty and Belief: Aesthetics and Religion in Victorian Literature* (New York, NY: Cambridge UP, 1986).

transcend the contents of religion so much as put them into a new kind of circulation within the modern world; it pictures a secular world in which religion is present but also distributed in a new way.

This alternative secular imaginary interests me because it finds a number of resonances within contemporary criticism. On one level, as I argued in my introduction, it echoes a desire among recent critics to imagine modes of secularism that are not Protestant, since the version of aesthetics that it up-ends very much turns upon a Protestant dichotomy between inward contents and outward form, sincerely believing and "going through the motions." Within literary studies, meanwhile, it speaks to the current project of bringing formalism and historicism more closely together by exploring how politics itself can have an aesthetic logic.[2] Tracing how writers like Arnold and Eliot used the ethos of many-sidedness to rethink the modern self's relationship to religion allows the new formalism and the new secularism studies to cooperate in considering how aesthetic concepts may open up alternate political imaginaries. For a conceptual touchstone, we can turn to the work of Jacques Rancière, who describes art's business as that of "constructing spaces and relations to reconfigure materially and symbolically the territory of the common."[3] The aesthetic, for Rancière, is political less because of its "message" than "because of the type of space and time it institutes"—the way in which it entails "the framing of a particular space of experience" and of objects and subjects in common.[4] Here Rancière cites Schiller's concept of free play, which sees aesthetic experience as "suspend[ing] the ordinary connections not only between appearance and reality, but also between form and matter, activity and passivity, understanding and sensibility."[5] Like the many-sidedness of Arnold and Pater, Schiller's free play keeps contradictory possibilities open rather than obliging us to choose between them.

Yet in fact the aesthetic secularism sketched out by Arnold, Pater, Eliot, and Lang also resonates with accounts of more ordinary cultural life in the Victorian period. For instance, it amplifies Christine Bolus-Reichert's argument that the nineteenth century represented an "age of eclecticism" in which the fracturing of cultural consensus along sectarian and class lines produced new ways of engaging with the past though mixing and matching.[6] Far from representing the obsession of a few disenchanted

---

[2] See, for example, Caroline Levine, *Forms: Whole, Rhythm, Hierarchy, Network* (Princeton, NJ: Princeton UP, 2015).
[3] Jacques Rancière, *Aesthetics and Its Discontents*, trans. Stephen Concoran (Cambridge, UK: Polity, 2009), 22.
[4] Ibid., 23–4.   [5] Ibid., 30.
[6] Christine Bolus-Reichert, *The Age of Eclecticism: Literature and Culture in Britain, 1815–1885* (Columbus, OH: Ohio State UP, 2009).

intellectuals, Bolus-Reichert suggests, the aesthetic practice of balancing contraries became a key Victorian strategy for dealing with disagreement beyond the liberal compartmentalization of private and public. In this context one might also invoke Simon During's argument that the modern relationship to fictionality emerged as part of a new way of relating to belief made possible by mass culture. Drawing a parallel between the rising capital of literary fiction and the emergence of the secular magic show during the nineteenth century, During argues that audiences for both were not seeking "surrogates for supernaturalism" but rather "engage[d] with performances through secular and heterogeneous skills and pleasures."[7] For During, the "willing suspension of disbelief" enabled by literary fiction and secular magic alike evinces a modernity in which people seek to entertain multiple ideas simultaneously.[8]

Most intriguingly of all, Arnold's and Eliot's aesthetic secularism, with the central role it affords to involuntary inheritance, would provide a template for early theorists of cultural pluralism in the United States. Horace Kallen, who studied under William James at Harvard and would go on to teach philosophy at the New School for Social Research, first coined the phrase "cultural pluralism" in *The Nation* in 1915 and developed the concept further in 1924's *Culture and Democracy in the United States*.[9] As the title of that volume suggests, Kallen's work was deeply informed by Arnold's, and used an Arnoldian understanding of aesthetic play to argue that a plurality of distinct cultures could enhance both American individualism and the democratic state.[10] He compared the interactions between different ethnic groups to an orchestra and maintained that the individual could only become "fully rounded" by "interact[ing] with cultural groups... within the larger society of which he and his own ethnic group were parts."[11] Kallen's friend John Dewey, himself a reader of both Arnold and Eliot, came even closer to echoing Arnold's description of the individual and the nation as a harmony of diverse pasts.[12] Just as Arnold had modeled

---

[7] Simon During, *Modern Enchantments: The Cultural Power of Secular Magic* (Cambridge, MA: Harvard UP, 2002), 64.

[8] Ibid., 44.

[9] Ronald Kronish, "John Dewey and Horace M. Kallen on Cultural Pluralism: Their Impact on Jewish Education," *Jewish Social Studies* 44.2 (1982): 135–6; Sidney Ratner, "Horace M. Kallen and Cultural Pluralism," *Modern Judaism* 4.2 (1984): 187.

[10] For Kallen and Arnold, see Milton R. Konvitz, "Horace Kallen and the Hebraic Idea," in Konvitz (ed.), *The Legacy of Horace M. Kallen* (London, UK/Toronto, Canada: Associated U Presses, 1987), 64–75.

[11] Ratner, 187, 188–9.

[12] For Dewey and Eliot, see Louis Feuer, "John Dewey's Reading at College," *Journal of the History of Ideas* 19.3 (1958): 415–21. For the relationship between Dewey's aesthetics and his social thought, see Jason Kosnoski, "John Dewey's Social Aesthetics," *Polity* 37.2 (2005): 193–215.

his state upon a "*harmonious* perfection, developing all sides of our humanity ... [and a] *general* perfection, developing all parts of our society," so did Dewey argue, in "Nationalizing Education" (1916), that American democracy was ideally a unity "created by drawing out and composing into a harmonious whole the best, the most characteristic, which each contributing race and people has to offer."[13] "A state which shall give play to diversity of human powers," he wrote, "is a state in which the multitude of human groups and associations do *not* dissolve. It is a mechanism ... for arranging terms of interplay among the indefinite diversity of groups in which men associate and through active participation in which they become socially-minded."[14] Tracing a through-line from Arnold to Kallen and Dewey reveals both the centrality of aesthetics to modern pluralism and the crucial function of fixed identity in such thinking. What multiculturalism learned from aestheticism, we might say, is that valorizing involuntary identity can keep pluralism open by transforming the political problem of insoluble difference into the aesthetic virtue of free play. Ethnic inheritance, although a stumbling block for the liberalism of individual choice and decision, can also preserve the possibility of a non-totalizing totality that is eclectic rather than homogenizing.

Or that is the hope. For in fact, as I have tried to show, this aesthetic secularism brings with it a unique set of difficulties. Most notably, although it purports to suspend the entire question of religious belief, such a secularism actually comes to fetishize belief in a highly ambivalent way. It sees "strong belief" and unconscious inheritance as vital elements of modernity that are also its competitors in organizing human life. Arnoldian culture finds itself needing to out-muscle a Hebraism whose "fire and strength" it wishes to internalize. Paterian free play, in order to reject the moment of ascetic sacrifice, must become stringently ascetic in its own right. Lang's primitivism imagines ancient folk tales as key ingredients of a catholic reading practice, even though part of their attraction is that they are tragically backward and unable to be modernized. In this way, as we have seen, Lang ends up essentializing savagery in spite of himself, sliding into a dogmatic primitivism that misses the more generous eclecticism envisioned by Jacobs and his thesis of textual diffusion.

For Charles Taylor, this dynamic in which pluralism becomes narrow itself tells us that the secularist desire for an ethos that affirms all sides of human life equally "may be a mission impossible": to attain it, "we either have to scale down our moral aspirations in order to allow our ordinary human life to flourish; or we have to agree to sacrifice some of this

---

[13] Arnold, *Complete Prose Works*, 5: 235; Dewey is quoted in Ratner, 193.
[14] Quoted in Beth J. Singer, "Pragmatism and Pluralism," *The Monist* 75.4 (1992): 487.

ordinary flourishing to secure our higher goals."[15] For David Russell, it shows how the liberal ethos of self-cultivation implies, ambiguously, both playful self-expansion and streamlining progress. Many-sidedness insists that we avail ourselves of the full range of human experience, yet also demands that this process pay off in some kind of teleological development.[16]

For our purposes, the key takeaway may be that this paradox is endemic to the attempt to make aesthetics into a working blueprint for politics. As Rancière points out, while aesthetics are always implicitly political in offering alternative arrangements of persons and powers, the moment at which these alternatives become implemented is one that sees the aesthetic risk losing its essential quality of distance. There may be an irreducible gap, for Rancière, between "the politics of resistant form" and "the politics of the becoming-life of art," "a type of art that makes politics by eliminating itself as art and a type of art that is political on the proviso that it retains its purity, avoiding all forms of political intention."[17] This is, we might say, the limit of aesthetic secularism that Arnold, Eliot, Pater, and Lang discover. Many-sidedness, for them, offers a different distribution of commitments in the world, but that difference often vanishes when they try to give flesh to spirit through a character like Marius or an ethos like Arnoldian culture. These writers like the fixity of racial or cultural inheritance because it appears to forestall this moment by positing differences as things that can never be subsumed into one totalizing vision. That attempt, however, produces an even starker set of alternatives as, frustrated with the difficulty of maintaining this ideal balance, they find themselves obliged to enter into a more direct strife with narrow commitments. Their broad ideal of inclusion, with its refusal to sacrifice anything, cannot always abide what it has internalized.

---

[15] Charles Taylor, *A Secular Age* (Cambridge, MA: Harvard UP, 2007), 640.
[16] David Russell, "Aesthetic Liberalism," *Victorian Studies* 56.1 (2013): 16.
[17] Rancière, 44, 40.

Bibliography

Aarsleff, Hans. *From Locke to Saussure: Essays on the Study of Language and Intellectual History.* Minneapolis, MN: U of Minnesota P, 1982.

Ackerman, Robert. *The Myth and Ritual School: J. G. Frazer and the Cambridge Ritualists.* New York, NY: Garland P, 1991.

Adams, James Eli. *Dandies and Desert Saints: Styles of Victorian Masculinity.* Ithaca, NY: Cornell UP, 1995.

Albrecht, Thomas. "'The Balance of Separateness and Communication': Cosmopolitan Ethics in George Eliot's *Daniel Deronda*." *ELH* 79.2 (2012): 389–416.

Alexander, Edward. *Matthew Arnold and John Stuart Mill.* New York, NY: Columbia UP, 1965.

Allott, Kenneth. "Matthew Arnold's Reading-Lists in Three Early Diaries." *Victorian Studies* 2.3 (1959): 254–66.

Amigoni, David. *Colonies, Cults, and Evolution: Literature, Science, and Culture in Nineteenth-Century Writing.* New York, NY: Cambridge UP, 2010.

Anderson, Amanda. "George Eliot and the Jewish Question." *Yale Journal of Criticism* 10.1 (1997): 39–61.

Anderson, Amanda. *The Powers of Distance: Cosmopolitanism and the Cultivation of Detachment.* Princeton, NJ: Princeton UP, 2001.

Anderson, Amanda. "Victorian Studies and the Two Modernities." *Victorian Studies* 47.2 (2005): 195–203.

Anger, Suzy. *Victorian Interpretation.* Ithaca, NY: Cornell UP, 2005.

Anon. *Correspondence Relating to the Establishment of an Oriental College in London.* 1857. London, UK: Williams and Norgate, 1858.

Appiah, Kwame Anthony. "Identity, Authenticity, Survival: Multicultural Societies and Social Reproduction." *Multiculturalism: Examining the Politics of Recognition.* Ed. Amy Gutmann. Princeton, NJ: Princeton UP, 1994. 149–64.

ApRoberts, Ruth. *Arnold and God.* Berkeley, CA: U of California P, 1983.

Arata, Stephen. *Fictions of Loss in the Victorian Fin de Siècle.* New York, NY: Cambridge UP, 1996.

Armstrong, Nancy. "Contemporary Culturism: How Victorian Is It?" *Victorian Afterlife: Postmodern Culture Rewrites the Nineteenth Century.* Eds. John Kucich and Diane Sadoff. Minneapolis, MN: U of Minnesota P, 2000. 310–26.

Arnold, Matthew. *The Complete Prose Works of Matthew Arnold.* 11 vols. Ed. R. H. Super. Ann Arbor, MI: U of Michigan P, 1960–77.

Arnold, Matthew. *The Letters of Matthew Arnold, 1848–1888.* 2 vols. Ed. George W. E. Russell. London, UK: Macmillan, 1895.

Arnold, Matthew. *The Poems of Matthew Arnold.* New York, NY: Oxford UP, 1950.

Asad, Talal. "Comment on Conversion." *Conversion to Modernities: The Globalization of Christianity.* Ed. Peter van der Veer. New York, NY: Routledge, 1996. 263–73.

Asad, Talal. *Formations of the Secular: Christianity, Islam, Modernity*. Stanford, CA: Stanford UP, 2003.

Asad, Talal. *Genealogies of Religion*. Baltimore, MD: Johns Hopkins UP, 1991.

Ashcroft, Bill. "Primitive and Wingless: the Colonial Subject as Child." *Dickens and the Children of Empire*. Ed. Wendy S. Jacobson. London, UK: Palgrave, 2000. 184–202.

Barksdale, Richard K. "Thomas Arnold's Attitude Toward Race." *The Phylon Quarterly* 18.2 (1957): 174–80.

Baudelaire, Charles. *The Painter of Modern Life and Other Essays*. Ed. and trans. Jonathan Mayne. New York, NY: Phaidon, 1995.

Beaty, Jerome. "*Daniel Deronda* and the Question of Unity in Fiction." *Victorian Newsletter* 15 (1959): 16–20.

Bebbington, D. W. *Evangelicalism in Modern Britain*. Boston, MA: Unwin Hyman, 1989.

Beiner, Ronald. *Liberalism, Nationalism, Citizenship: Essays on the Problem of Political Community*. Vancouver, Canada: U of British Columbia P, 2003.

Bell, Bill. "The Function of Arnold at the Present Time." *Essays in Criticism* 47.3 (1997): 203–19.

Bell, Michael. *Primitivism*. London, UK: Methuen, 1972.

Benedict, Ruth. *Patterns of Culture*. 1934. New York, NY: Houghton-Mifflin, 2005.

Berger, Peter. *The Sacred Canopy: Elements of a Sociological Theory of Religion*. Garden City, NY: Doubleday, 1967.

Berlin, Isaiah. *The Roots of Romanticism*. Princeton, NJ: Princeton UP, 1999.

Best, Stephen and Sharon Marcus. "Surface Reading: An Introduction." *Representations* 108.1 (2009): 1–21.

Bishop, Jonathan. "The Identities of Sir Richard Burton: The Explorer as Actor." *Victorian Studies* 1.2 (1957): 119–35.

Blair, Kirstie. *Form and Faith in Victorian Poetry and Religion*. New York, NY: Oxford UP, 2012.

Boes, Tobias. *Formative Fictions: Nationalism, Cosmopolitanism, and the Bildungsroman*. Ithaca, NY: Cornell UP, 2012.

Bolus-Reichert, Christine. *The Age of Eclecticism: Literature and Culture in Britain, 1815–1885*. Columbus, OH: The Ohio State UP, 2009.

Brand, John. *Observations on Popular Antiquities*. Newcastle-upon-Tyne, UK: T. Saint, 1777.

Brantlinger, Patrick. *Rule of Darkness: British Literature and Imperialism, 1830–1914*. Ithaca, NY: Cornell UP, 1988.

Brilmyer, S. Pearl. "'The Natural History of My Inward Self': Sensing Character in George Eliot's *Impressions of Theophrastus Such*." *PMLA* 129.1 (2014): 35–51.

British Association for the Advancement of Science. *Report of the Thirty-Sixth Meeting of the British Association for the Advancement of Science; Held at Nottingham in August 1866*. London, UK: John Murray, 1867.

British Association for the Advancement of Science. *Report of the Thirty-Ninth Annual Meeting of the British Association for the Advancement of Science*. London, UK: John Murray, 1870.

Brown, Callum. *The Death of Christian Britain: Understanding Secularisation, 1800–2000*. New York, NY: Oxford UP, 2001.

Brown, Michael F. "Cultural Relativism 2.0." *Current Anthropology* 49.3 (2008): 363–83.

Brown, Richard. *Church and State in Modern Britain, 1700–1850*. London, UK: Routledge, 1991.

Brown, Wendy. *Regulating Aversion: Tolerance in the Age of Identity and Empire*. Princeton, NJ: Princeton UP, 2006.

Bunsen, C. C. J. "On the Results of the Recent Egyptian Researches in Reference to Asiatic and African Ethnology, and the Classification of Languages." *Report of the Seventeenth Meeting of the British Association for the Advancement of Science; Held at Oxford in June 1847*. London, UK: John Murray, 1848. 254–99.

Burne, Glenn S. "Andrew Lang's *The Blue Fairy Book*: Changing the Course of History." *Touchstones: Reflections on the Best in Children's Literature*. 3 vols. West Lafayette, IN: Children's Literature Association, 1987, 2:140–50.

Burrow, J. W. "Evolution and Anthropology in the 1860's: The Anthropological Society of London, 1863–71." *Victorian Studies* 7.2 (1963): 137–54.

Burrow, J. W. *Evolution and Society*. New York, NY: Cambridge UP, 1966.

Burrow, J. W. *Whigs and Liberals: Continuity and Change in English Political Thought*. New York, NY: Oxford UP, 1988.

Burton, Antoinette and Isabel Hofmeyr (eds.). *Ten Books That Shaped the British Empire: Creating an Imperial Commons*. Durham, NC: Duke UP, 2015.

Burton, Richard. *A Mission to Gelele, King of Dahome*. 2 vols. London, UK: Tinsley Brothers, 1864.

Burton, Richard. *Personal Narrative of a Pilgrimage to Al-Medinah and Meccah*. 3 vols. London, UK: Longman, Brown, Green, and Longmans, 1855.

Burton, Richard, and Verney Lovett Cameron. *To the Gold Coast for Gold: A Personal Narrative*. 2 vols. London, UK: Chatto and Windus, 1883.

Buurma, Rachel and Laura Heffernan. "Interpretation, 1980 and 1880." *Victorian Studies* 55.4 (2013): 615–28.

Buzard, James. *Disorienting Fiction: The Autoethnographic Work of Nineteenth-Century British Novels*. Princeton, NJ: Princeton UP, 2005.

Calinescu, Matei. *Five Faces of Modernity*. 1977. Durham, NC: Duke UP, 1987.

Carpenter, Mary Wilson. "The Apocalypse of the Old Testament: Daniel Deronda and the Interpretation of Interpretation." *PMLA* 99.1 (1984): 56–71.

[Carpenter, William B.] "Ethnology, or the Science of Races." *Edinburgh Review* 88 (1848): 429–87.

Carter, Stephen L. *The Culture of Disbelief*. New York, NY: Anchor, 1994.

Casanova, José. *Public Religions in the Modern World*. Chicago, IL: U of Chicago P, 1994.

Castle, Gregory. *Modernism and the Celtic Revival*. New York, NY: Cambridge UP, 2001.

Castle, Gregory. *Reading the Modernist Bildungsroman*. Gainesville, FL: UP of Florida, 2006.

Cecil, David. *Walter Pater. The Scholar-Artist*. New York, NY: Cambridge UP, 1955.

Chaudhuri, Nirad C. *Scholar Extraordinary: The Life of Professor the Rt. Honorable Friedrich Max Müller*. New York, NY: Oxford UP, 1974.

Cheyette, Bryan. *Constructions of "The Jew" in English Literature and Society: Racial Representations, 1875–1945*. New York, NY: Cambridge UP, 1993.

Chidester, David. *Empire of Religion: Imperialism and Comparative Religion*. Chicago, IL: U of Chicago P, 2014.

Clifford, James. *The Predicament of Culture: Twentieth-Century Ethnography, Literature, and Art*. Cambridge, MA: Harvard UP, 1988.

Clodd, Edward. "Presidential Address." *Folk-Lore* 6 (1895): 78–81.

Clouston, W. A. *Popular Tales and Fictions: Their Migrations and Transformations*. 2 vols. London, UK: Blackwood, 1887.

Colenso, J. W. "On the Efforts of Missionaries among Savages." *Journal of the Anthropological Society* 3 (1865): 248–79.

Collini, Stefan. *Arnold*. New York, NY: Oxford UP, 1988.

Collini, Stefan. *Liberalism and Sociology*. New York, NY: Cambridge UP, 1979.

Collini, Stefan. *Public Moralists: Political Thought and Intellectual Life in Britain*. Oxford, UK: Clarendon, 1991.

Comaroff, John L. and Jean. *Ethnicity, Inc.* Chicago, IL: U of Chicago P, 2009.

Connolly, William. *Why I Am Not a Secularist*. Minneapolis, MN: U of Minnesota P, 1999.

Cottom, Daniel. *Social Figures: George Eliot, Social History, and Literary Representation*. Minneapolis, MN: U of Minnesota P, 1987.

Court, Franklin E. "The Critical Reception of Pater's *Marius*." *English Literature in Transition, 1880–1920*. 27.2 (1984): 124–39.

Cox, Harvey. *The Secular City*. 1965. New York, NY: Macmillan, 1966.

Crawford, Robert. *Devolving English Literature*. 1992. Edinburgh, UK: Edinburgh UP, 2000.

Crawford, Robert. "Pater's *Renaissance*, Andrew Lang, and Anthropological Romanticism." *ELH* 53.4 (1986): 849–79.

Crawfurd, John. "On the Plurality of the Races of Man." *Transactions of the Ethnological Society of London* 6 (1868): 49–58.

Creppell, Ingrid. *Toleration and Identity: Foundations in Early Modern Though*. London, UK: Routledge, 2003.

Dahl, Curtis. "Pater's *Marius* and Historical Novels on Early Christian Times." *Nineteenth-Century Fiction* 28.1 (1973): 1–24.

Daly, Nicholas. *Modernism, Romance and the Fin de Siècle: Popular Fiction and British Culture, 1880–1914*. New York, NY: Cambridge UP, 1999.

Darwin, Charles. *The Descent of Man, and Selection in Relation to Sex*. 1871. New York, NY: D. Appleton, 1878.

De Vries, Hent. "Introduction." *Political Theologies: Public Religions in a Post-Secular World*. Eds. de Vries and Lawrence E. Sullivan. New York, NY: Fordham UP, 2006. 1–88.

DeLaura, David. *Hebrew and Hellene in Victorian England.* Austin, TX: U of Texas P, 1969.

Dentith, Simon. *George Eliot.* Sussex, UK: Harvester, 1986.

Derrida, Jacques. *Writing and Difference.* 1967. Trans. Alan Bass. Chicago, IL: U of Chicago P, 1978.

Desmond, Adrian J. *The Politics of Evolution.* Chicago, IL: U of Chicago P, 1989.

Dobbeleare, Karel. "Secularization: A Multi-Dimensional Concept." *Current Sociology* 29.2 (1981): 1–216.

Donoghue, Dennis. *Walter Pater: Lover of Strange Souls.* New York, NY: Knopf, 1995.

Dorson, Richard. *The British Folklorists: A History.* Chicago, IL: U of Chicago P, 1968.

Dowling, Linda. *Hellenism and Homosexuality in Victorian Oxford.* Ithaca, NY: Cornell UP, 1994.

Dowling, Linda. *Language and Decadence in the Victorian Fin de Siècle.* Princeton, NJ: Princeton UP, 1986.

Duncan, Ian. "George Eliot and the Science of the Human." *A Companion to George Eliot.* Eds. Amanda Anderson and Harry E. Shaw. Oxford, UK: Wiley-Blackwell, 2013. 471–85.

During, Simon. "George Eliot and Secularism." *A Companion to George Eliot.* Eds. Amanda Anderson and Harry E. Shaw. Oxford, UK: Wiley-Blackwell, 2013. 428–41.

During, Simon. *Modern Enchantments: The Cultural Power of Secular Magic.* Cambridge, MA: Harvard UP, 2002.

Durkheim, Émile. *The Elementary Forms of the Religious Life.* 1912. Trans. J. W. Swain. London, UK: Allen and Unwin, 1915.

Eliot, George. *Adam Bede.* 1859. Ed. Valentine Cunningham. New York, NY: Oxford UP, 1996.

Eliot, George. *Daniel Deronda.* 1876. Ed. Graham Handley. New York, NY: Oxford UP, 1986.

Eliot, George. "Evangelical Teaching: Dr. Cumming." *Westminster Review* 64 (1855): 436–62.

Eliot, George. *The George Eliot Letters.* 9 vols. Ed. Gordon S. Haight. New Haven, CT: Yale UP, 1954–55.

Eliot, George. *Impressions of Theophrastus Such.* 1879. Ed. Nancy Henry. London, UK: Pickering, 1994.

Eliot, George. "Introduction to Genesis." 1856. *Essays of George Eliot.* Ed. Thomas Pinney. New York, NY: Columbia UP, 1963. 255–60.

Eliot, George. "Mackay's Progress of the Intellect." *Westminster Review* 54 (1851): 353–68.

Eliot, George. *Middlemarch: A Study of Provincial Life.* 1871–72. Ed. David Carroll. New York, NY: Oxford UP, 1996.

Eliot, George. "The Natural History of German Life." *Westminster Review* 66 (1856): 28–44.

Eliot, George. *Poems: Together with Brother Jacob and The Lifted Veil*. New York, NY: Harper & Brothers, 1885.

Eliot, T. S. "Arnold and Pater." 1930. *Selected Essays, 1917–1932*. New York, NY: Harcourt, Brace, 1932. 346–57.

Eliot, T. S. "Ulysses, Order, and Myth." *The Dial* 75.5 (1932): 480–3.

Ellis, Havelock. "Introduction." J. K. Huysmans. *Against the Grain (À Rebours)*. 1884. Trans. John Howard. New York, NY: Lieber and Lewis, 1922. vii–xvi.

Esty, Jed. *Unseasonable Youth: Modernism, Colonialism, and the Fiction of Development*. New York, NY: Oxford UP, 2011.

Evangelista, Stefano. "'Outward Nature and the Moods of Men': Romantic Mythology in Pater's Essays on Dionysus and Demeter." *Walter Pater: Transparencies of Desire*. Eds. Laurel Brake, Lesley Higgins, Carolyn Williams. Greensboro, NC: ELT P, 2002. 107–18.

Evans, Brad. *Before Cultures: The Ethnographic Imagination in American Literature, 1865–1920*. Chicago, IL: U of Chicago P, 2005.

Evans-Pritchard, E. E. *Theories of Primitive Religion*. Oxford, UK: Clarendon P, 1965.

Fabian, Johannes. *Time and the Other: How Anthropology Makes Its Object*. New York, NY: Columbia UP, 1983.

Farrar, F. W. "Language and Ethnology." *Transactions of the Ethnological Society of London* 4 (1866): 196–203.

Farrar, F. W. "On Fixity of Type." *Transactions of the Ethnological Society of London* 3 (1865): 394–9.

Faverty, Frederic. *Matthew Arnold the Ethnologist*. Evanston, IL: Northwestern UP, 1951.

Feltes, N. N. *Literary Capital and the Late Victorian Novel*. Madison, WI: U of Wisconsin P, 1993.

Ferguson, Christine. *Language, Science, and Popular Fiction in the Victorian Fin-de-Siècle: The Brutal Tongue*. Burlington, VT: Ashgate, 2006.

Feuer, Louis. "John Dewey's Reading at College." *Journal of the History of Ideas* 19.3 (1958): 415–21.

Feuerbach, Ludwig. *The Essence of Christianity*. 1841. Trans. Marian Evans. London, UK: John Chapman, 1854.

Fielding, Penny. *Writing and Orality: Nationality, Culture, and Nineteenth-Century Scottish Fiction*. Oxford, UK: Clarendon P, 1996.

Fisher, Philip J. *Making Up Society: The Novels of George Eliot*. Pittsburgh, PA: U of Pittsburgh P, 1981.

Fitzgerald, Timothy. *The Ideology of Religious Studies*. New York, NY: Oxford UP, 2000.

Fleishman, Avrom. *The English Historical Novel*. Baltimore, MD: Johns Hopkins UP, 1971.

Fleishman, Avrom. *George Eliot's Intellectual Life*. New York, NY: Cambridge UP, 2010.

Forbes, Duncan. *The Liberal Anglican Idea of History*. New York, NY: Cambridge UP, 1952.

Foster, R. F. "Protestant Magic: W. B. Yeats and the Spell of Irish History." *Paddy and Mr. Punch: Connections in Irish History and English History*. London, UK: Penguin, 1993. 83–105.

Foucault, Michel. "On the Genealogy of Ethics: An Overview of a Work in Progress." *The Foucault Reader*. Ed. Paul Rabinow. New York, NY: Pantheon, 1984. 340–72.

Fraser, Hilary. *Beauty and Belief: Aesthetics and Religion in Victorian Literature*. New York, NY: Cambridge UP, 1986.

Frederickson, Kathleen. *The Ploy of Instinct: Victorian Sciences of Nature and Sexuality in Liberal Governance*. New York, NY: Fordham UP, 2014.

Freeden, Michael. *The New Liberalism: An Ideology of Social Reform*. New York, NY: Cambridge UP, 1978.

Freedman, Jonathan. *Professions of Taste: Henry James, British Aestheticism and Commodity Culture*. Stanford, CA: Stanford UP, 1990.

Frei, Hans. *The Eclipse of Biblical Narrative: A Study in Eighteenth and Nineteenth Century Hermeneutics*. New Haven, CT: Yale UP, 1974.

Gagnier, Regenia. *Individualism, Decadence, and Globalization: On the Relationship of Part to Whole, 1859–1920*. London, UK: Palgrave, 2012.

Gallagher, Catherine. "George Eliot: Immanent Victorian." *Representations* 90.1 (2005): 61–74.

Gandhi, Leela. *Affective Communities: Anticolonial Thought, Fin-de-Siècle Radialism, and the Politics of Friendship*. Durham, NC: Duke UP, 2006.

Gaster, Moses. *Ilchester Lectures on Greeko-Slavonic Literature*. London, UK: Trübner, 1887.

Gaster, Moses. "The Modern Origin of Fairy-Tales." *Folk-Lore Journal* 5 (1887): 339–51.

Gates, Sarah. "'A Difference of Native Language': Gender, Genre, and Realism in *Daniel Deronda*." *ELH* 68.3 (2001): 699–724.

Geertz, Clifford. *The Interpretation of Cultures*. New York, NY: Basic Books, 1973.

Gettelman, Debra. "Reading Ahead in George Eliot." *Novel: A Forum on Fiction* 39.1 (2005): 25–47.

Gikandi, Simon. *Maps of Englishness: Writing Identity in the Culture of Colonialism*. New York, NY: Columbia UP, 1996.

Goodheart, Eugene. "Arnold Among the Neoconservatives." *Clio* 25.4 (1996): 455–8.

Goodlad, Lauren M. E. "Liberalism and Literature." *The Oxford Handbook of Victorian Literary Culture*. Ed. Juliet John. New York, NY: Oxford UP, 2016.

Goodlad, Lauren M. E. *Victorian Literature and the Victorian State: Character and Governance in a Liberal Society*. Baltimore, MD: Johns Hopkins UP, 2003.

[Goodwin, D. R.] "The Unity of Language and of Mankind." *North American Review* 73 (1851): 163–89.

Goodyear, Sara Suleri. *The Rhetoric of English India*. Chicago, IL: U of Chicago P, 2012.

Gordon, George. "Andrew Lang." 1927. *Concerning Andrew Lang: Being the Andrew Lang Lectures Delivered Before the University of St. Andrews, 1927–1937*. Oxford, UK: Clarendon P, 1949.

Gorski, Philip and Ateş Altınordu. "After Secularization?" *Annual Review of Sociology* 34 (2008): 55–85.

Gossman, Lionel. "Philhellenism and Antisemitism: Matthew Arnold and his German Models." *Comparative Literature* 46.1 (1994): 1–39.

Graff, Gerald. "Arnold, Reason, and Common Culture." Matthew Arnold. *Culture and Anarchy*. Ed. Samuel Lipman. New Haven, CT: Yale UP, 1994. 186–201.

Graver, Suzanne. *George Eliot and Community: A Study in Social Theory and Fictional Form*. Berkeley, CA: U of California P, 1984.

Green, Martin. *Dreams of Adventure, Deeds of Empire*. London, UK: Routledge, 1980.

Green, Roger Lancelyn. *Andrew Lang*. Leicester, UK: Ward, 1946.

Greiner, Rae. *Sympthetic Realism in Nineteenth-Century British Fiction*. Baltimore, MD: Johns Hopkins UP, 2012.

Grillo, R. D. *Pluralism and the Politics of Difference: State, Culture, and Ethnicity in Comparative Perspective*. New York, NY: Oxford UP, 1998.

Habermas, Jürgen. *Postmetaphysical Thinking: Philosophical Essays*. Trans. Fred Lawrence. Cambridge, UK: Polity, 1992.

Habermas, Jürgen. *Religion and Rationality*. Ed. Eduardo Mendieta. Cambridge, MA: Polity P, 2002.

Hadley, Elaine. *Living Liberalism: Practical Citizenship in Mid-Victorian Britain*. Chicago, IL: U of Chicago P, 2010.

Hadot, Pierre. *What is Ancient Philosophy?* 1995. Trans. Michael Chase. Cambridge, MA: Harvard UP, 2002.

Haggard, H. Rider. "About Fiction." *Contemporary Review* 51 (1887): 172–80.

Haight, Gordon. *George Eliot: A Biography*. New York, NY: Oxford UP, 1968.

Haight, Gordon. *George Eliot and John Chapman*. New Haven, CT: Yale UP, 1969.

Hale, Piers J. *Political Descent: Malthus, Mutualism, and the Politics of Evolution in Victorian England*. Chicago, IL: U of Chicago P, 2014.

Hall, Catherine. "Missionary Stories: Gender and Ethnicity in England in the 1830s and 1840s." Eds. Lawrence Grossberg, Cary Nelson, Paula Treichler. *Cultural Studies*. New York, NY: Routledge, 1992. 240–70.

Harris, Marvin. *The Rise of Anthropological Theory*. New York, NY: Crowell, 1968.

Harrison, Peter. *"Religion" and the Religions in the English Enlightenment*. New York, NY: Cambridge UP, 1990.

Hartland, E. S. *Folklore: What Is It, and What Is the Good of It?* London, UK: David Nutt, 1904.

Heaney, Seamus. "A Tale of Two Islands: Reflections on the Irish Literary Revival." *Irish Studies* 1 (1980): 1–20.

Heath, Dunbar. "Anniversary Address." *Journal of the Anthropological Society* 6 (1868): lxxxiv–xcv.

Heath, Dunbar. "On the Great Race-Elements in Christianity." *Journal of the Anthropological Society* 5 (1867): xix–xxxi.

Heath, Dunbar. "On the Primary Anthropoid and Secondary Mute Origin of the European Races, versus the Theory of Migration from an External Source." *Journal of the Anthropological Society* 4 (1866): xxxiii–xlviii.

Heelas, Paul. *The New Age Movement: The Celebration of the Self and the Sacralization of Modernity.* Oxford, UK: Blackwell, 1996.

Helmstadter, Richard J. and Bernard Lightman (eds.). *Victorian Faith in Crisis: Essays on Continuity and Change in Nineteenth-Century Religious Belief.* Stanford, CA: Stanford UP, 1990.

Henderson, Philip. *Swinburne: Portrait of a Poet.* New York, NY: Macmillan, 1974.

Henriques, Ursula. *Religious Toleration in England, 1787–1833.* Toronto, Canada: U of Toronto P, 1961.

Henry, Nancy. "George Eliot and the Colonies." *Victorian Literature and Culture* 29.2 (2001): 413–33.

Hensley, Nathan. "What is a Network? (And Who Is Andrew Lang?)." *Romanticism and Victorianism on the Net* 64 (October 2013).

Henville, Letitia. "Andrew Lang's 'Literary Plagiarism': Reading Material and the Material of Literature." *Romanticism and Victorianism on the Net* 64 (October 2013).

Herbert, Christopher. *Culture and Anomie: Ethnographic Imagination in the Nineteenth Century.* Chicago, IL: U of Chicago P, 1991.

Herder, Johann Gottfried. *Reflections on the Philosophy of the History of Mankind.* 1784–91. Trans. Frank Manuel. Chicago, IL: U of Chicago P, 1968.

Higgins, Lesley. "A 'Thousand Solaces for the Modern Spirit: Walter Pater's Religious Discourse." *Victorian Religious Discourse: New Directions in Criticism.* Ed. Jude V. Nixon. New York, NY: Palgrave, 2004. 189–204.

Hill, Susan E. "Translating Feuerbach, Constructing Morality: The Theological and Literary Significance of Translation for George Eliot." *Journal of the American Academy of Religion* 65.3 (1997): 635–53.

Hillard, Molly Clark. "Trysting Genres: Andrew Lang's Fairy Tale Methodologies." *Romanticism and Victorianism on the Net* 64 (October 2013).

Hilton, Boyd. *The Age of Atonement: The Influence of Evangelicalism on Social and Economic Thought, 1795–1865.* Oxford, UK: Clarendon P, 1988.

Hines, Sarah. "Collecting the Empire: Andrew Lang's Fairy Books (1889–1910)." *Marvels and Tales* 24.1 (2010): 39–56.

Hobsbawm, E. J. *Nations and Nationalism since 1780: Programme, Myth, Reality.* New York, NY: Cambridge UP, 1990.

Hodgkin, Thomas. "Biographical Sketch of James Cowles Prichard." *The Edinburgh New Philosophical Journal* 47 (1849): 205–24.

Hollinger, David. *Postethnic America: Beyond Multiculturalism.* New York, NY: Harper Collins, 1995.

Holloway, John. *The Victorian Sage: Studies in Argument.* London, UK: Archon, 1962.

Honan, Park. *Matthew Arnold: A Life.* New York, NY: McGraw-Hill, 1981.

Horowitz, Evan. "George Eliot: The Conservative." *Victorian Studies* 49.1 (2006): 7–32.

Houghton, Walter E. "Victorian Periodical Literature and the Articulate Classes." *Victorian Studies* 22.4 (1979): 389–412.

Howells, W. D. "Henry James, Jr." 1882. *Selected Literary Criticism.* 3 vols. Eds. Ulrich Halfmann, Donald Pizer, and Ronald Gottesman. Bloomington, IN: Indiana UP, 1993. 1:317–23.

Humboldt, Wilhelm von. *The Limits of State Action.* 1791–92. Trans. and ed. J. W. Burrow. New York, NY: Cambridge UP, 1969.

Humboldt, Wilhelm von. *The Sphere and Duties of Government.* 1791–92. Trans. Joseph Coulthard. London, UK: John Chapman, 1854.

Hunt, James. "On the Doctrine of Continuity Applied to Anthropology." *Anthropological Review* 5 (1867): 110–20.

Hunt, James. "On the Negro's Place in Nature." *Memoirs Read before the Anthropological Society of London, 1863–64.* 2 vols. London, UK: Trübner and Company, 1865. 1:1–64.

Hunt, James. "On Physio-Anthropology: Its Aims and Methods." *Journal of the Anthropological Society of London* 5 (1867): cclvi–cclvii.

Hunt, James. "President's Address." *Journal of the Anthropological Society* 5 (1867): xliv–lxx.

Hunt, James. "Race in Religion." *Anthropological Review* 4 (1866): 289–320.

Hunt, James. *Stammering and Stuttering, Their Nature and Treatment.* London, UK: Longman, Green, Longman and Roberts, 1861.

Hutchinson, John. *The Dynamics of Cultural Nationalism: The Gaelic Revival and the Creation of the Irish Nation State.* London, UK: Allen and Unwin, 1987.

Hyde, Douglas. *Beside the Fire: A Collection of Irish Gaelic Folk Stories.* London, UK: David Nutt, 1910.

Inman, Billie Andrew. "The Organic Structure of *Marius the Epicurean.*" *Philological Quarterly* 41.2 (1962): 475–91.

Inman, Billie Andrew. *Walter Pater's Reading: A Bibliography of His Library Borrowings and Literary References, 1858–1873.* New York, NY: Garland, 1981.

Iser, Wolfgang. *Walter Pater: The Aesthetic Moment.* 1960; New York, NY: Cambridge UP, 1987.

Jacobs, Joseph. "Cinderella in Britain." *Folk-Lore* 4 (1893): 269–84.

Jacobs, Joseph. "The Science of Folk-Tales and the Problem of Diffusion." *The International Folk-Lore Congress, 1891: Papers and Transactions.* Ed. Joseph Jacobs and Alfred Nutt. London, UK: David Nutt, 1892. 76–86.

Jager, Colin. *The Book of God: Secularization and Design in the Romantic Era.* Philadelphia, PA: U of Pennsylvania P, 2007.

James, Henry. "The Art of Fiction." 1884. *Partial Portraits.* London, UK: Macmillan, 1899. 375–408.

James, William. *The Varieties of Religious Experience: A Study in Human Nature.* 1902. London, UK: Longmans, Green, 1920.

Jones, Tod E. *The Broad Church: A Biography of a Movement.* Lanham, MD: Lexington Books, 2003.

Jordan, Louis Henry. *Comparative Religion: Its Genesis and Growth.* Edinburgh, UK: T & T Clarke, 1905.

Kant, Immanuel. *Religion Within the Limits of Reason Alone.* 1793. Trans. Theodore M. Greene and Hoyt H. Hudson. New York, NY: Harper, 1960.

Kaufmann, Michael W. "The Religious, the Secular, and Literary Studies: Rethinking the Secularization Narrative in Histories of the Profession." *New Literary History* 38.4 (2007): 607–28.

Keane, Webb. *Christian Moderns: Freedom and Fetish in the Mission Encounter.* Berkeley, CA: U of California P, 2007.

Kennedy, Dane. *The Highly Civilized Man: Richard Burton and the Victorian World.* Cambridge, MA: Harvard UP, 2005.

Kidd, Colin. *The Forging of Races: Race and Scripture in the Protestant Atlantic World, 1600–2000.* New York, NY: Cambridge UP, 2006.

King, Joshua. *Imagined Spiritual Communities in Britain's Age of Print.* Columbus, OH: Ohio State UP, 2015.

King, Richard. "Address to the Ethnological Society of London, Delivered at the Anniversary, 25th May 1844." *Journal of the Ethnological Society of London* 2 (1850): 9–16.

Kissane, James. "Victorian Mythology." *Victorian Studies* 6.1 (1962): 5–28.

Knight, Mark and Emma Mason. *Nineteenth-Century Religion and Literature: An Introduction.* New York, NY: Oxford UP, 2006.

Knoepflmacher, U. C. "George Eliot, Feurerbach, and the Question of Criticism." *Victorian Studies* 7.3 (1964): 306–9.

Knoepflmacher, U. C. *Religious Humanism and the Victorian Novel: George Eliot, Walter Pater, and Samuel Butler.* Princeton, NJ: Princeton UP, 1965.

Knox, Robert. "Abstract of Observations on the Assyrian Marbles, and on their Place in History and Art." *Transactions of the Ethnological Society* 1 (1861): 146–54.

Knox, Robert. *The Races of Men.* Philadelphia, PA: Lea and Blanchard, 1850.

Konvitz, Milton R. "Horace Kallen and the Hebraic Idea." *The Legacy of Horace M. Kallen.* Ed. Konvitz. London, UK/Toronto, Canada: Associated U Presses, 1987. 64–75.

Kosnoski, Jason. "John Dewey's Social Aesthetics." *Polity* 37.2 (2005): 193–215.

Kronish, Ronald. "John Dewey and Horace M. Kallen on Cultural Pluralism: Their Impact on Jewish Education." *Jewish Social Studies* 44.2 (1982): 135–48.

Kuenen, Abraham. *National Religions and Universal Religions.* London, UK: Macmillan, 1882.

Kuper, Adam. *Culture: The Anthropologists' Account.* Cambridge, MA: Harvard UP, 1999.

Kurnick, David. "An Erotics of Detachment: *Middlemarch* and Novel-Reading as Critical Practice." *ELH* 74.3 (2007): 583–608.

Lang, Andrew. *Alfred Tennyson.* Edinburgh, UK: Blackwood, 1901.

Lang, Andrew. "Andrew Lang on Rudyard Kipling." *The Review of Reviews* 2 (1890): 217.

Lang, Andrew. "The Art of Mark Twain." *The Illustrated London News* 98 (1891): 222.

Lang, Andrew. "The Celtic Renascence." *Blackwood's Edinburgh Magazine* 161 (1897): 181–91.

Lang, Andrew. "Charles Dickens." *Fortnightly Review* 6 (1898): 944–60.

Lang, Andrew. "Charles Kingsley." *Essays in Little*. New York, NY: Scribner, 1891. 153–9.

Lang, Andrew. *Cock Lane and Common-Sense*. London, UK: Longmans, Green, 1894.

Lang, Andrew. *The Crimson Fairy Book*. London, UK: Longmans, Green 1903.

Lang, Andrew. *Custom and Myth*. London, UK: Longmans, Green, 1884.

Lang, Andrew. "A Dip in Criticism." *Contemporary Review* 54 (1888): 495–503.

Lang, Andrew. "Edward Burnett Tylor." *Anthropological Essays Presented to Edward Burnett Tylor in Honour of His 75th Birthday, Oct. 2, 1907*. Oxford, UK: Clarendon, 1907. 1–15.

Lang, Andrew. "The End of Phaecia." *In the Wrong Paradise, and Other Stories*. London, UK: Kegan Paul, Trench, 1886. 3–107.

Lang, Andrew. "The Evolution of Literary Decency." *Blackwood's Edinburgh Magazine* 167 (1900): 363–70.

Lang, Andrew. "French Peasant Songs." *Cornhill* 33 (1876): 596–608.

Lang, Andrew. "Introduction." *Cinderella: Three Hundred and Forty-five Variants*. Ed. Marian Roalfe Cox. London, UK: The Folk-Lore Society, 1893. vii–xxiv.

Lang, Andrew. "Introduction. Household Tales; Their Origins, Diffusion, and Relation to the Higher Myths." *Grimm's Household Tales*. 2 vols. Ed. Margaret Hunt. London, UK, 1884. 1:ix–lxxv.

Lang, Andrew. *The Lilac Fairy Book*. London, UK: Longmans, Green, 1910.

Lang, Andrew. "Literary Fairy Stories." *Little Johannes*. 1887. Ed. Frederick Van Eeden. Trans. Clara Bell. London, UK: William Heinemann, 1895. v–xix.

Lang, Andrew. "Mr. Kipling's Stories." *Essays in Little*. New York, NY: Scribner, 1891. 198–205.

Lang, Andrew. "Mr. Stevenson's Works." *Essays in Little*. New York, NY: Scribner, 1891. 24–35.

Lang, Andrew. "Mythology and Fairy Tales." *Fortnightly Review* 13 (1873): 618–31.

Lang, Andrew. *Myth, Ritual and Religion*. 2 vols. London, UK: Longmans, Green, 1887.

Lang, Andrew. "Notes on Ghosts." *Forum* 10 (1890): 452–62.

Lang, Andrew. *The Orange Fairy Book*. London, UK: Longmans, Green, 1906.

Lang, Andrew. "The Poems of Walter Scott." *Essays in Little*. New York, NY: Scribner, 1891. 171–81.

Lang, Andrew. *Prince Prigio*. Bristol, UK: J. W. Arrowsmith, 1889.

Lang, Andrew. "Protest of a Psycho-Folklorist." *Folklore* 6 (1895): 236–48.

Lang, Andrew. "Realism and Romance." *Contemporary Review* 52 (1887): 683–93.

Lang, Andrew. "The Sagas." *Essays in Little*. New York, NY: Scribner, 1891. 141–52.

Lang, Andrew. "She." *The Academy* 83 (1912): 274–5.

Lang, Andrew. "Superstition and Fact." *Contemporary Review* 64 (1893): 882–92.

Lang, Andrew. *The Violet Fairy Book*. London, UK: Longmans, Green, 1901.

Langstaff, Eleanor De Selms. *Andrew Lang*. Boston, MA: Twayne, 1978.

LaPorte, Charles. *Victorian Poets and the Changing Bible*. Charlottesville, VA: U of Virginia P, 2012.

Larsen, Timothy. *Crisis of Doubt*. New York, NY: Oxford UP, 2006.

Larsen, Timothy. *The Slain God: Anthropologists and the Christian Faith*. New York, NY: Oxford UP, 2014.

Latham, Robert Gordon. *Man and His Migrations*. London, UK: John Van Voorst, 1851.

Latour, Bruno. *We Have Never Been Modern*. 1991. Trans. Catherine Porter. Cambridge, MA: Harvard UP, 1993.

Leerssen, Joep. "Ossian and the Rise of Literary Historicism." *The Reception of Ossian in Europe*. Ed. Howard Gaskill. New York, NY: Continuum, 2004. 109–25.

Lerer, Seth. *Children's Literature: A Reader's History, from Aesop to Harry Potter*. Chicago, IL: U of Chicago P, 2008.

Levine, Caroline. *Forms: Whole, Rhythm, Hierarchy, Network*. Princeton, NJ: Princeton UP, 2015.

Levine, George. *Realism, Ethics and Secularism: Essays on Victorian Literature and Science*. New York, NY: Cambridge UP, 2008.

Levine, Philippa. *The Amateur and the Professional: Antiquarians, Historians and Archaeologists in Victorian England, 1838–1886*. New York, NY: Cambridge UP, 1986.

Lewis, Bernard. *What Went Wrong?* New York, NY: Oxford UP, 2002.

Li, Hao. *Memory and History in George Eliot*. London, UK: Macmillan, 2000.

Lightman, Bernard. "Darwin and the Popularization of Evolution." *Notes and Records of the Royal Society* 64.1 (2010): 5–24.

Lincoln, Bruce. *Theorizing Myth: Narrative, Ideology, and Scholarship*. Chicago, IL: U of Chicago P, 2000.

Linke, Uli. "Folklore, Anthropology, and the Governance of Social Life." *Comparative Studies in Society and History* 32.1 (1990): 117–48.

Lloyd, David and Paul Thomas. *Culture and the State*. New York, NY: Routledge, 1998.

Locke, John. *Two Treatises of Government and a Letter Concerning Toleration*. Ed. Ian Shapiro. New Haven, CT: Yale UP, 2003.

Logan, Peter Melville. *Victorian Fetishism: Intellectuals and Primitives*. Albany, NY: SUNY P, 2009.

Lorimer, Douglas A. *Colour, Class, and the Victorians: English Attitudes to the Negro in the Mid-Nineteenth Century*. Leicester, UK: Leicester UP, 1978.

Love, Heather. "Close But Not Deep: Literary Ethics and the Descriptive Turn." *New Literary History* 41.2 (2010): 371–91.

Love, Heather. "Forced Exile: Walter Pater's Queer Modernism." *Bad Modernisms*. Eds. Douglas Mao and Rebecca L. Walkowitz. Durham, NC: Duke UP, 2006.

Low, Gail Chang-Liang. *White Skins/Black Masks: Representation and Colonialism*. New York, NY: Routledge, 1996.

Luckhurst, Roger. "Knowledge, Belief and the Supernatural at the Imperial Margin." *The Victorian Supernatural*. Eds. Nicola Bown, Carolyn Burdett, and Pamela Thurschwell. New York, NY: Cambridge UP, 2004. 197–217.

Luckmann, Thomas. *The Invisible Religion*. New York, NY: Macmillan, 1967.

Lukács, Georg. *The Historical Novel*. 1937. Trans. Hannah and Stanley Mitchell. 1962. Lincoln, NE: U of Nebraska P, 1983.

Lukács, Georg. *Theory of the Novel*. 1916/1920. Trans. Anna Bostock. Cambridge, MA: MIT P, 1971.

Lyons, Sara. *Algernon Swinburne and Walter Pater: Victorian Aestheticism, Doubt, and Secularization*. London, UK: Legenda, 2015.

Macedo, Stephen. *Diversity and Distrust: Civic Education in a Multicultural Democracy* Cambridge, MA: Harvard UP, 2000.

Mahmood, Saba. *Politics of Piety: The Islamic Revival and the Feminist Subject*. Princeton, NJ: Princeton UP, 2005.

Mahmood, Saba. "Secularism, Hermeneutics, and Empire: The Politics of Islamic Reformation." *Public Culture* 18.2 (2006): 323–47.

Maistre, Joseph de. *The Works of Joseph de Maistre*. Trans. Jack Lively. 1965. New York, NY: Shocken, 1971.

Maitland, Brownlow. "Lord Shaftesbury's Life and Work." *Littell's Living Age* 57 (1887): 515–32.

Malachuk, Daniel S. "George Eliot's Liberalism." *A Companion to George Eliot*. Eds. Amanda Anderson and Harry E. Shaw. Oxford, UK: Wiley-Blackwell, 2013. 370–84.

Malachuk, Daniel S. *Perfection, the State, and Victorian Liberalism*. New York, NY: Palgrave Macmillan, 2005.

Manganaro, Marc. *Culture, 1922: The Emergence of a Concept*. Princeton, NJ: Princeton UP, 2002.

Mao, Douglas. *Fateful Beauty: Aesthetic Environments, Juvenile Development, and Literature 1860–1960*. Princeton, NJ: Princeton UP, 2010.

Marcus, Steven. "Culture and Anarchy Today." Matthew Arnold. *Culture and Anarchy*. Ed. Samuel Lipman. New Haven, CT: Yale UP, 1994. 165–85.

Markovits, Stefanie. *The Crisis of Action in Nineteenth-Century English Literature*. Columbus, OH: The Ohio State UP, 2006.

Martin, David. *A General Theory of Secularization*. New York, NY: Harper and Row, 1978.

Masuzawa, Tomoko. *The Invention of World Religions: Or, How European Universalism Was Preserved in the Language of Pluralism*. Chicago, IL: U of Chicago P, 2006.

Masuzawa, Tomoko. "Our Master's Voice: F. Max Müller after a Hundred Years of Solitude." *Method and Theory in the Study of Religion* 15.4 (2003): 305–28.

Mattar, Sinéad Garrigan. *Primitivism, Science, and the Irish Revival.* New York, NY: Oxford UP, 2004.

Maurice, Frederick Denison. *The Religions of the World and Their Relations to Christianity.* 1847. London, UK: Macmillan, 1877.

McClintock, Anne. *Imperial Leather: Race, Gender, and Sexuality in the Colonial Contest.* New York, NY: Routledge, 1995.

McClure, John. *Late Imperial Romance.* New York, NY: Verso, 1994.

McGowan, John. "From Pater to Wilde to Joyce: Modernist Epiphany and the Soulful Self." *Texas Studies in Literature and Language* 32.3 (1990): 417–45.

McGrath, F. C. *The Sensible Spirit: Walter Pater and the Modernist Paradigm.* Tampa, FL: U of South Florida P, 1986.

McKelvy, William R. *The English Cult of Literature: Devoted Readers, 1774–1880.* Charlottesville, VA: U of Virginia P, 2007.

McLaughlin, Kevin. "Culture and Messianism: Disinterestedness in Arnold." *Victorian Studies* 50.4 (2008): 615–39.

McLennan, J. F. "The Worship of Plants and Animals." *Fortnightly Review* 6 (1869): 407–27.

Mehta, Uday. *Liberalism and Empire: A Study in Nineteenth-Century British Liberal Thought.* Chicago, IL: U of Chicago P, 1999.

Meyer, Susan. "'Safely to their own borders': Proto-Zionism, Feminism, and Nationalism in *Daniel Deronda.*" *ELH* 60.3 (1993): 733–58.

Michalski, Robert. "Towards a Popular Culture: Andrew Lang's Anthropological and Literary Criticism." *Journal of American Culture* 18.3 (1995): 13–17.

Mill, John Stuart. *On Liberty.* London, UK: Parker, 1859.

Miller, J. Hillis. *The Disappearance of God: Five Nineteenth-Century Writers.* 1963. New York, NY: Schocken Books, 1965.

Miller, J. Hillis. "Optic and Semiotic in *Middlemarch.*" *The Worlds of Victorian Fiction.* Ed. Jerome Hamilton Buckley. Cambridge, MA: Harvard UP, 1975. 125–48.

Modern, John Lardas. *Secularism in Antebellum America.* Chicago, IL: U of Chicago P, 2010.

Molendijk, Arie L. *Friedrich Max Müller & the Sacred Books of the East.* New York, NY: Oxford UP, 2016.

Montenyohl, Eric L. "Andrew Lang's Contribution to English Folk Narrative Scholarship." *Western Folklore* 47.4 (1988): 269–84.

Moore, James R. "Deconstructing Darwinism: The Politics of Evolution in the 1860s." *Journal of the History of Biology* 24.3 (1991): 353–408.

Moran, Maureen. "Pater's 'Great Change': *Marius the Epicurean* and the Historical Conversion Romance." *Walter Pater: Transparencies of Desire.* Eds. Laurel Brake, Lesley Higgins, Carolyn Williams. Greensboro, NC: ELT P, 2002. 170–88.

Moretti, Franco. *Distant Reading.* London, UK: Verso, 2013.

Moretti, Franco. *The Way of the World: The Bildungsroman in European Culture.* 1987. London, UK: Verso, 2000.

Morgan, Benjamin. "Aesthetic Freedom: Walter Pater and the Politics of Autonomy." *ELH* 77.3 (2010): 731–56.

Morris, William. "The Revival of Architecture." *Fortnightly Review* 43 (1888): 665–74.

Mott, Lewis F. "Renan and Matthew Arnold." *Modern Language Notes* 33.2 (1918): 65–73.

Mufti, Aamir. *Enlightenment in the Colony: The Jewish Question and the Crisis of Postcolonial Culture.* Princeton, NJ: Princeton UP, 2007.

Müller, F. Max. "Comparative Mythology." 1856. *Chips from a German Workshop.* 4 vols. London, UK: Longmans, Green, 1867. 2:1–143.

Müller, F. Max. *Contributions to the Science of Mythology.* 2 vols. London, UK: Longmans, Green, 1897.

Müller, F. Max. "Forgotten Bibles." *Nineteenth Century* 15 (1884): 1004–22.

Müller, F. Max. *Introduction to the Science of Religion: Four Lectures Delivered at the Royal Institution in February and March 1870.* London, UK: Spottiswoode, 1870.

Müller, F. Max. "Lectures on Mr. Darwin's Philosophy of Language." *Fraser's Magazine* 7–8 (1873): 525–41, 659–79, 1–24.

Müller, F. Max. *Lectures on the Origin and Growth of Religion, as Illustrated by the Religions of India.* London, UK: Longmans, Green, 1878.

Müller, F. Max. *Lectures on the Science of Language Delivered at the Royal Institution of Great Britain in April, May, and June, 1861. First Series.* London, UK: Longman, Green, Longman, and Roberts, 1861.

Müller, F. Max. *Lectures on the Science of Language Delivered at the Royal Institution of Great Britain in February, March, April, and May, 1863. Second Series.* London, UK: Longman, Green, Longman, Roberts, and Green, 1864.

Müller, F. Max. *The Life and Letters of the Right Honourable Max Müller.* 2 vols. Ed. Georgina Adelaide Müller. London, UK: Longmans, Green, 1902.

Müller, F. Max. "Literary Recollections." Part 2 of 4. *Cosmopolis* 4 (1896): 626–48.

Müller, F. Max. "Literary Recollections." Part 3 of 4. *Cosmopolis* 5 (1897): 642–67.

Müller, F. Max. "Literary Recollections." Part 4 of 4. *Cosmopolis* 6 (1897): 324–47.

Müller, F. Max. *My Autobiography: A Fragment.* New York, NY: Scribners, 1901.

Müller, F. Max. "On Freedom." *Contemporary Review* 36 (1879): 369–97.

Müller, F. Max. "On the Relation of the Bengali to the Arian and Aboriginal Languages of India." *Report of the Seventeenth Meeting of the British Association for the Advancement of Science; Held at Oxford in June 1847.* London, UK: John Murray, 1848. 319–51.

Müller, F. Max. "The Parliament of Religions, Chicago, 1893." *Last Essays.* London, UK: Longmans, Green, 1901. 324–45.

Müller, F. Max. "The Savage." *Nineteenth Century* 18 (1885): 109–32.

Müller, F. Max. "Semitic Monotheism." 1860. *Chips from a German Workshop.* 4 vols. London, UK: Longmans, Green, 1867. 1:341–79.

Nongbri, Brent. *Before Religion: A History of a Modern Concept.* New Haven, CT: Yale UP, 2013.

Numbers, Ronald L. and John Stenhouse. *Disseminating Darwinism*. New York, NY: Cambridge UP, 1999.

Nutt, Alfred. "Recent Archaeological Research II." *Archaeological Review* 3 (1889): 73–88.

Oliphant, Margaret. "New Books." *Blackwood's Edinburgh Magazine* 114 (1873): 596–617.

Orel, Harold. *Victorian Literary Critics*. London, UK: Macmillan, 1984.

Osborne, Catherine Dunagan. "Inherited Emotions: George Eliot and the Politics of Heirlooms." *Nineteenth-Century Literature* 64.4 (2010): 465–93.

Osborne, R. V. "*Marius the Epicurean*." *Essays in Criticism* 1 (1951): 387–403.

Owen, Alex. *The Place of Enchantment: British Occultism and the Culture of the Modern*. Chicago, IL: U of Chicago P, 2007.

Owen, Ralph Albert. *Christian Bunsen and Liberal English Theology*. Montpelier, VT: Capital City P, 1924.

Paine, Thomas. *The Age of Reason*. Amherst, NY: Prometheus, 1984.

Parry, J. P. *Democracy and Religion: Gladstone and the Liberal Party, 1867–1875*. New York, NY: Cambridge UP, 1986.

Pater, Walter. *The Works of Walter Pater*. 8 vols. London, UK: Macmillan, 1900–01.

Pecora, Vincent. *Secularization and Cultural Criticism: Religion, Nation, and Modernity*. Chicago, IL: U of Chicago P, 2006.

Pethica, James. "Yeats, Folklore, and Irish Legend." *The Cambridge Companion to W. B. Yeats*. Eds. Marjorie Howes and John Kelly. New York, NY: Cambridge UP, 2006. 129–43.

Pfau, Thomas. "From Mediation to Medium: Aesthetic and Anthropological Dimensions of the Image (*Bild*) and the Crisis of *Bildung* in German Modernism." *Modernist Cultures* 1.2 (2005): 141–80.

Pfleiderer, Otto. *Religion and Historic Faiths*. 1906. Trans. Daniel A. Heubsch. New York, NY: B. W. Heubsch, 1907.

Piggott, Stuart. *Ruins in a Landscape: Essays in Antiquarianism*. Edinburgh, UK: Edinburgh UP, 1976.

Pike, Luke Owen. "On the Place of the Sciences of Mind and Language in the Science of Man." *Anthropological Review* 2 (1864): cxciii–ccviii.

Pippin, Robert. *Modernity as a Philosophical Problem*. Cambridge, MA: Basil Blackwell, 1991.

Potolsky, Matthew. "Fear of Falling: Walter Pater's *Marius the Epicurean* as a Dangerous Influence." *ELH* 65.3 (1998): 701–29.

Pratt, Mary Louise. *Imperial Eyes: Travel Writing and Transculturation*. New York, NY: Routledge, 1992.

Preus, J. S. *Explaining Religion: Criticism and Theory from Bodin to Freud*. New Haven, CT: Yale UP, 1996.

Preyer, Robert. "Bunsen and the Anglo-American Literary Community in Rome." *Der Gelehrte Diplomat: zum Wirken Christian Carl Josias Bunsens*. Ed. Erich Geldbach. Leiden, Germany: Brill, 1980. 35–64.

Price, Leah. *How to Do Things With Books in Victorian Britain*. Princeton, NJ: Princeton UP, 2013.

Prichard, James Cowles. *The Eastern Origin of the Celtic Nations: Proved by a Comparison of Their Dialects with the Sanskrit, Greek, Latin and Teutonic Languages.* London, UK: Sherwood, Gilbert, and Piper, and J and A Arch, 1831.

Prichard, James Cowles. *The Natural History of Mankind; Inquiries into the Modifying Influence of Physical and Moral Agencies on the Different Tribes of the Human Family.* Ed. Edwin Norris. 1843. London, UK: H. Baillière, 1855.

Prichard, James Cowles. "Of the Relations of Ethnology to Other Branches of Knowledge." *Journal of the Ethnological Society of London* 1 (1848): 301–29.

Prichard, James Cowles. *Researches into the Physical History of Mankind.* 2 vols. London, UK: John and Arthur Arch, 1813.

Propp, Vladimir. *Morphology of the Folktale.* 1958. Ed. Louis A. Wagner. Trans. Lawrence Scott. Austin, TX: U of Texas P, 1968.

Psomiades, Kathy Alexis. "Hidden Meaning: Andrew Lang, H. Rider Haggard, Sigmund Freud, and Interpretation." *Romanticism and Victorianism on the Net* 64 (October 2013).

Qualls, Barry V. *The Secular Pilgrims of Victorian Fiction: The Novel as Book of Life.* New York, NY: Cambridge UP, 1982.

Ragussis, Michael. *Figures of Conversion: "The Jewish Question" and English National Identity.* Durham, NC: Duke UP, 1995.

Ramos, Alice. "Technologies of the Self: Truth, Asceticism, and Autonomy." *Journal of French and Francophone Philosophy* 6.1–2 (2010): 20–9.

Ratner, Sidney. "Horace M. Kallen and Cultural Pluralism." *Modern Judaism* 4.2 (1984): 185–200.

Rawls, John. *Political Liberalism.* New York, NY: Columbia UP, 1993.

Redinger, Ruby V. *George Eliot: The Emergent Self.* New York, NY: Knopf, 1975.

Regan, Stephen. "W. B. Yeats and Irish Cultural Politics in the 1890s." *Cultural Politics at the Fin de Siècle.* Eds. Sally Ledger and Scott McCracken. London, UK: Routledge, 1995. 66–84.

Reid, Julia. *Robert Louis Stevenson, Science, and the Fin de Siècle.* London, UK: Palgrave, 2006.

Renan, Ernest. *Studies in Religious History.* 1857. Trans. William M. Thomson. London, UK: Mathieson, 1893.

Rose, Jacqueline. *The Case of Peter Pan, or The Impossibility of Children's Fiction.* London, UK: Macmillan, 1984.

Rosenberg, Sheila. "The 'Wicked Westminster': John Chapman, His Contributors and Promises Fulfilled." *Victorian Periodicals Review* 33.3 (2000): 225–46.

Rosenblum, Nancy L. *Another Liberalism: Romanticism and the Reconstruction of Liberal Thought.* Cambridge, MA: Harvard UP, 1987.

Ruskin, John. "The Nature of Gothic" (selection from *The Stones of Venice*). *The Genius of John Ruskin.* Charlottesville, VA: U of Virginia P, 1964. 170–96.

Russell, David. "Aesthetic Liberalism." *Victorian Studies* 56.1 (2013): 7–30.

Said, Edward. *The World, the Text, and the Critic.* Cambridge, MA: Harvard UP, 1983.

Saler, Michael. "Modernity and Enchantment: A Historiographic Review." *The American Historical Review* 111.3 (2006): 692–716.

Schaefer, Donovan. *Religious Affects: Animality, Evolution, and Power*. Durham, NC: Duke UP, 2015.

Schlegel, W. F. *The Philosophy of History in a Course of Lectures, Delivered at Vienna*. 1829. Trans. James Burton Robertson. London, UK: Henry G. Bohn, 1852.

Schmitt, Carl. *Political Theology: Four Chapters on the Concept of Sovereignty*. 1922. Trans. George Schwabb. Cambridge, MA: MIT P, 1985.

Schwab, Raymond. *Oriental Renaissance: Europe's Rediscovery of India and the East, 1680–1880*. 1950. Trans. Gene Patterson-Black and Victor Reinking. New York, NY: Columbia UP, 1984.

Seagar, Richard H. *The World's Parliament of Religions: The East/West Encounter, Chicago, 1893*. Bloomington, IN: Indiana UP, 1995.

Seigel, Jerrod. *Between Cultures: Europe and Its Others in Five Exemplary Lives*. Philadelphia, PA: U of Pennsylvania P, 2016.

Semmel, Bernard. *George Eliot and the Politics of National Inheritance*. New York, NY: Oxford UP, 1994.

Shaffer, E. S. *"Kubla Khan" and* The Fall of Jerusalem*: The Mythological School in Biblical Criticism and Secular literature, 1770–1880*. New York, NY: Cambridge UP, 1975.

Sharpe, Eric. "Andrew Lang and the Making of Myth." *Ethnography is a Heavy Rite: Studies of Religion in Honor of Juha Pentikäinen*. Eds. Juha Pentikäinen, Nils G. Holm, and Hannu Kilpeläinen. Helskinki, Finland: Åbo Akademi, 2000. 52–63.

Sharpe, Eric. *Comparative Religion: A History*. La Salle, IL: Open Court, 1986.

Shuter, William F. *Rereading Walter Pater*. New York, NY: Cambridge UP, 1997.

Siegel, Jonah. "Lang's Survivals." *Romanticism and Victorianism on the Net* 64 (October 2013).

Singer, Beth J. "Pragmatism and Pluralism." *The Monist* 75.4 (1992): 477–91.

Smail, Daniel Lord. *On Deep History and the Brain*. Berkeley, CA: U of California P, 2008.

Smith, Christian. *The Secular Revolution: Power, Interests, and Conflict in the Secularization of American Public Life*. Berkeley, CA: U of California P, 2003.

Smith, W. Robertson. *Lectures on the Religion of the Semites*. New York, NY: D. Appleton, 1889.

Smol, Anna. "The 'Savage' and the 'Civilized': Andrew Lang's Representation of the Child and the Translation of Folklore." *Children's Literature Association Quarterly* 21.4 (1996–97): 177–83.

Spencer, Herbert. *The Principles of Biology*. 2 vols. London, UK: Williams and Norgate, 1864.

Stark, Susanne. *"Behind Inverted Commas": Translation and Anglo-German Cultural Relations in the Nineteenth Century*. Clevedon, UK: Multilingual Matters, 1999.

Stepan, Nancy. *The Idea of Race In Science: Great Britain, 1800–1960*. London, UK: Macmillan, 1982.

Stevenson, Robert Louis. "A Gossip on Romance." *Longman's Magazine* 1 (1882): 69–79.

Stocking, George. *After Tylor: British Social Anthropology, 1888–1951*. Madison, WI: U of Wisconsin P, 1995.

Stocking, George. "From Chronology to Ethnology: James Cowles Prichard and British Anthropology, 1800–1850." James Cowles Prichard. *Researches into the Physical History of Mankind*. 1813. Ed. George Stocking. Chicago, IL: U of Chicago P, 1973. xii–xxiv.

Stocking, George. "Matthew Arnold, E. B. Tylor, and the Uses of Invention." 1968. *Race, Culture, and Evolution: Essays in the History of Anthropology*. Chicago, IL: U of Chicago P, 1982. 69–90.

Stocking, George. *Victorian Anthropology*. New York, NY: Free P, 1987.

Stocking, George. "What's in a Name? The Origins of the Royal Anthropological Institute." *Man* 6 (1971): 369–90.

Stone, Jon R. "Introduction." *The Essential Max Müller*. Ed. Jon R. Stone. New York, NY: Macmillan, 2002. 1–23.

Strauss, D. F. *The Life of Jesus Critically Examined*. 1835. 3 vols. Trans. Marian Evans. London, UK: John Chapman, 1846.

Taves, Anne. *Religious Experience Reconsidered*. Princeton, NJ: Princeton UP, 2009.

Taylor, Charles. *A Secular Age*. Cambridge, MA: Harvard UP, 2007.

Tennyson, G. B. "The *Bildungsroman* and Nineteenth-Century English Literature." *Medieval Epic to the "Epic Theater" of Brecht: Essays in Comparative Literature*. Eds. Rosario P. Armato and John M. Spalek. Los Angeles, CA: U of Southern California P, 1968. 135–46.

Teukolsky, Rachel. *The Literate Eye: Victorian Art Writing and Modernist Aesthetics*. New York, NY: Oxford UP, 2009.

Thomas, David Wayne. *Cultivating Victorians: Liberal Culture and the Aesthetic*. Philadelphia, PA: U of Pennsylvania P, 2004.

Thuente, Mary Helen. *W. B. Yeats and Irish Folklore*. Dublin, Ireland: Gill and Macmillan, 1980.

Tolkien, J. R. R. "On Fairy Stories." *The Tolkien Reader*. New York, NY: Ballantine, 1966. 31–99.

Treitel, Corinna. *A Science for the Soul*. Baltimore, MD: Johns Hopkins UP, 2004.

Trilling, Lionel. *Matthew Arnold*. 1939. New York, NY: Columbia UP, 1949.

Trumpener, Katie. *Bardic Nationalism: The Romantic Novel and the British Empire*. Princeton, NJ: Princeton UP, 1997.

Trumpener, Katie. "Paratext and Genre System: A Response to Franco Moretti." *Critical Inquiry* 36.1 (2009): 159–71.

Tucker, Herbert. "Arnold and the Authorization of Criticism." *Knowing the Past: Victorian Literature and Culture*. Ed. Suzy Anger. Ithaca, NY: Cornell UP, 2001. 100–20.

Tucker, Herbert. *Epic: Britain's Heroic Muse, 1790–1910*. New York, NY: Oxford UP, 2008.

Turner, Frank. *Contesting Cultural Authority: Essays in Victorian Intellectual Life*. New York, NY: Cambridge UP, 1993.

Turner, Frank. *The Greek Heritage in Victorian Britain*. New Haven, CT: Yale UP, 1981.

Tylor, E. B. *Anthropology: An Introduction to the Study of Man and Civilization*. 1881. New York, NY: D. Appleton, 1898.

Tylor, E. B. "On the Traces of the Early Mental Condition of Man." *Proceedings of the Royal Institution* 5 (1867): 83–93.

Tylor, E. B. "Phenomena of the Higher Civilisation Traceable to a Rudimental Origin Among Savage Tribes." *Anthropological Review* 5 (1867): 304–5.

Tylor, E. B. *Primitive Culture: Researches into the Development of Mythology, Philosophy, Religion, Language, Art, and Custom*. 2 vols. London, UK: John Murray, 1871.

Tylor, E. B. "Remarks on Buschman's Researches in North American Philology." *Transactions of the Ethnological Society of London* 2 (1863): 130–6.

Tylor, E. B. "Wild Men and Beast-Children." *Anthropological Review* 1 (1863): 21–32.

van den Bosch, Lourens P. *Friedrich Max Müller: A Life Devoted to the Humanities*. Leiden, Germany: Brill, 2002.

van der Veer, Peter. *Imperial Encounters: Religion and Modernity in India and Britain*. Princeton, NJ: Princeton UP, 2001.

van der Veer, Peter. "Introduction." *Conversion to Modernities: The Globalization of Christianity*. Ed. Peter Van der Veer. New York, NY: Routledge, 1996. 1–21.

Vance, Norman. *Bible and Novel: Narrative Authority and the Death of God*. New York, NY: Oxford UP, 2013.

Vaninskaya, Anna. "The Late Victorian Romance Revival: A Generic Excursus." *English Literature in Transition, 1880–1920* 51 (2008): 57–79.

Vickery, John B. *The Literary Impact of the Golden Bough*. Princeton, NJ: Princeton UP, 1973.

Villin, Edouard. "Discussion" of "On Phallic Worship." *Anthropological Review* 8 (1870): cxliii.

Viswanathan, Gauri. *Outside the Fold: Conversion, Modernity, and Belief*. Princeton, NJ: Princeton UP, 1998.

Viswanathan, Gauri. "Secularism in the Framework of Heterodoxy." *PMLA* 123.2 (2008): 466–76.

Vogeler, Martha S. "George Eliot and the Positivists." *Nineteenth Century Fiction* 35.3 (1980): 406–31.

Wake, C. S. "The Aim and Scope of Anthropology." *Journal of Anthropology* 1 (1870): 1–18.

Waldron, Jeremy. *God, Locke, and Equality: Christian Foundations in Locke's Political Thought*. New York, NY: Cambridge UP, 2002.

Wallace, Jo-Ann. "De-Scribing *The Water-Babies*: 'The Child' in Post-Colonial Theory." *De-Scribing Empire: Post-colonialism and Textuality*. Eds. Chris Tiffin and Alan Lawson. London, UK: Routledge, 1994. 171–93.

Ward, Mrs. Humphry (Mary Arnold Ward). *A Writer's Recollections*. London, UK: W. Collins, 1918.

Warner, Michael. "Is Liberalism a Religion?" *Religion: Beyond a Concept.* Ed. Hent de Vries. New York, NY: Fordham UP, 2008. 610–17.

Warner, Michael. "Uncritical Reading." *Polemic: Critical or Uncritical.* Ed. Jane Gallop. New York, NY: Routledge, 2004. 13–38.

Watson, Tim. *Caribbean Culture and British Fiction in the Atlantic World, 1780–1870.* New York, NY: Cambridge UP, 2008.

Weintraub, Joseph. "Andrew Lang: Critic of Romance." *English Literature in Transition* 18.1 (1975): 5–15.

Wheeler-Barclay, Marjorie. *The Science of Religion in Britain, 1860–1915.* Charlottesville, VA: U of Virginia P, 2010.

Wilde, Jane Francesca. *Ancient Legends, Mystic Charms, and Superstitions of Ireland.* London, UK: Ward and Downey, 1888.

Wilde, Oscar. *The Major Works.* New York, NY: Harper Collins, 1966.

Williams, Carolyn. *Transfigured World: Walter Pater's Aesthetic Historicism.* Ithaca, NY: Cornell UP, 1989.

Williams, Daniel G. *Ethnicity and Cultural Authority: From Arnold to DuBois.* Edinburgh, UK: Edinburgh UP, 2006.

Williams, Raymond. *Culture and Society, 1780–1950.* New York, NY: Columbia UP, 1958.

Williams, Raymond. *Keywords: A Vocabulary of Culture and Society.* 1976. New York, NY: Oxford UP, 2011.

Williamson, Eugene L. *The Liberalism of Thomas Arnold: A Study of His Religious and Political Writings.* Tuscaloosa, AL: U of Alabama P, 1964.

Wilson, Bryan. *Contemporary Transformations of Religion.* New York, NY: Oxford UP, 1976.

Wilson, William A. "Herder, Folklore, and Romantic Nationalism." *The Journal of Popular Culture* 6.4 (1973): 819–35.

Winter, Sarah. "Mental Culture: Liberal Pedagogy and the Emergence of Ethnographic Knowledge." *Victorian Studies* 41.3 (1998): 427–54.

Wolin, Sheldon. *Politics and Vision: Continuity and Innovation in Western Political Thought.* Boston, MA: Little, Brown, 1960.

Wright, Thomas. *The Life of Walter Pater.* 2 vols. London, UK: Everett, 1907.

Yeats, W. B. "The Celtic Element in Literature." *Cosmopolis* 10 (1898): 675–87.

Yeats, W. B. *The Celtic Twilight.* 1893. London, UK: A. H. Bullen, 1902.

Yeats, W. B. "Irish Fairies, Ghosts, Witches, Etc." *Lucifer* 3 (1899): 399–404.

Young, Julian. *Nietzsche's Philosophy of Religion.* New York, NY: Cambridge UP, 2006.

Young, Robert J. C. *Colonial Desire: Hybridity in Theory, Culture, and Race.* New York, NY: Routledge, 1995.

Index